TRAVERSING THE
TRACTION
GAP

TRAVERSING THE

TRACTION GAP

BRUCE CLEVELAND

& W|LDCAT
VENTURE PARTNERS

RADIUS BOOK GROUP
NEW YORK

Distributed by Radius Book Group
A Division of Diversion Publishing Corp.
443 Park Avenue South, Suite 1004
New York, NY 10016
www.RadiusBookGroup.com

Library of Congress Control Number: 2018958128

First edition: February 2019
Hardcover ISBN: 978-1-63576-573-1
Trade Paperback ISBN: 978-1-63576-624-0
eBook ISBN: 978-1-63576-574-8

Manufactured in the United States of America

10 9 8 7 6 5 4 3 2 1

Cover design by Mark Karis
Interior design by Pauline Neuwirth, Neuwirth & Associates

I, along with the Wildcat Venture Partners team, wrote this book for you; the brave entrepreneurs who dare to change the world and make it a better place for us all.

CONTENTS

FOREWORD

by Geoffrey Moore

The whole point of this book, as Bruce makes clear in his introduction, is to radically reduce the failure rate of venture-backed startups, specifically during their metamorphosis from promising product in a potential blockbuster category to scalable business highly attractive to later-stage investment. This is the murky territory of detecting and securing market-product fit, a term Bruce introduces and defines in the book, at a time when it is critical for the entrepreneur and the sponsoring venture capitalists to be on exactly the same page.

Traversing the Traction Gap shines a very bright light on this transition in two important ways. First, it prescribes objective, quantifiable milestones that guide the journey through four stages, from Initial Product Release to Minimum Viable Traction. Second—and this is the unique contribution of the book in my view—each stage directly equates to a step-function change in valuation for the budding enterprise. That is, not only are these market-development milestones, they are venture-funding milestones as well. As a result, the framework directly aligns the entrepreneur with the investor on how a specific funding event translates into a subsequent uplift in company valuation.

This connection between entrepreneurial innovation and venture valuation has never before been made this clear, and, as a result, far too many venture-backed startups wandered off course, not because they were doing poor work, but because they weren't doing the right work at the right time. As a result, when they went to get their next round of funding, what they heard from investors was "You've done some very fine work here, but we'd like to see you get a bit more traction before we invest."

Traction. That was the word that haunted their fundraising lives. What is it? Why is it so elusive? How do you get it? How do you demonstrate it? These are the questions that the Traction Gap Framework helps management teams and their investing sponsors address.

At Wildcat Venture Partners, where both Bruce and I work, we have been using this framework with every single one of our investments, first informally, and now formally via the Traction Gap Institute. It is proving invaluable both as a navigational device to chart courses through the unpredictable currents of disruptive innovation and as a communication device to keep us aligned with our funded CEOs and their teams. Along with Bruce and the rest of the partners of Wildcat, we hope that you too can leverage this guidance to entrepreneurial success.

PART

LEARNING THE CONCEPTS

The Traction Gap Framework

INTRODUCTION

This is an unusual business book.

Unusual because unlike many business books, we have set out to provide you with a set of prescriptive techniques and tactics you can leverage with your own startup—or with your portfolio companies if you are a venture investor. We are venture capitalists and entrepreneurs, not academics; our orientation is toward real-life business success, not interesting theories. We will always choose messy successes over elegant failures.

This book contains valuable lessons that my Wildcat partners and I have learned in our careers, combined with tried, tested, and proven techniques used by teams to successfully traverse one of the most challenging phases in a startup's life cycle: we call it the "Traction Gap." As you will see, this journey is almost never smooth. That's why this is a guide, not a bible. Every entrepreneur's experience will be different.

Why should you value the advice in this book? Well, I, along with the members of the Wildcat Venture Partners team who have contributed to its contents, have been involved with successful Silicon Valley companies and the technology industry in some manner for at least twenty years.

I have held operating roles in several Silicon Valley technology companies that were small startups at the time I joined them. At Oracle, I began as a mid-level manager when it was a private company of 100+ employees located on Sand Hill Road in Menlo Park. At 27, I was given the opportunity to build a division, and in less than four years we grew from a "startup" inside Oracle to a major contributor to Oracle's top line. After Oracle, I joined Apple and ran its Unix and object technology divisions. In 1996, I joined Siebel Systems as a member of its senior executive team just after it completed a $2M year; five years later, we generated $1.7B in revenue. All three companies are among the most transformational technology companies in Silicon Valley history.

After we sold Siebel to Oracle in 2006, I elected to try my hand at investing in startups as a member of a venture firm. One of my first investments was in Marketo, when it was essentially just an idea with three talented people. This small team was led by Phil Fernandez, who went on to transform the marketing function as we know it. With C3, I was invited by Tom Siebel to participate in helping the company form its original business plan and then subsequently invest in it; and when Doximity's founder, Jeff Tangney, sat in the offices of my former venture firm as an Executive in Residence, I had the privilege of watching him work his way through the process of selecting one among three ideas he was contemplating and go on to create a market-leading application for physicians and the healthcare industry.

My Wildcat partners have each had similar experiences, helping to either build or advise startups to go on to become successful market-leading companies.

As such, we have had a front-row seat where we have learned what is required to take an idea from startup to category leader. These invaluable experiences, working with incredible people, serve as the foundation for the principles developed and documented as part of the Traction Gap Framework.

What compelled me—and my Wildcat partners to encourage me—to write this book? It was a troubling statistic. *More than 80 percent of all startups fail,* according to Dow Jones VentureSource, Correlation Ventures, CB Insights, and other sources. And the percentage may be even greater than that.

I am talking about thousands of failed companies every year. Many entrepreneurs believed they had valuable, important new products . . . and yet they failed, in spite of their belief and their best all-out efforts.

These companies either failed outright or failed to return at least the capital invested. This is a tremendous waste: lost capital, lost jobs, and lost dreams. Some of the smartest people in our economy invest significant amounts of time, effort, and capital that ultimately produce no tangible result. And here's the worst of it.

Most startups can engineer a product; but, sadly, the vast majority stumble when it comes to engineering a market for that product. Just as important as the product itself is accurately assessing and validating market need for that product, then defining or redefining that market, so that their beautifully engineered product has a chance to succeed. To do any less is a colossal wasted effort.

As early-stage investors, we wanted to expose the reasons behind that 80 percent failure rate, especially when venture firms widely proclaim their ability to "add value" as a core competency.

What we have discovered—what I will discuss in depth in the pages that follow—is that every startup must pass through three distinct phases:

1. Go-to-Product,
2. Go-to-Market, and
3. Go-to-Scale.

For negotiating the go-to-product phase, founders have a tremendous amount of information and support for their startup. Incubators, accelerators, angel investors—all are ready and eager to help. For example, Steve Blank's excellent book, *The Startup Owner's Manual*, is a phenomenal reference for any startup team seeking to navigate the go-to-product phase.

That said, I have elected to devote a significant portion of this book—the first four chapters—to exploring some critical issues in the go-to-product period. The issues I discuss have not been dealt with as readily, yet are mission-critical; and if you do not address these issues satisfactorily, they will at a minimum compromise your success or, worse, lead to an early shutdown.

I will introduce you to terms, concepts, and strategies that will enable you to navigate and exit the go-to-product phase, prepared to take on and success-fully traverse the Traction Gap, the meat of this book, what I later term "Slide 29." You'll read a lot about Slide 29 in Chapter 1 and throughout this book.

For those relatively few startups that actually make it to the third—go-to-scale—phase, a significant amount of information and support exists for them as well. Consultants and books abound with information that can help found-ers "cross that chasm" (to paraphrase Geoffrey Moore's title of his best-selling book) and begin to scale. We are privileged to have Geoff, the master of mar-keting challenges, as one of our partners here at Wildcat Venture Partners, and I know he agrees with what I am about to tell you:

While there is a substantial amount of information and support for the first and third phases, there is very little data or support for teams making their way through the second—go-to-market—phase.

———————

Very few business metrics exist at this point in a startup's life cycle. So spread-sheet analysis offers little help to the management team as it attempts to de-velop a category, define it, and create sophisticated demand-generation and revenue-conversion programs.

This lack of internal and external support could not come at a worse time. Startups in the go-to-market stage face tremendous financial risk. They have a limited amount of time to figure things out and get them right. In many ways, they are never more vulnerable.

It is this dangerous and tumultuous period that we have labeled the "Trac-tion Gap" and presented as the main topic of this book. Fail to generate suffi-cient traction during this phase, and your startup will never get the opportunity to cross the chasm to its next era of growth. More likely instead, it will come to a sad and dismal end. However optimistic your beginnings, you will end up on the scrap heap of the 80+ percent.

1

SLIDE 29

New technology startup companies have been getting it wrong for decades—and it is not their fault.

Venture capital firms not only make the same mistake, but they reward it.

Business schools that teach entrepreneurialism exacerbate the problem with future generations of entrepreneurs by not just teaching this mistake, but by concentrating on it.

What is it? An intense focus on creating great new products without an equally great go-to-market strategy that includes "market-engineering" tasks such as category creation and market validation.

As we are an early-stage venture capital firm, the vast majority of the entrepreneurs we meet have as yet few customers or consumers using their product when we first consider making an investment. In fact, in some cases there is no product at all, just a concept or prototype.

In a first meeting with an entrepreneur, I usually sit through a presentation of—on average—thirty slides. The presentation typically, in the first 28 of those slides, sets up the problem, the product, and the assessment of the market opportunity, though the latter is seldom thoroughly validated.

In this part of the presentation, entrepreneurs can—and often do—go into great detail about Product Architecture, product features, product roadmaps, and a theoretical Total Addressable Market (TAM). To their credit, most have invested a great deal of time thinking about these issues.

Slide 30 is usually the "ask" slide: that is, it covers how much the startup is raising and what it intends to do with the capital. Most entrepreneurs actually make a rational argument for the amount of capital they want; others just put down a number they hope to get. I typically ignore this request for the time being, as the investment we make must be calculated and linked to reaching key future value inflection points. To determine this amount is an exercise we like to go through with the team, using Traction Gap principles.

It is the penultimate slide, number 29, where things get dicey. I call it the "a miracle occurs" slide after the famous Sidney Harris cartoon, seen here.

Then a Miracle Occurs

"I THINK YOU SHOULD BE MORE EXPLICIT HERE IN STEP TWO."

FIGURE 2[1]

Slide 29 inevitably shows a "hockey stick" graph of dramatic five-year usage or revenue projections. And where the first 28 slides went into extensive detail regarding the product, team, and TAM, Slide 29 almost never precisely articulates how the team expects to generate that spectacular growth. The "a miracle occurs" slide always seems to suggest that the presence of the new widget or application in the marketplace will magically attract thousands of customers or millions of users simply by its very existence.

If only that were true. However, as startup failure rates demonstrate, usage or revenue don't just happen on their own. The history of the tech revolution is littered with thousands of dead products—and companies—that look brilliant on paper but failed to attract paying customers or rabid users. I have been, at various times in my career, an entrepreneur and an investor—and I have learned the hard way that just as a product must be physically well engineered, usage and revenue must be engineered as well.

In my experience, creating a powerful "growth engine" demands significant planning and a thorough and detailed go-to-market plan. This process requires a team with significant related expertise—yet the majority of the teams I meet with, while having great product-engineering skills, seldom have equally great market-engineering skills to adequately prepare their startup for the critical go-to-market stage in its life cycle. Most don't even recognize that Slide 29 is a sign of likely failure, not the road map to victory.

A lack of requisite market-engineering skills, such as knowing how to define or redefine a category, develop powerful positioning or competitor de-positioning, and perform in-depth market research to confirm or reject proposed products and features—which must all be accomplished well in advance of entering the go-to-market phase—will invariably compromise a startup's ability to demonstrate the traction it needs to secure its next round of financing. Unless it can grow quickly and profitably without that financing, it will be unlikely to scale. And that is the kiss of death.

So, while I am always excited by new ideas and products (that's why I love this profession!), I have learned to be sober and pragmatic about the herculean effort and abundant capital required to successfully take a product to market and subsequently capture leadership of that market. That's why, often to the dismay of startup teams that meet with me, I will seem to all but ignore those glorious opening slides . . . and instead focus on the young company's market-engineering plans. I know better than to trust in miracles.

This stage is so important, I will spend the first chapters of this book telling you what you need to do to address market-engineering issues, as well as some key product-engineering issues.

The failure of most startup teams and their investors to invest in market-engineering, while still in the go-to-product phase, so they are well prepared to enter the go-to-market phase, takes a terrible toll.

The number of reported startups that begin each year is approximately 4,000 to 5,000 companies. Based upon industry data from Mattermark, of those thousands only *800* startups will ever actually raise their first, Series A, investment round. That's an 84 percent failure rate. And the likelihood of those 800 firms getting to the next stage of investment is less than 10 percent—just *80* companies of the thousands that started down this path.

The result is this heartbreaking graph:

• • •

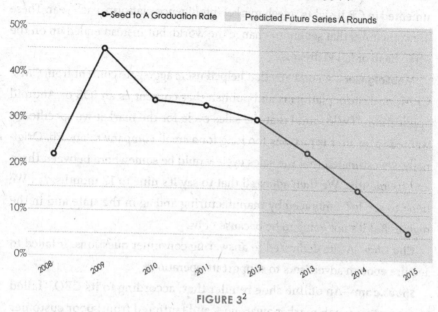

Startup Graduation Seed to Series A

FIGURE 3[2]

Data from firms such as Correlation Ventures and Dow Jones Venture-Source confirms these dismal statistics.

To put a finer point on these failure rates, according to Professor Shikhar Ghosh of the Harvard Business School, roughly 75 percent of US venture-backed startups—the cream of the crop among new companies—fail. Ghosh's research also has found that 30 to 40 percent of quality startups end up liquidating *all* their assets—in other words, nothing of them survives. Ghosh further suggests that if startup failure is defined as "not delivering the projected return on investment," then 95 percent of VC-backed companies are failures.

▪ Startup Failure Definitions and Rates[3] ▪

STARTUP FAILURE DEFINITION	FAILURE RATE
Liquidating all assets, with investors losing most or all the money they put into the company	30%–40%
Failing to see the projected return on investment	70%–80%
Declaring a projection and then falling short of meeting it	90%–95%

Here are just five examples, taken from hundreds of defunct startups documented in CB Insights, a tech market intelligence platform, each year. These are companies that set out to change the world, but instead ended up on the scrap heap of failed dreams.

MobileIgniter—A company that helped users aggregate content from CMS, CRM, or custom platforms and publish that content as an iOS or Android application. "[W]e found that the sales cycle for the market we specifically wanted to go after is just way too long for a small company to absorb. Originally, we estimated that the sales cycle would be somewhere between three and six months. We then adjusted that to say it's nine to 12 months. . . . We hope to see IoT embraced by manufacturing and ag in the state and in the region. But it's not going to be because of us."

Cha Cha—A site dedicated to answering consumer questions. It failed to acquire enough advertisers to support its operations.

Shoes.com—An online shoe retailer that, according to its CEO, "failed to generate enough market awareness and [suffered from] poor customer service."

Rendeevoo—A dating app company. One of its veterans explained "We never managed to raise the next round in time; so . . . the ugly reality slapped us hard. Bills were piling up on the business but also on our personal lives."

Hivebeat—This startup developed a way for student organizations to promote and manage events on campus. "We never hit a real product/market fit," recalled one of its founders. "Our product was great, but it wasn't a 10x product. We had a much prettier product than the competition, but we were always lacking features in every niche."

CB Insights has captured statements from hundreds of failed startups that tell similar tales of woe.

I am a founding partner at Wildcat Venture Partners. We are a relatively new venture firm, formed in 2015, but each of us has been a successful venture investor with other firms for at least a decade. So, when we came together to form

Wildcat Venture Partners, we spent a significant amount of time discussing and planning how we wanted to run our firm, the areas of investment interest we shared, and the investment decision-making processes we wanted to adopt. We also conducted an in-depth analysis of the successes, failures, and lessons we had learned along the way, in order to avoid making the mistakes again.

As a part of that process, we examined our personal investment records and—in stark contrast to dreary industry statistics—we were pleasantly surprised to discover that nearly 70 percent of the very early-stage startups—more than 2 out of 3—we had backed over our individual venture careers had made it through this challenging go-to-market phase.

The problem was that we weren't sure why. We liked to think we were just smart. But everybody in venture capital is smart—otherwise investors wouldn't entrust them with billions of dollars to invest. So we set out to explore what our careers had in common. Perhaps the secret lay hidden there.

The closer we looked, the more we realized—to our surprise—that while we didn't necessarily use the same language, all of us had had similar experiences and used similar approaches when working with our startup teams.

In one of our Wildcat planning sessions, I introduced an investing and operating framework I had developed over the previous few years at my former venture firm. I called it the "Traction Gap Framework." As I took us through its concepts, everyone was quick to recognize its relevance, embrace its terminology, and begin contributing new concepts based upon their own individual experiences.

Today, the Traction Gap Framework is a composite of my own and the Wildcat team's collective experiences, along with some great contributions from others as well. At our firm, we now all use Traction Gap vernacular and principles with our portfolio companies as both an operational and financing strategy.

Traversing the Traction Gap

In their seminal works on startups, authors Steve Blank (*The Startup Owner's Manual*) and Eric Ries (*The Lean Startup*) do an outstanding job of explaining the challenges associated with the first phase of a company—what I have labeled as the go-to-product phase. They coined the term "lean startup," based upon lean manufacturing concepts and principles originally developed by Toyota, to reflect a startup team's need to quickly identify the market opportunity, validate that opportunity, and reach "product/market fit" with a Minimum Viable Product (MVP).

In Chapter 4, "Getting to Initial Product Release," I build upon their key concepts by introducing and explaining what it means to be "market-first"; why it's critically important to test products and features with statistically validated market research *before* committing to build them. I also introduce new terms, concepts, and tactics you can use both to ensure that you are building a product the market wants and to show you how to plan for getting it cost-effectively and efficiently into market—before you officially enter the go-to-market—Slide 29—phase.

I mentioned Geoffrey Moore earlier. He is an iconic business author and speaker, and one of my partners at Wildcat Venture Partners. Through his many books and lectures, he has shown companies how to think about markets, "cross the chasm," and begin to successfully scale a product—what I have labeled the *go-to-scale* phase.

Yet, surprisingly, very little practical and prescriptive advice has been captured and published discussing what startups should do to successfully make it through that middle *go-to-market* phase. This is the devastatingly critical period of time between the go-to-product and go-to-scale phases—the phase that destroys the vast majority of startups and even kills new products within existing companies.

I have observed that most startups are able to create a first product on the initial capital they raise. Yet time and again, these companies falter when they take those initial products to market.

This challenging go-to-market phase is the *Traction Gap*.

The Traction Gap Framework

FIGURE 4

Over my more than 25 years as an entrepreneur and early-stage venture investor, I have tackled these problems head-on. My goal in the pages that follow is to provide practical advice any startup—or new-product team in an existing company—can use to help successfully traverse the Traction Gap. I will provide you with the "missing link" between the "lean launchpad" and "crossing the chasm."

In each chapter, I will showcase how—and when—you should move from one phase to the next, complete with valuable insights, tips, and tricks others have used to successfully traverse the Traction Gap and go on to scale.

TRACTION GAP FRAMEWORK OVERVIEW

To begin, I lay out the Traction Gap Framework so you can become familiar and comfortable with its terminology.

The Traction Gap Framework is broader than just the Traction Gap alone. It begins with the go-to-product phase. As you will read in these first four chapters, you have a lot of work to do in the go-to-product phase to prepare yourself for the go-to-market phase. This is why I spend some time on the go-to-product end of the spectrum. But the actual Traction Gap spans from a startup's Initial Product Release (IPR) to Minimum Viable Traction (MVT), which we define as a point in a company's maturity—whether it is a certain level of revenue growth, engagement, downloads, usage, or other variables—that demonstrates market validation and signals a positive growth trajectory.

(These milestones also apply to a new product launched from within an existing company.)

TRACTION GAP VALUE INFLECTION POINTS

A quick word about the acronyms you see on this graph, as I will be using them throughout this text.

Startups must successfully reach a series of increasing value inflection points in their path along the Traction Gap. These points include:

Minimum Viable Category (MVC): Reaching this value inflection point is a critical part of the market-engineering process. You must develop and validate the name and definition of the category your startup is attempting to create or redefine—and provide evidence that it is capable of supporting a startup. MVC is a key part of the Traction Gap Framework. Before you even start developing your product, you need to think about the category you must create (or disrupt) and define. Playing in someone else's category is fraught with peril and results in many startup failures. This marketing milestone must be reached well before entering the Traction Gap.

Initial Product Release (IPR): First publicly deployed product iteration. IPR is when the startup first makes its product generally available to the public. In many cases, this is the "Beta" version of the product. At this stage, the team is seeking customer validation metrics to prove it has developed an MVP. This milestone signals entry into the Traction Gap.

Minimum Viable Product (MVP): The product has achieved minimal customer validation metrics and product/market fit. Marc Andreessen defines product/market fit as follows: "Product/market fit means being in a good market with a product that can satisfy that market."[4] MVP is a debated term, but at Wildcat we subscribe to the following definition:

Minimum Viable Product is the most pared-down version of a product that will be purchased or used by customers. And, as you will read, we believe that MVP goes beyond basic product-engineering: it must also include market-engineering elements.

Minimum Viable Repeatability (MVR): My Wildcat partner Bryan Stolle identified and named this critical value inflection point. At MVR, you should have a solution-grade product, business model, and repeatable sales/marketing. We define MVR as the smallest amount of repeatability a startup can execute to demonstrate its business-model feasibility and product/market fit. MVR is a critical value inflection point for most startups. At MVR, the startup has demonstrated that it has some understanding as to "how" and "why" customers and users are acquired. It now knows a significant amount about its target market, has semi-effective product positioning, a reasonable sales pitch, a handle on the primary sales objections, and rational responses to them. It also has a few reference customers. The startup is now safe to hire a small number of salespeople, can invest in marketing and lead generation, and can expect them to be fairly effective. That said, repeatability is not just about sales. The startup should have also demonstrated product-release repeatability, implementation-success repeatability (real customers or consumers using the product and getting real value), and some marketing and lead generation repeatability.

Minimum Viable Traction (MVT): MVR + multiple quarters of growth. MVT is a point in time when many—if not most—of the mid- to late-stage venture firms will begin to aggressively reach out to find out more about your startup and compete to invest in it. To reach the point of Minimum Viable Traction (MVT), startups must build upon the lessons they learned reaching MVR. They now must scale successively quarter over quarter for the next 12 to 18 months. Reaching MVT signals the company's exit from the Traction Gap and entry into the go-to-scale phase.

These milestones represent critical moments in time for a startup. As you will see, in the fast-moving world of business in the 21st century, there is only a brief amount of time to go from one Traction Gap value inflection point to the next. I spend a significant amount of time in the beginning of this book explaining each Traction Gap value inflection point and its importance, so that we are speaking the same language before we get there.

Ultimately, startups must raise enough capital to ensure that they do not fall short of reaching the next Traction Gap value inflection point using the capital raised in the prior round. Otherwise, they will face significant challenges or even potential dissolution.

THE FOUR CORE ARCHITECTURAL PILLARS

So far, we've looked only at the milestones in the early-stage development of a new startup (or corporate new-product initiative). But, in fact, it is not a monolithic enterprise that marches down this path. Rather, as this chart shows, it is the four core architectures of an enterprise—product, revenue, team, and systems—that must successfully complete this journey, including traversing the Traction Gap.

Architectural Pillars

| PRODUCT | REVENUE | TEAM | SYSTEMS |

FIGURE 5

All startups—at all stages—must develop competencies in these four architectures, then continue to measure, refine, and optimize each of them along the entire path to MVT and beyond.

I want to make a critical point here: that for each Traction Gap milestone, you must satisfy the revenue, product, team, and systems requirements associated with that specific milestone before you begin moving to the next. Failure to do so can, and often does, lead to excessive delays and use of capital, thereby significantly compromising your ability to reach the next value inflection point with the amount of capital you have in the bank. And failure to reach that next value inflection point on your current capital can substantially compromise your ability to raise any future capital. Better to take a little extra time to make sure you are ready—across all four architectures—before taking off to the next value inflection point.

Let's look at each of these architectures in turn:

Product Architecture

A startup's Product Architecture includes the set of technologies, applications, and features that comprise its offerings. A well thought-out Product Architecture enables a startup to achieve rapid product/market fit through customer validation, as well as to sign on the partners needed to complete the whole product offering.

Sometimes, in spite of early product acceptance, a team may discover that it needs to pivot its product, change positioning, or add significant capabilities in order to secure sustainable fit in a viable market category. This pivot is neither rare nor a sign of failure—some great companies started out intending to be entirely different enterprises.

For example, Slack began its life as a company called Tiny Speck. It built a massive multiplayer online game called Glitch. After nearly four years from its founding, it threw in the towel on Glitch for a variety of business and technical reasons.

But Tiny Speck, in order to provide its team with better internal communications, had created a collaboration application built on top of Internet Relay Chat (IRC) technology. Using the application, their team could easily post, view, and respond to content and conversations exchanged over a variety of channels.

The team decided this collaboration application worked so well for themselves that they should bring it to market. They began working in earnest to do this in November 2012 and, based on user downloads and usage, they won the support of their investors and persuaded them to stick with this "pivot."

Tiny Speck launched Slack—which stands for Searchable Log of All Communication and Knowledge—to a small number of companies in May 2013. In August 2013, the company opened access up to a wider audience. Within 24 hours, Slack signed up 8,000 companies, and the total increased to 15,000 companies in two weeks. Slack officially launched in February 2014, and the company was renamed Slack Technologies in August 2014.

As of the writing of this book, Slack was valued at more than $7B. Nice pivot, Slack team!

In such cases, early-stage investors must be prepared to provide more time and capital if they believe significant value creation is likely. Startup teams must ensure that true customer validation has been achieved to avoid premature expansion and the accompanying dangerous waste of capital. Instead, they must have the patience to postpone expensive go-to-market scaling until such a fit has been confirmed.

Of the four elements critical to MVR, the Product Architecture is where early-stage startups tend to have the most well-developed plans and expertise. That's not surprising, given that most of these entrepreneurs start a company in the first place to pursue a product idea.

Revenue Architecture

A startup's Revenue Architecture is defined by its business model and its ability to monetize awareness, engagement, and sustained usage. When a startup reaches a Minimum Viable Product (MVP), it has validated a set of value propositions, but it will likely still be experimenting with business models and processes that convert awareness and interest into revenue.

For B2C (or B2B2C) startups, this process normally translates into testing techniques that:

- Optimize Lifetime Value (LTV) to Customer Acquisition Cost (CAC) ratios (including organic as well as paid acquisition);

- Create efficient supply-side acquisition in the case of marketplaces;
- Experiment with margin on transaction fees, subscriptions, etc., building toward positive unit economics and contribution margins;
- Increase engagement of Monthly Active Users (MAU) and Daily Active Users (DAU); and
- Build repeatable and scalable geographic or market segment roll-out strategies for multiple consumer marketplaces and services.

For B2B, Revenue Architecture involves strategies to:

- Lower Customer Acquisition Costs (CAC);
- Identify up-sell opportunities;
- Increase usage rates; and
- Optimize Top of the Funnel (TOTF), Middle of the Funnel (MOTF), and Bottom of the Funnel (BOTF) conversion rates.

B2B Funnel

INQUIRY

MARKETING QUALIFICATION

SALES QUALIFICATION

CLOSE

FIGURE 6

Whatever the product and business model, entrepreneurs must build critical momentum. That's because a deficiency in Revenue Architecture poses the greatest near-term risk of failure. It is this momentum that enables start-ups to exit from the Traction Gap with sustained, significant growth and usage rates that exceed the competition and your target expectations.

As I mentioned previously, despite the desire of most startups to begin scaling prior to reaching MVR, such a tactic can be disastrous both for the startup and its investors, consuming a significant amount of capital with little growth to show for it. This premature scaling can result in a material down-round, layoffs, significant employee ownership dilution, and even shutdown due to lack of investor interest. This is why entrepreneurs must carefully evaluate and objectively decide when their startup has truly reached its MVR.

Between MVR and MVT, the challenge for entrepreneurs is to determine when, where, and how to optimally scale: should they look at new geographies, move into new industries, or a new market segment (e.g., from small to medium businesses into large enterprises)?

Team Architecture

Early-stage startups often have small product-oriented teams, and have not yet hired a complete management team or other personnel needed to scale the company. Competition for A-level employees is fierce, further impeding a startup's ability to scale. Many times, the wrong people are hired for the wrong role, or early team members are unable to scale with the startup. Other times, the founding team may pull together a good core management team, but then lack a comprehensive strategy to address the extended team of the board of directors, customer advisory board, products council, employee advisory group, etc.

Getting the Team Architecture right is key to reaching MVR on the path to MVT. We have seen this play out in startups countless times. Entrepreneurs must learn how to systematically build up their teams and dramatically reduce the team dynamic risk.

Experienced investors know that one of the biggest risks leading to startup failure is associated with dysfunctional teams. For example, these teams might include people who were great contributors early on but fail to scale or, under increasing pressure, become toxic to other team members. The more you can fill out your management team and the longer you work together, the less risk there is in the eyes of the investment community.

I want to spend some time on the topic of team here, because team is the number one issue of concern cited by every CEO and founder we interviewed via the Traction Gap Institute.

The Traction Gap Institute (TGI)—www.tractiongap.com—was founded by Wildcat Venture Partners to help entrepreneurs traverse the Traction Gap. Anyone can become a member, at no cost. One of the benefits of the TGI is the networking events where we interview successful founders, hear from industry experts, and explore topics and issues related to product, revenue, team, and systems.

One of the TGI's partners is Velocity, a research and consulting firm located in Silicon Valley. Velocity worked with the TGI and our Wildcat team to interview founders/CEOs of technology companies such as CouchBase, Egnyte, Eloqua, Marketo, Medallia, ServiceMax, Veeva, and many others.

The interviews focused on the founding CEOs and executives and their journeys from Initial Product Release to Minimum Viable Traction, specifically looking at the four Architecture Pillars of the Traction Gap.

Given the startup community's fascination with product and issues surrounding Minimum Viable Product, you might have expected these CEOs and/or founders to say that product is everything. If so, you would be wrong. The fact is, you can't win with product unless you are supported by good people, a clear customer focus, and a path to profit, revenue, and growth.

Overwhelmingly, the entrepreneurs interviewed said that having the right team and culture in place played a bigger role in their company's success. Velocity found that 82 percent of those surveyed *started building their culture on day one*, looking for individuals who were willing to make similar sacrifices, had a strong work ethic and an intellectual curiosity, shared the same values, and were top-performing "A players."

This was definitely the case for Marketo, a poster child for making it through the Traction Gap. I was fortunate to be a first investor in Marketo, a board member of the company from inception through IPO, and had the opportunity to work with Marketo chairman, CEO, and founder Phil Fernandez.

I can attest to the team and focus on culture that Phil placed from the earliest days.

In our interviews with Phil and other successful startup teams, most told us they believed that the founders are the ones responsible for building culture from day 1. While I don't recall whether Marketo had a formal written playbook describing its culture, I do recall that the Marketo management team had a strong belief system that focused on diversity, gender equality, and a passion for customers.

The Velocity survey data showed that focusing on team issues too late slowed down progress for 18 percent of the companies. In hindsight, those companies realized that they needed to act faster to make corrections if their hires didn't fit the company culture.

In our interviews, one executive commented that there's no "perfect team," and changing requirements in a fast-growing company may make it difficult for some individuals to keep up. He explained that in one case he hired, then fired, his first head of sales within that person's first six weeks on the job, as soon as he realized the fit wasn't right.

Some of the biggest disappointments were the times a CEO had to tell an executive that they weren't the right person for that stage of the company. Knowing that the team is what's important in the end, meant doing what was right for the company.

This experience was echoed in the responses heard again and again from the CEOs we interviewed. In fact, one executive surveyed admitted that waiting too long to get rid of a "toxic" person cost the company 18 months in delays. That's right, he thought they could have reached Minimum Viable Traction—the monumental stage when a company is ready to scale and has traversed the Traction Gap—18 months earlier had they quickly eliminated just one employee.

Other interesting takeaways from the TGI research included:

- ► 75 percent of the successful companies cultivated a customer-centric culture, which entailed learning what customers wanted before building any product. Executives said discovering customers' pain points is key because they will be willing to pay for you to ease that pain. In the next chapter, I'm going to show you why being customer-centric alone is insufficient to succeed.
- ► 60 percent focused on building a sales-oriented culture in the early stages. That culture must embrace experimentation and continuous improvement, so the company can deliver a product that customers are ready to pay for, even before the official launch.

One executive explained how they developed a strong feedback loop between their customers and the sales group. This close relationship resulted in a core group of loyal users who were instrumental in evangelizing the company's solution and building a paid user base. This circle of friends grew to include others not connected to the company, such as analysts and press. A piece of advice we were given from one executive: conduct yourself in a way where people want you to be successful . . . and remember, you don't have to win every battle to win the war.

Systems Architecture

The systems and processes of a startup can either help it accelerate growth or hold it back. A successful Systems Architecture must integrate front and back offices, establish transparent performance metrics, and cultivate the progressive cultures needed to succeed.

When we invest in early-stage startups, many of them are using a rudimentary CRM implementation for sales and support, a basic development system, perhaps a simple e-commerce platform for the web, and most typically outsource their back-office functions such as payroll. Once we invest, we ask them to architect—not necessarily yet implement—back and front office systems and processes they will require for the kind of growth they will ultimately need to support.

By the time they reach Minimum Viable Traction, startups should be using relatively sophisticated platforms with refined business processes.

In addition to operational systems, startups must ensure that they have a well-designed development stack: the suite of applications that a startup uses to manage its development process. We have found that the type of engineering management infrastructure a startup elects to use can negatively impact margins and prevent the company from scaling later on. This upgrading process must be thoughtful and systematic, with one eye on the future.

Having worked with so many high-growth technology startups, we counsel founders and teams to build systems and processes with the right foundation early so that operational efficiency can fuel, as well as keep pace with, growth—while also minimizing the amount of financing required.

Once a startup has demonstrated mastery over these four architecture areas, acquired a meaningful cohort of customers using its now-proven go-to-market strategy, and executed four or more quarters of successive growth, it is prepared to declare MVT.

HOW TO USE THE TRACTION GAP FRAMEWORK

The Traction Gap stretches from a startup's Initial Product Release—typically a year or so into its existence—to Minimum Viable Traction, which can occur as much as three years later, when it has achieved a certain level of revenue growth, engagement, downloads, or usage. These variables signify market validation and positive growth.

In other words, the Traction Gap is the all-important 36-month span that determines whether the company will thrive or die.

As already noted, there is little data or advisory support available for teams entering the Traction Gap. Worse, we have discovered that while many startups typically apply rigor and discipline to the development of their products, they more often rely upon myth and lore when it comes to team building, marketing, and sales.

Too many of these teams release a product and then squander valuable capital and time experimenting with a variety of marketing programs, positioning statements, user-acquisition strategies, pricing models, onboarding schemes, and sales tactics. Then, as the initial capital begins to dwindle, the team and its investors grow increasingly nervous as they realize that the company has failed to generate sufficient traction to secure interest from new—or even current—investors. At this point, the company faces a shutdown or is forced to sell its assets at a substantial loss.

What is going on? Why is a process involving billions of dollars of investment and run by some of the smartest people in the business world operating at such a low level of success?

———

In the chapters that follow, I am going to show you how to navigate the perils of the Traction Gap—using a new set of milestones, processes, and tactics—to emerge successfully on the other side.

I end subsequent chapters by introducing the "Traction Gap Hack," the anecdotal, how-to-do-it section you will find following the information in each subsequent chapter. Here is a commentary by the founder of a company that has adopted the Traction Gap model—and that wishes to share some of the techniques it learned along the way.

———

Jamie Miller is the CEO of Amplero. Amplero positions itself as an "Artificial Intelligence Marketing (AIM) company that enables business-to-consumer (B2C) marketers at global brands to build lasting customer relationships at a scale not humanly possible. Amplero's award-winning AIM technology experiments, learns, and optimizes each interaction as customer relationships evolve."

Here is how Jamie describes their use of the Traction Gap Framework:

The management team was first introduced to Bill Ericson and Bruce Cleveland at Wildcat Venture Partners through a joint relationship at RocketFuel, where Bill Ericson sat on the board. When I joined the company as CEO, I was introduced to the Traction Gap Framework and its concepts. The approach immediately made sense to me.

I was impressed with the simplicity of the model and its relevance, and have used it to align our objectives top to bottom throughout the company. In fact, we have organized our board meetings around the four Traction Gap Architecture Pillars—product, revenue, team, and systems—to explain to the board what we've done, where we are, where we need to go, and what we need to do to get there.

For our board meetings, we make the board aware of several high-level accomplishments/issues. We typically do this with a slide called "Bottom 3/Top 3." These include the three biggest challenges or downside developments in the business, such as product delays, deal slippage, customer issues, or even negative team dynamics, and three of the most positive accomplishments, such as new customers, product shipments, and staff members, that have affected Amplero since the last board meeting. We use this as a way to inform the board of our most pressing matters and focus conversation in the board meeting.

The slide immediately after "Bottom 3/Top 3" is the "FY Goals" slide. We break this slide into four quadrants—Product Architecture and Revenue Architecture on the upper/bottom left of the slide. Team Architecture and Systems Architecture are on the upper/bottom right of the slide.

In each quadrant, we list out the high-level FY goals/objectives we have set for ourselves for that particular Traction Gap architectural pillar. To the right of the text that identifies the goal/objective, we use a rectangle colored red, green, or yellow—based upon the executive team's assessment of where we are against the goal.

This approach allows us to quickly convey to our team and the board where we believe we are succeeding and where we are not, relative to our operating plan for the year. We spend little time on the green rectangles; we focus the board meeting on the yellow and red ones. This allows us to talk about key issues and get the board's input efficiently and effectively. We use a similar approach in our weekly executive staff meetings.

We have found the Traction Gap Framework taxonomy and principles to be an invaluable way to think about and manage Amplero. Companies of any size developing a new product and business to address an emerging market opportunity would be well served to use the Traction Gap Framework.

PART

GETTING THERE

Slides 1–28 "Go-to-Product"

2

APPLYING THE TRACTION GAP FRAMEWORK

Alas, time is not a luxury that startups have if they want or need to raise venture capital. Venture investors seek traction—increasing growth rates—over anything else. In general, profitability only becomes a factor for investors once a company has become a market leader and growth begins to taper off. Even then, profitability takes a back seat, as investors have learned that they are rewarded for growth over nearly any other business metric.

As a result, traction is a powerful investment decision factor for venture investors. You must show increasing traction at each Traction Gap value inflection point.

Your mission is to use early-stage venture capital to achieve product/market fit as rapidly as possible, and then raise additional venture capital at each successive value inflection point by demonstrating increased traction through metrics such as revenue, usage rates, downloads, etc.

————

As I explained in the beginning of this book, if you are in search of venture capital, you need to build two products—one a business or consumer offering, and the other a financial offering for investors.

The Traction Gap Framework is designed to help you develop a well-grounded operating plan with strategies and tactics that enable you to build traction and scale. More importantly, the Traction Gap Framework will help you build a financial product, one specifically that venture investors will back.

You may wonder why, if you can grow organically through your profits, you might consider taking venture capital. If you have no competition—and don't expect to have any in the foreseeable future—then self-financing through your profits might be a perfectly viable strategy. But if a competitor emerges in your category, and that competitor is better capitalized than you, that entity may be able to grow more quickly, having the financial capacity to invest more than you can in engineering, sales, and marketing, and thereby diminish your ability to compete and survive.

Additionally, depending upon the industry you are in and the products you are creating, many venture investors can help you; most have networks that you can tap into for hiring needs, customer introductions, and other key resources that you may require. These are some of several legitimate reasons to take venture capital even if you believe you can grow organically without it.

Venture capital is the most expensive source of capital you will secure—you have to give up ownership in your company in exchange for it. Therefore, it is important to understand why you want it, when you want it, what you are going to use it for, who you want to take it from, and how you'll spend it: as wisely and miserly as you can!

Once you've made the decision that you want to raise venture capital, your objective from that point onward should be to maximize the probability of

ing the amount of

are so popular. They are
apital to see if they can
rate significant returns
what excites entrepre-

ore than 30,000 new
hem fail. If you are
even higher: more
m Viable Category,
go to market in the

need to reach the
and even the tim-

understand the
to attract ven-
ftware startups,
imilar for start-

lic software
Salesforce,

about one
e (getting
place in
year) to
as data-
to reach

k the CEO can dele-
This requires relation-
—which takes time.
ount of time and effort
building your business.

es a factor. The amount of
ap value inflection point to
to generate interest by ven-

cessfully raise capital have not
h a venture firm, few will have
to share with you here. But the
od back-of-the-envelope metrics
ey just have not been forthcoming

and meet with a venture firm with
concludes the meeting with some-
making a lot of progress. Let's circle
e doing," then you don't yet have trac-
citing enough for the firm to consider

flection points are valid for any startup, the
een those value inflection points will vary,
you are building and the markets you serve.
mount of time between Ideation and Initial
ignificantly between a consumer mobile appli-
ase company. The former can usually get to an
n take several years and will require a lot more
arket fit.

This is just one reason why consumer applications
relatively fast to build, don't typically require much c
achieve product/market fit, and, if successful, can gene
more quickly than most business applications. This is
neurs and investors alike.

That said, according to a recent blog post, each year n
consumer products are launched—and 80 percent of
building a consumer software product, the numbers are
than 90 percent fail.[1] This is why defining your Minimu
doing statistically valid market research, and preparing to
go-to-product phase are so critical to your success.

Startups building products for businesses and consumer
same Traction Gap value inflection points, but the metrics
ing tend to be different.

What I am about to share with you should help you bette
metrics—the velocity of growth—you need to achieve in ord
ture investors. The examples I show are primarily for B2B so
but the timing between value inflection points is surprisingly s
ups with other offerings and business models.

THE METRICS

The following metrics come from examining the data from pub
companies—the ones we are all familiar with, such as Marketo,
and Workday—when they were small private companies.

As I pointed out previously, most B2B software startups take
year to one and a half years from Ideation to Initial Product Releas
to MVC is part of "market-engineering"; this process should take
parallel with creating your IPR), and another half a year (up to one
reach Minimum Viable Product. For more complex offerings—such
base or platform software—it can take two, three, or more years just

Traction Gap Timeline

FIGURE 7

These time frames can vary dependent upon the complexity of the product and market.

IPR. The amount of time to IPR and the capital required to build the product can and does vary greatly during this go-to-product phase.

Consumer software startups often can get to IPR with a few people and in a few months and with far less capital. B2B startups typically require much longer to get to IPR, as the products are more complex and they require people with significant computer science and domain expertise. That said, consumer products aren't cheap downstream; once they reach product/market fit, they require significant amounts of capital to scale.

The most difficult question startups must answer during the go-to-product phase is whether they can develop tangible proof that if they successfully build a product—even if their initial market feedback is positive—will consumers or businesses actually purchase and use it?

Angel and venture investors who invest in startups during the go-to-product phase must rely mainly upon their intuition rather than copious evidence of a market or actual business metrics. I like to call early-stage investors "slideshow investors," because for the most part that's all there typically is to go on when making an investment decision! In contrast, I call the mid- to later-stage investors "spreadsheet investors," because they have the advantage of being able to look at spreadsheets and evaluate actual business performance. Early-stage investors tend to be informed (well . . . sometimes not that informed) speculators who believe that a potentially large addressable market exists for a particular product and that the product team they are investing in are rock stars.

Many of the best-known venture firms employ growth-sniffers (people who track websites, social media, and other sources of digital data to identify start-ups that are gaining traction) and analysts who meet with entrepreneurs to track startups early, but hold off from investing until they see that the startup is close to MVR or MVT.

They can wait because they have "brand power" that enables them to get into and win competitive investment opportunities. Lesser-known venture firms many times must invest in startups at an earlier stage—with more as-sumed risk—or lose out to firms with more significant brands.

This is just one of the several reasons the better-known venture firms can generate better returns than other venture firms; their reputation (brand) affords them the opportunity to see more startups when they are working— that is, generating traction. Even if they have to invest at higher valuations, by investing in the best of the startups, they benefit from correspondingly lower failure rates.

This doesn't mean that the best-known venture firms won't invest in the early go-to-product phase, even at Ideation. They absolutely will—and often do—if they have a deep conviction about a certain market opportunity and the founders have great credentials.

TICK TOCK

In general, the Traction Gap clock—the amount of time it takes to get from Initial Product Release to Minimum Viable Traction—doesn't begin to run in earnest until a startup reaches Minimum Viable Product. And the good news is that the startup is in control over when it decides to declare MVP.

The bad news is that public software companies have generated a fairly well-known revenue growth curve from Ideation that private startups need to match or beat if they want venture investors to get excited about them.

Most real revenue growth doesn't begin until a startup reaches MVP, so that is where I will begin.

From when they declared MVP, the most successful public software companies using a subscription model (SaaS) on average were able to generate $1M annual recurring revenue (ARR) by the end of their first year in market. By the end of the second year, they were able to generate at least $3M in ARR. At the end of year 3, these companies were generating at least $10M in ARR.

It looks like this:

■ ARR Per Year After Reaching MVP ■

ANNUAL RECURRING REVENUE (ARR)			
MVP	Year 1	Year 2	Year 3
$0	$1M	$3M	$10M

So if you want to be on an equal or better revenue growth path than these successful predecessors, this is the model upon which you need to build your operating plan.

Let's assume you believe your average Annual Contract Value (ACV) for each customer will be $30K. To match the better SaaS companies' revenue growth model, you need to reach $1M ARR by the end of Y1 from MVP with a total of 33 paying customers.

ARR GOAL: Desired ARR / ACV = # of needed accounts

For most SaaS companies, the value inflection point of MVR is about $2M ARR and, to be on model, you should reach this critical value inflection point within one and a half years from MVP. Assuming that a typical deal generates an average of $30K in Annual Contract Value, this means you will have approximately 66 paying customers.

By this time, you should have delivered several releases of your product, hired multiple people for various business functions, and begun to have a sense of your sales cycle. The metrics of your business should now emerge so you understand what type of pipeline coverage you need to generate monthly new customer targets, revenues, and what your customer acquisition costs average.

Just prior to reaching MVR is the time when you should expect to invest in developing full-scale marketing and sales functions. As I noted previously, scaling before reaching MVR is ill advised. The cost of building a growth engine is expensive; and if you don't have well-honed value propositions, and absolute product/market fit, you can rapidly deplete cash reserves with little revenue to show for it.

Prior to MVR, the *entire* management team should be actively involved in selling activities and focused on learning which value propositions, demonstrations, features, et al. are persuasive with potential buyers/users. Knowing this enables the product marketing, marketing, and sales teams to build marketing and sales enablement content and tools that everyone can have some confidence will work in preparation for scaling.

By the end of the second year after MVP, to be on a similar growth model to the best public software companies when they were at your stage, you should be at $3M ARR; and by end of the third year from MVP, assuming your average ACV per customer remains at $30K, you will need at least 333 customers to be generating $10M ARR. You can easily close 33 customers without a growth engine in place, but once you double this and reach MVR, you will need to have a well-functioning growth team in place if you want to reach MVT ($6M ARR) on your way to $10M ARR by the end of your third year in market.

If you can reach MVT ($6M ARR) within two and a half years from the time you declare MVP, the best known—and for sure the unknown—venture firms will take notice of your company. They will have heard about you and will reach out. Guaranteed.

BUILDING YOUR OPERATING MODEL

You can build your operating model around these "facts" and use your assumed average Annual Contract Value, Customer Acquisition Cost (CAC), and Customer Acquisition Cost Ratio to determine how much capital you will need to reach each of the Traction Gap value inflection points.

I would model Worst, Expect, and Best CAC Ratios of two, one, and one half for this exercise, implying a two-year, one-year, and one-half-year payback respectively, built off your assumed average Annual Contract Value.

A good "rule of thumb" for early-stage startups that haven't yet reached MVT is that sales and marketing expenses should be about half the cost of running your company per month/year. So, if you want to drive the formula using this logic, then you should budget half of your monthly expenditures on engineering, GA, systems, etc., and the other half on sales and marketing expenditures.

Average net monthly burn is best kept to $150K to $250K or less while you get from MVP to MVR, and no more than $500K per month post-MVR but pre-MVT. After MVT, your net burn may be allowed to increase if you can demonstrate to your investors that this investment is generating faster growth and market share. But at this high net burn rate, you are rapidly burning a lot of valuable capital. So you need to ensure that you monitor your key growth metrics (e.g., CAC, CAC ratio, bookings backlog, billings) every month; and if your growth rate diminishes, that you are prepared and able to take swift action to curb the net burn.

Again, the top public SaaS companies have established a revenue growth model that other SaaS companies must meet or beat.

On average, they have grown from MVP as follows:

Y1 = $1M ending ARR
Y2 = $3M ending ARR
Y3 = $10M ending ARR
Y4 = $25M ending ARR
Y5 = $50M ending ARR

I will expand on this topic in Chapter 7, "The Final Sprint to Minimum Viable Traction."

DEVELOPING A CAPITALIZATION STRATEGY

You need capital to hire a team, develop a product, take that product to market, and invest in the systems that support all your business functions. In other words, capital is the foundation that girds the four Traction Gap Architecture Pillars—product, revenue, team, and systems. Where you get your capital may be optional, but going without it is not.

Consequently, you need to develop a capitalization strategy from the inception of your startup.

One of the many questions I'm asked about this topic is "How much capital should I raise?" The simplest answer is: as much as you can, at a valuation you can live with, and at least enough to reach the next successive Traction Gap value inflection point and slightly beyond.

To address this, I constructed this chart, generated from industry data, to give you a better idea of what you can expect:

■ **Startup Capital Needs for Each Value Inflection Point** ■

	IDEA/MVC /IPR	MVP	MVR	MVT
Capital Raised at This TG Inflection Point	$1M	$5M	$11M	$20M
Pre-Money Valuation	$5.3M	$14.2M	$40M	$77M
Valuation Step Up from Ideation	N/A	3x	8x	15x
Dilution from Prior Round	16%	26%	22%	21%

The data suggests that from Ideation through MVT, a successful technology startup can expect to raise about $37M and give up 38 percent of ownership through dilution—if it does everything right. This calculation does not account for dilution from increases to employee stock option pools.

These are *median* values—and these funding rounds (Seed, Series A, B, C, etc.) are not precisely tied to Traction Gap value inflection points. But these funding rounds are linked to startups that are, for the most part, successfully generating traction—or else they would be unlikely to raise new capital.

The main point here is that if you hit all the Traction Gap value inflection points on the time scale I've laid out, you should be able to raise similar amounts or more of capital at equal or potentially higher pre-money valuations. A word of advice: until you are beyond MVT, I would not concentrate as much on valuation. Yes, it's important, but at this stage the more important issue for you is securing the capital you need to continue.

RISK MANAGEMENT

Your focus should be on having enough capital to reach a value inflection point where your startup is viewed as "less risky"—and therefore more valuable—than it was the last time you sought capital.

What does "less risky" mean? It varies based upon stage. It can mean you built the product you said you would in the time frame you set for yourself. You found multiple customers or consumers who would buy/use your product. You demonstrated that you could acquire new users cost-effectively. Or you are rapidly scaling quarter over quarter.

My Wildcat partner, Geoffrey Moore, wrote the following, which I think sums up the "risk" issue nicely:

> There are no hard and fast rules here, but one way to calibrate a venture valuation model is by what risks you have taken off the table. For example:
>
> Technology risk is often the first one to tackle. A seed round of funding might go to proving technical feasibility for a product idea. If proof of concept is achieved, then technology risk can be said to have been taken off the table, and the company's valuation should reflect that.
>
> Product risk is another step in the journey—can you deliver a

minimum viable product, and can you get at least a few customers to buy it, use it, and be a reference for it going forward? If so, that takes another risk off the table.

Market risk is a third category—can you cross the chasm from early adopters and find at least one target market segment that will adopt your new offer with enthusiasm? If so, your company is well on its way to being a going concern, and that takes a whole bunch of risk off the table.

Team risk is a fourth area—can you successfully recruit high-quality leaders with strong resumes that demonstrate they know what they are doing when it comes to building out a new company? Will they come work for you? If so, that sends a great signal to the next-round investor.

Financing and systems risk is a fifth area—having proven you can make the top line, can you make the rest of the P&L work as well? Can you put the systems in place needed to operate effectively and efficiently at scale? Can you get to escape velocity on the capital plan in place? If so, you protect your current investors' ownership from further dilution.

Execution risk is a sixth area—have you consistently demonstrated that you are able to do what you said you were going to do? Can you forecast accurately and then meet or beat your numbers quarter after quarter? That's what it takes to do a successful IPO and to keep your valuation in the quarters thereafter.

Now every one of these risks is something that keeps a venture investor up at night, so the sooner you can take any one of them off the table and do so definitively, the better. That said, "definitive progress" is often in the eye of the beholder. Given such ambiguity, it is critical to get agreement with your prospective investors as to what state change they think they are funding, what milestones they think will clearly demonstrate to a new investor that it has been achieved, and then together with them make a bet on that model being right. The more experienced your prospective investors, the better your odds will be, for these are the folks that have seen this movie many times before.[2]

CAPITAL MANAGEMENT

Earlier in the chapter, I provided you with a chart that outlined the approximate median values raised by startups at various Traction Gap value inflection points. But that doesn't tell you exactly how much you should raise or how much you should be spending at any given stage. Again, venture capital is expensive. You are exchanging points of ownership for dollars that you can apply against your product, revenue, team, and systems requirements. So it's critical that you make significant progress with that capital and that you spend it wisely.

So, how should you think about spending this capital? Well, the answer to that question depends upon how much you were able to successfully raise, what stage you are in, and what risk you're willing to assume. What I'm about to share with you is not solely based on industry data; it also includes my personal experience working with many different startups over the prior decade. Thus, this information has some subjective opinion heaped on top, so use it accordingly.

▪ Capital Expenditures ▪

	IDEA/MVC /IPR	MVP	MVR	MVT
Revenue (ARR)	$0	$0	$2M	$6M
Max Monthly Net Cash Burn	$100K	$250K	$500K	$750K
% R&D Spend	80%	80%	70%	50%
% Sales & Marketing Spend	0%	0%	10%	35%
% Sales/Marketing Split	0%	0%	70/30%	70/30%
% G&A Spend	20%	20%	20%	15%

(continues)

	IDEA/MVC /IPR	MVP	MVR	MVT
CAC Ratio (Median)	0	0	2	1.2
% Gross Margin (License)	0%	0%	78%	78%
% Churn Rate (Median)	0%	0%	10%	10%
Headcount	4–6	10–12	15–25	35–50

Depending on where you are located geographically, you should expect to pay about $15K to $20K per month per Full Time Equivalent (FTE) employee. Once you have reached Minimum Viable Repeatability, you should be generating revenue (e.g., $2M ARR), which should give you additional operating capital on top of the capital you raised previously to invest in more R&D, Sales & Marketing resources, or to simply extend your cash run-out date to remove more risk from the business before raising your next round of funding.

With respect to spending, for SaaS business models there is a generally agreed-upon concept called "The Rule of 40%." This rule requires you to add your annual growth rate to your EBITDA percent (which can be, and most often is, negative). If the result is 40 percent or greater, you're in good shape. The purpose of this metric is to prevent "growth at all costs" operating models.

That said, McKinsey issued a report a few years ago that looked at more than 3,000 software companies over a 32-year period and determined that growth rate was the single most important variable, by a wide margin, in determining value. And while you may have a small startup, as I stated earlier, the truth is that venture investors value growth over almost anything else.

When you are an early-stage startup, investors are primarily concerned about whether you can continue to scale at previous rates (e.g., will your growth taper out due to competition?) or you can manage external growth so that your internal systems and governance scale accordingly and don't cause customer, employee, and/or other related issues.

If you're growing more than 100 percent per year, continuously, investors will help you finance that growth. They may ask you to try to improve your CAC ratio, gross margins, and a few other metrics, but for the most part they will be cheering you on.

KEY TAKEAWAYS

At the Ideation stage of your startup, we believe team members should be focused on statistically verifying that any product or service concept has merit in the market and that the product or service can be developed and brought to market cost-effectively and with relative certainty.

PRODUCT

Product—The company should perform quantitative and qualitative market research and document that research to statistically validate the overall market opportunity. In addition, the team should have a really good idea of how it will build the product or service and how much time and personnel are required to reach IPR.

REVENUE

Revenue—The management team should explore potential business models—and remain flexible—along with a few hypotheses regarding what it believes it will take to identify consumers/customers and to monetize them. This exploration process should

(continues)

include basic assumptions regarding the total addressable market size, customer/consumer acquisition techniques, pricing models, customer/consumer acquisition costs, sales cycles, etc.

TEAM

Team—At this stage, members of the team should have relevant subject-matter expertise and consist only of people who can determine what product/service needs to be developed and people who can actually develop the product/service. There should be a rough organization chart of what additional product/service skills need to be hired at subsequent Traction Gap value inflection points. Anyone who isn't contributing significantly to getting to an IPR should be replaced as rapidly as possible.

SYSTEMS

Systems—Not much needs to happen at this stage with respect to systems. The team should acquire basic tools that enable them to communicate and collaborate effectively and share information easily. Applications such as email, spreadsheets, collaboration software, word processing and engineering applications (e.g., build/QA system, bug database, user stories) are typically sufficient at this point. Once the team becomes a legal entity, it should also have systems in place to track expenses, payments, equity, hiring, payroll, benefits, etc.

• • •

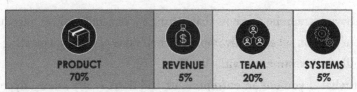

TRACTION GAP ARCHITECTURAL PILLARS

—————— IDEATION ——————

PRODUCT	REVENUE	TEAM	SYSTEMS
70%	5%	20%	5%

FIGURE 8

Percentage of emphasis at this stage.

The following are the key principles Wildcat Venture Partners looks for at Ideation.

▪ Traction Gap Principles ▪
IDEATION

Product	Focus on product-engineering tasks: Perform statistically valid market research and prioritize initial product features based upon that market research.
Revenue	Focus on market-engineering tasks: Build draft business model and initial value propositions—estimate customer acquisition costs and marketing/sales funnel conversion rates.
Team	Invest solely in people who can specify and build the product.
Systems	Implement basic systems for engineering, collaboration, and back-office functions.

• • •

TRACTION GAP HACKS ▶ IDEATION

Raising Venture Capital

Most savvy entrepreneurs know that getting a warm and positive introduction to a venture firm substantially improves their odds of getting a meeting—and hopefully an investment—with that firm.

But what if you are an entrepreneur and don't really know anyone at a venture firm?

Many startups are now using LinkedIn to initially contact potential venture investors. I get a lot of unsolicited requests from entrepreneurs this way. I pass on almost all of them for a variety of reasons, but I always try to quickly scan the opportunity and provide thoughtful reasons for why I'm passing.

So if you don't have a relationship with a venture firm or specific venture investor, or know anyone who does—how do you get an opportunity to present your startup idea?

Here's an approach—along with some simple modern tools you can use—to increase the likelihood of getting that meeting. Note that this is a multi-step process.

First, you need to target the right firm. Venture firms and their partners tend to invest across two dimensions—investment stage and investment type. Seldom do firms invest in all stages across all investment types—only the largest firms can afford to do that.

In particular, venture firms may invest from very early stage (e.g., ideation/pre-revenue) to late stage (e.g., scaling)—and across a variety of investment types around key markets, technologies, and business models.

Further, some venture firms raise funds to go after specific areas such as early-stage, late-stage, technology-centric (e.g., blockchain), market-centric (e.g., fintech), or geo-specific (e.g., China) startups.

Each of these funds has been marketed to limited partners by the venture firm, each of whom has agreed with the venture firm's investment theses, unique insights, strategies, expertise, and projected returns.

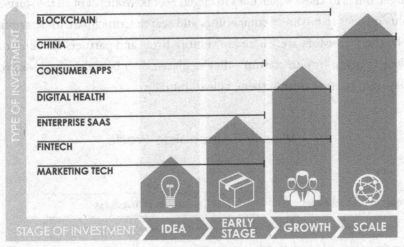

FIGURE 9

Note that the vertical arrows represent the magnitude of the investment at each of these stages.

So, how do you find the right firm on this matrix with the right fund and/ or the right partner that aligns with your startup?

First, you need to understand who you are. What kind of company, at which stage of development, and targeted at which markets? If you can't answer the following two questions with both confidence and data, you aren't yet ready to reach out to investors:

1. At what stage is your startup?
2. Which companies participate in your market?
   - Competitors?
   - Companies in the same market but in a different sector and not a direct competitor?

That was easy. Now, you are ready to use Crunchbase.

It's just as important to know which firms and partners you aren't going to target as it is to know which ones to target. So, take your list of all the startups you consider to be direct competitors and search Crunchbase to determine who their investors are. These are venture firms and partners that *aren't* as likely to invest in your startup—they've placed their bets elsewhere—so you may want to steer clear of them, at least initially.

Vlocity Crunchbase Profile

Investors			
Number of Lead Investors	2	**Number of Investors**	7

Vlocity is funded by 7 investors. Sutter Hill Ventures and TDF Ventures are the most recent investors.

Which investors participated in the most funding rounds?			Show

Investor Name	Lead Investor	Funding Round	Partners
Sutter Hill Ventures	Yes	Series B - Vlocity	–
TDF Ventures	No	Series B - Vlocity	–
New York Life Investment Management	No	Series B - Vlocity	–
Wildcat Venture Partners	No	Series B - Vlocity	Bruce Cleveland
Kennet Partners	No	Series B - Vlocity	–
Accenture	No	Series B - Vlocity	–
Salesforce Ventures	No	Series B - Vlocity	–
Accenture	–	Series A - Vlocity	–
Salesforce Ventures	Yes	Series A - Vlocity	–

FIGURE 10[3]

Note that if a firm hasn't taken the time to update its Crunchbase profile, then the partner who made the investment may not be named. Therefore, you may need to go to the venture firm's website to discover which specific partner made the investment.

Next, make a list of startups that you believe operate in the same market as your startup but you *don't* consider to be direct competitors. Now, go into Crunchbase and find out which venture firms, and which partner in those firms, invested in these companies and at which stage they did so. It may not seem so, but this is key information.

Mid- to late-stage investors, for example, don't typically invest in early-stage startups. So spending any effort trying to convince those firms and partners that don't invest at your current stage is a waste of your valuable time. Don't forget them, however; they may be the first people you want to visit when you reach that later stage.

Now, you have your initial target list of venture firms and partners and are ready for the next phase.

Developing Your Message

Okay, you know the firms and the partners you want to target. What's next?

You need to develop a "native ad" for LinkedIn with a compelling visual, message, and call to action (CTA) that encourages your prospective investor to click. It is that straightforward—you are creating attractive bait for potential investors.

You don't need a design team or marketing agency to do any of this; the tools you will use are inexpensive, easy to learn, and, in most cases, built into the platform you will use to distribute the ad.

Your ad always should include a link. Typically this is to the homepage of your website. Better yet, the link can be to a unique landing page that quickly informs your prospective investor about what you do and what you are seeking. This isn't the time or place to tell your complete story; all you are trying to accomplish is to get a meeting.

Your digital ad should always include imagery to induce interest and speed perception. At the very least, this should include your company logo and a graphic or image that best represents the market you serve or the product you've developed.

Multimedia is even better. If you have a short video clip that you can overlay with your logo, all the better. Video has been demonstrated to perform better—higher click-through rates—than static images. You can easily purchase all types of stock ('b-roll'), short video clips.

Your message should be brief and cogent, and it should compel your prospective investor to want to learn more about you. You don't need, or want, to tell them everything in the digital ad—that would be overload. You just want them to click on the ad.

Your message might be something like:

VC Targeted Ad

FIGURE 11

These ads will be seen only by prospective investors who have demonstrated an investment interest in your company's category. So don't be afraid to make the initial ask: you can be direct about the fact that you are seeking an investment.

Finally, your call to action is simple: click here to learn more.

While you can opt to just take someone to your website—if you have one—you are far better served if your ad takes the reader to a custom landing page that tells the investor exactly what you are seeking.

There are many low-cost products on the market to develop a landing page, and you can find them in a simple search. Far more important than the medium is the message: what it is you say on your investor-specific landing page.

Your objective here is to get a prospective investor to meet with you so you can tell your story. So, you want to say just enough to be compelling but not so much that the prospective investor feels he or she knows enough to make a decision about you.

Here is what your landing page should contain:

- *A graphic, photo, or video clip*—something that is visually interesting and relevant to what you do, your logo, and your website URL.
- *A short narrative about your company*—a few sentences that tell the investor:
  - Who you are,
  - What category you are creating or redefining [this book as well as the book titled *Play Bigger* discuss category creation],
  - What "big problem" you are solving, and
  - Some preliminary results, if you have any.
- *Your "digital warm introduction."* This is a positive quote about you or your idea from someone who has credibility (an executive in a notable company or a professor from a good school).
- *Your ask—simple.* You want to meet with your correspondent to:
  - Tell your story,
  - Explain how much capital you are raising, and
  - How you will use it to accomplish key objectives.

The landing page should be written from the point of view of the CEO/founder and provide his or her direct contact information. Keep in mind that investing in your company is personal. You are asking the investor to stake his or her reputation and potentially put their career on the line by making an investment in you. For that reason, raising capital is not a task the CEO can delegate to others.

Getting Your Ad in Front of the Right People

Fortunately, everything you will need to execute your ad campaign is on LinkedIn. All you need is a company page.

Once you have your company page and created your native ad—or a few versions of them—you can use LinkedIn's LI Audience Network, and its account and contact targeting, to cost-effectively target specific companies and people in those companies with your message.

These tools allow you to directly target your ads to specific firms and even specific partners in those firms (if you have their email addresses) with LinkedIn sponsored posts. In addition, you can use these tools to target the same firms and people on key third-party publisher apps and websites outside of LinkedIn.

You also can limit the amount you spend on any given day either from direct clicks (CPC) or ad impressions (CPM). The tools will tell you the typical bid/ask range for similar ad campaigns, so you can budget accordingly.

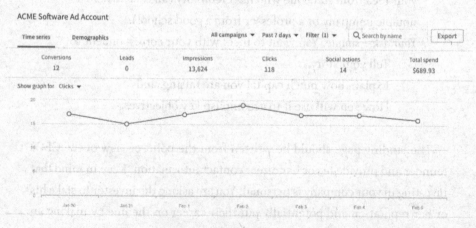

FIGURE 12

Further, these tools offer basic analytics on how your ads are performing—conversions, impressions, clicks, social actions, and what you spend.

Adding Email to the Mix

If you want to take your campaign to the next level and make it more effective, you can follow up your ads with targeted emails.

Companies, such as discover.org, can provide you with the specific email addresses of everyone you want to target. However, these solutions can be expensive and require someone on your team to set them up (as if you have such resources at this point in your history).

A far less expensive route is to use one or more of the tools such as Clearbit, SellHack, or LeadFuze, along with an intern (or you), to find all the email addresses you are seeking.

Then you should use an inexpensive app, such as MailChimp, to create a targeted email to every partner in the firm, reference the digital ad with which you've been targeting them, and ask for a meeting. Don't forget to include that "digital warm introduction" you used on your landing page. The reason you want to use a product like MailChimp is that it allows you to easily track delivery and open rates and by whom.

Venture investing is a relationship business. If you want a 21st-century venture investor to invest in your company and you don't have personal relationships with that person, don't rely on 20th-century techniques. Take advantage of these low-cost approaches to get in front of that person by convincing her that even in personal communications, you are on top of your game.

A few final words here. When you do get that meeting, be sure you are well prepared for it. Find out which partners you are meeting with and get background information on them before the meeting: the college(s) they attended, the places they've worked, the startups they've invested in previously (type and stage), etc. See if you can determine how many successful investments the investor you are meeting with has made; that will determine her "power"—her reputation—within the firm. This is an enterprise sales call, and you need to know as much as you can about the firm and partner(s) you are meeting with so you can tailor your presentation accordingly. And don't rely on intermediaries to help you raise capital. Early-stage venture capitalists seldom respond well to these groups. Venture investors expect you, not a banker, to figure out how to get their attention.

3

THE ROAD TO CATEGORY KING

THE
TRACTION GAP

GO-TO-PRODUCT ›   GO-TO-MARKET ›   GO-TO-SCALE ›

IPR   MVP   MVR   MVT   SCALE

IDEATION   MVC

The focus of this chapter is on a critical element of market-engineering, "category design"—that is, why trying to compete in an existing category already ruled by a "category king" is fraught with significant challenges. In other words, why "me-too" usually leads to "me-dead."

I will provide evidence why a failure to create a new category for your startup—or to redefine an existing one—is a recipe for disaster.

> In a well-honed category-driven strategy, the company designs the category, evangelizes the problem, offers its solution to the problem, and then the category makes the company its king. . . . A self-determined king that isn't made by the

category is a hollow despot destined to be overthrown at the first sign of weakness."

—

CHRISTOPHER LOCHHEAD, coauthor, *Play Bigger: How Pirates, Dreamers, and Innovators Create and Dominate Markets*; host, *Legends & Losers* podcast

THE IMPORTANCE OF CATEGORY DESIGN

So, you have an idea for a new product and/or new company? That's awesome. Your next step is to realize that ahead of you is a long journey from Ideation to a scalable, successful market-leading company.

The first critical step in that journey is category design and reaching the Minimum Viable Category (MVC) value inflection point on the Traction Gap Framework. In particular, you must design a new category—or redefine an existing one—by naming it and developing a well-conceived plan to overtake it and then own it. Then, if you expect to survive and thrive as a company, you must install your company as the king of that new sector. This process needs to happen early in a startup's life cycle. Very early.

Why is category design so important? Because humans naturally compare and contrast new concepts, ideas, and products against what they already know. We respect novelty, but fear the utterly new. We like to categorize. We need to organize. This innate human talent allows us to quickly determine where innovative concepts and products fit into our sense of the world.

That's why, when a company emerges with a new offering, we humans immediately try to determine how it compares with what we already understand.

If a new company with its new offering doesn't explain who it is and what it does in an elementary, comprehensible way (what a friend of mine likes to call "in crayon," to capture the simplicity of this message), then potential investors and customers will attempt to impose their own description on the company. Thus, if the company offers complex products bereft of a simple message to explain them, outsiders will often end up confused and move on to something else less confusing.

You often hear the term "elevator pitch," that brief description of a business that can be told to an interested party over the course of a brief elevator ride. Yet you would be astonished how many CEOs—even those of established companies—are unable to give a precise description of what distinguishes their company in the marketplace.

B2B startups that fail to adequately explain the category they are in find themselves in delayed sales cycles. Even worse, they end up with poor win/loss ratios because potential customers/clients tend to want to buy from existing category kings, even if those products aren't quite as good, cool, etc.

For B2C or even B2B2C startups, it's worse. Consumers will just ignore the new company and its products entirely. That's because the company/consumer contact (typically over the Internet) is so quick that there is no sales cycle, no opportunity for a human to convince them that they need the product. In an instant, lacking a quick understanding of what is being offered, the consumer is clicking off to another company or product.

In their ground-breaking book, *Play Bigger: How Pirates, Dreamers, and Innovators Create and Dominate Markets*, a group of several veteran Silicon Valley entrepreneurs explain how and why "category kings" capture, on average, 76 percent of all profits in their category. And they show why trying to displace a king in an existing category is expensive, time-consuming, and rarely successful.

Play Bigger makes a compelling and statistically relevant case for why new startups and products must either redefine an existing category or create a new one. So, your challenge is either to redefine an existing category so that the current king is left ruling a deserted kingdom (think iPhone and Blackberry), or it is to create a new category (think cloud computing and perpetual enterprise software) with a large and addressable market and with you as the new category king to rule over it.

The following are a couple of examples of B2B technology startups. They both understood the importance of category design:

> ❝ When you innovate, you've got to be prepared for every-
> one telling you you're nuts."

LARRY ELLISON, Cofounder, Executive Chairman & CEO, Oracle
Corporation

Oracle was founded in 1977 by Larry Ellison, Bob Miner, and Ed Oates. Oracle was not the first database company. Oracle wasn't even the first relational database company. But Oracle was the first *portable*, SQL relational database company.

Before Oracle, most databases were inextricably linked to the operating system and hardware they ran on. Applications written for one platform were not easily "portable" to another, if at all. Companies experienced "vendor lock-in" once they made a hardware/OS decision and were forced to endure ever-increasing price increases from their vendor because the cost of moving the application to an entirely different platform vastly exceeded the annual price increases.

Oracle positioned itself as the only commercial, portable SQL relational database with the tagline: *Portability. Compatibility. Connectability. Capability.*

Let's look at each word in the tagline more closely and the marketing message it conveyed to potential customers:

Portability—Implying Oracle runs on virtually any hardware/operating system combination.

Compatibility—Oracle supports the industry-standard Structured Query Language (SQL).

Connectability—Oracle supports connecting two or more databases.

Capability—Oracle uses a technology architecture that addresses performance with techniques as "row-level locking" versus "page-level locking."

Regarding the latter, Oracle's marketing and sales organization extolled the virtues of supporting a truly relational model (messaging that IBM was simultaneously driving into its customer base, and off which Oracle was able to draft), Structured Query Language (SQL) compatibility, the ability to connect several databases together, and "row-level locking," the ability to lock and update a single row of data, versus locking an entire page or table in the database. The latter approach—in common use at the time—prevented multiple users from being able to quickly update information contained in the same area of the database at the same time.

By comparison, row-level locking enabled higher levels of "concurrency," the ability to support large numbers of users all attempting to update the database at the same time. Brilliantly, Oracle captured all of these technical concepts in a single word: "capability."

As IBM marketed the significant benefits of the relational model to its customers, Oracle was able to state that "IBM is right" and that Oracle was 100 percent compatible with IBM's offerings, but also offered the additional benefit that Oracle could run those applications on *any* vendor's hardware and operating system (not just IBM's).

By defining in the simplest possible terms what it meant to be a portable SQL relational database, and positioning itself as the only company offering such a solution—the category king, Oracle set itself on a path toward becoming one of the most influential and successful technology companies in the world.

> **"** The only constant in the technology industry is change."
>
> **MARC BENIOFF**, CEO, Salesforce.com

Salesforce develops business software products primarily for the Customer Relationship Management (CRM) category. Salesforce didn't actually define the CRM category. That distinction goes to Tom Siebel and Pat House, the cofounders of Siebel Systems. Siebel Systems was founded in late 1993 and grew to nearly $2B in revenue in just 5 years from its first product shipment. Siebel is still recognized by Deloitte as one of the fastest-growing companies in US history: more than 750,000 percent CAGR over 5 years.

At the time Siebel was founded, the state-of-the-art computing architecture for enterprise applications was called "client/server." This is an architecture in which the client application resides on a user's local desktop or laptop and the data and other services reside on a remote server. The two then are connected by a network.

A downside to this earlier model was that each time the application was modified or needed to be upgraded, every user needed to have his or her copy revised. This was a headache for IT personnel, who had to deal with local and remote users who owned laptops and desktops in myriad configurations.

If you own a smartphone, you are familiar with this concept because you own client/server applications. Every time a mobile app provider modifies its app, you are requested to update your phone's version via the app store. This similar updating process is cumbersome and difficult to manage in companies with hundreds or thousands of users.

Siebel's CRM solutions were built using this client/server model, and its pricing was based upon "perpetual licenses." Companies purchased a perpetual license to use Siebel for hundreds of thousands or even millions of dollars, along with a corresponding annual maintenance agreement. Customers were responsible for installing, configuring, and maintaining Siebel CRM solutions in their own data centers on their own hardware.

In 1999, Salesforce's founder and CEO, Marc Benioff, recognized that a new—and, to his mind, far superior—form of application software development, delivery, and pricing model was emerging. It turns out he was right. Really right.

This new model relied on browser technology from dominant companies of the era, such as Microsoft (Internet Explorer) or Netscape (Navigator), to render the application interface on a user's desktop or laptop, with shared servers and resources located in a remote location to process and store the application data. This model promised an easier way for application software companies to deploy their applications and an even easier way for their customers to consume and pay for them. Using this approach, companies no longer had to purchase servers, install software, and manage the entire system to keep it running.

This new approach offered an entirely new business model. Companies could subscribe to use the service through a relatively low cost-per-user monthly fee. This let companies of all sizes gain access to mission-critical business software for a fraction of the cost and time of traditional enterprise software solutions.

Benioff seized upon the opportunity to upend incumbent enterprise application software providers using this new computing model. And he chose a very clever way to discuss and position this new category. He didn't fall into the trap—as most technology startups do—of talking about "cool technology features." Instead, he decided to introduce and convey the significance of this new category by using an internationally recognized sign—a circle with a red line drawn diagonally through it—with the word "software" inside. The meaning—"No Software"—was obvious at a glance.

He did this to easily and quickly signal that there was no need for companies to buy "expensive," "bloated" enterprise software anymore. Just sign up and use what you need—just like a utility service such as water, gas, or electricity—and simply pay a monthly subscription fee.

His first target application? CRM. And the market leader in CRM in 1999—now nearly a $2B juggernaut—was Siebel. In an instant, Benioff was able to beautifully convey what Salesforce did vs. Siebel and every other enterprise application software provider.

Monte Zweben, former CEO of Blue Martini and current CEO of Splice Machine, provides an interesting anecdote from the era:

> At the time I was running Blue Martini, Tom Siebel was on my board. Another investor and advisor to my company was Marc Benioff. Marc was trying to convince Tom of this idea to create CRM in the Cloud (it wasn't called that back then, of course).
>
> But, according to Marc, Tom didn't bite.
>
> So Marc started this little dinky company to do CRM in the Cloud. Marc and I talked about it, and he offered me this great deal—it may have been free—to be their first customer.
>
> As a result, Blue Martini became the first customer of Salesforce.com and the first company to support a new category of CRM.[1]

The company's sales exploded—a lesson to other potential Salesforce customers.

So, did Tom Siebel, an astute technologist and businessman, fail to understand the potential benefits of Salesforce and what is now known as cloud computing? Unlikely. Tom recognized that a subscription-based pricing model could potentially disrupt Siebel's business model. He, along with other enterprise application software leaders—including Larry Ellison at Oracle and Hasso Plattner at SAP—intentionally derided the approach as a joke to undermine its image to their existing customers. At one point, Larry said, *"Maybe I'm an idiot, but I have no idea what anyone is talking about. What is it? It's complete gibberish. It's insane. When is this idiocy going to stop?"*[2]

And, in the early days, the product offerings from Salesforce and others using this new computer-science and business model were sufficiently immature, and the business buyers sufficiently skeptical, that few people gave the new approach significant credence.

But, as Blue Martini showed, Benioff's insights weren't a joke.

Benioff successfully created a new category and business model that we all now recognize as cloud computing and "Software as a Service" (SaaS). He chose to use this new computing and pricing model to verbally attack the market leader, Siebel, in the CRM category.

At the beginning, Salesforce's solution was not initially capable of competing in the enterprise market, so Benioff went after small businesses—the ones Siebel ignored—that wanted and needed CRM capabilities but couldn't afford Siebel.

In the process, Benioff shrewdly used Siebel as the poster child for the pains associated with client/server computing. In other words, he personalized the weaknesses of the current category king. In the meantime, he plotted to make a direct attack on Siebel's market.

As explained by Clayton Christensen in his book *The Innovator's Dilemma*, technology deficits can be overcome over time, by using profits from one market to fund entry into others. In that way, Salesforce eventually built better and better offerings that enabled the company to move from the small business category into the enterprise segment.

> " Breaking an old business model is always going to require leaders to follow their instinct. There will always be persuasive reasons not to take a risk. But if you only do what worked in the past, you will wake up one day and find that you've been passed by."
>
> **CLAYTON CHRISTENSEN,** Professor, Harvard Business School, author, *The Innovator's Dilemma*

At the same time, Salesforce moved horizontally as well into areas beyond classic CRM, such as offerings in development infrastructure, all using this new SaaS model. Weakened by the 2001 worldwide recession, which put a hold on all large, expensive "nonessential" enterprise application projects, in 2005 the Siebel board elected to accept an acquisition offer of nearly $6B from Oracle. Now the door was open: Salesforce was left virtually alone to gobble up CRM market share across the economy.

_____

Many startups don't understand the importance of doing category-creation work from the start. And many fail as a result. Perhaps the most tragic are those that have a ready-made new category waiting for them—and fail to recognize that fact, and don't distinguish themselves from the competition.

The data show that there are thousands of these failures each year. The fact is that unless you successfully create and define a new category—or redefine an existing one—and become the category king—even if your startup manages to traverse the Traction Gap—it is unlikely to generate significant returns for employees or the investors. Think about that. You could spend years building a company and scaling it . . . only to find that you are left only with "scraps."

THE CATEGORY-CREATION PROCESS

"Okay," you say, "I get it. We need to create or redefine a category. But how do we go about doing it?"

The answer is that no single act can establish a new category for a company to exploit and dominate. Rather, category creation is a multistep process that can, and likely will, take years and a significant investment in marketing and sales to develop.

To start, you must recognize that a category is nothing more than *a problem*. And it begins with identifying the nature of that problem, then unlocking the name of the category you want to create or redefine.

To show you how you might do this, I thought I would share with you the actual category-naming and definition process I personally went through with a startup I founded—GreenFig, a combination B2B and B2B2C company—before I arrived at its category name and definition.

GreenFig is in the educational technology space, and I was faced with the challenge of defining an alternative form of education in order to differentiate GreenFig from existing traditional education institutions and alternative education options (e.g., online education companies).

The following are excerpts from the actual document I developed as I explored a variety of issues regarding the problem with current education formats—before arriving at the final category name and definition.

I started by putting the problem into words. This process was more challenging—and more important—than you might imagine. It forced me to take what was in my head and structure the concepts so others would be able to quickly and easily understand them.

Here are some excerpts from the original document I drafted:

THE PROBLEM

Educational programs for professionals (e.g., doctor, lawyer, accountant), technical (e.g., engineering, computer science, scientist) and trade/vocational areas (e.g., nurse, mechanic, electrician) all combine an academic program with "hands-on" training and mentors.

Students are continuously tested and certified for subject-matter proficiency. Apprentices are paired with experienced journeymen who act as mentors to ensure that knowledge gained through years of experience is passed down to the next generation. This is a tried, tested, and proven approach to transfer complex knowledge and skills.

Yet this approach is seldom used in business; at least, not any longer. Due to rapid change and competition, most employers do not have the time or resources to adequately train and mentor newly hired workers.

Over the past several decades, packaged application software from companies such as Google, Oracle, Salesforce, SAP, and many others has emerged to enable business and government organizations of all sizes to optimize their operational functions. These areas include, but are not limited to: marketing, sales, sales operations, finance/accounting, customer success, and support. Businesses implement and use this software to power these various functions.

Businesses seek workers skilled in these operational functions and the use of business application software. If you go to any one of many job websites (e.g., Indeed.com), and enter search terms such as "sales operations," "marketing operations," etc., you will see hundreds of thousands of open requisitions for workers with the skills to operate business application software.

While business application software providers can train people in the mechanics of how to operate their products, they don't teach "business science"; how to perform the function. And no

(continues)

single vendor typically provides all the product capabilities that companies require; therefore, workers need to learn a variety of applications from various vendors to perform their jobs.

Traditional higher-ed programs are not well-suited to teach "business science." The applications and use cases change so rapidly that most professors are not up to speed on the latest techniques and applications. By the time a course is designed and peer-reviewed, it can be obsolete.

Businesses are looking for workers who have work-related experience. Neither business application software providers nor higher-ed are well equipped to offer practical work experience.

As a result, there is a need to create a new category of learning/education to address this vacuum in our current educational format.

After I completed the work of defining the "problem," I next set out to define the properties of the new education category I wanted to create:

Definition of NewCo Category

- Skills-based training that leads to jobs in areas of high demand by industry and government organizations,
- Hands-on business application software instruction designed to prepare students to perform specific operational functions,
- Combination of physical (on-premise) and online learning delivered in real-time,
- Work experience gained through real-world projects guided by industry experts,

- One semester or less from zero knowledge to basic proficiency, and
- Application software-provider certification preparation and testing to ensure employers that job applicants have achieved basic levels of proficiency.

The next step in the process was to compare education as it currently exists against a new education category I wanted to create:

THE FROM / TO	
From	**To**
Expensive	Affordable by most
Time consuming	Less than 6 months
Insufficient knowledge/skill	Domain-specific expertise
No work-related experience	Work experience
Physically constrained	Delivered anywhere
Slow/difficult to change	Rapidly change to address industry needs

Category Brand Promise

When you complete a "NewCo Category" program, you will gain enough proficiency in a functional area to secure an entry-level position in industry or government.

With this differentiation characterized, I next set out to give these differences a name:

CATEGORY DESCRIPTIONS		
Time	**Objective**	**Type**
Rapid	Job	Learning
Fast	Proficiency	Education
Quick	Skill	Training
Swift	Talent	Instruction
Express	Expertise	Teaching
Immersive		Schooling
Short		
Accelerated		

SOME EXISTING CATEGORIES

Rapid Learning

http://rapidlearninginstitute.com/training-insights/survey-surprising-reason-training-pros-want-bite-size-learning/

Short-Form Learning

https://www.intrepidlearning.com/blog/short-form-big-opportunities-challenges

SOME POTENTIAL COMBINATIONS FOR A NEWCO CATEGORY

2-Word Combinations		
Learning	**Education**	**Training**
Quick Learning [QL]	Quick Education [QE]	Quick Training [QT]
Rapid Learning [RL]	Rapid Education [RE]	Rapid Training [RT]
Immersive Learning [IL]	Immersive Education [IE]	Immersive Training [IT]
Skills Learning [SL]	Skills Education [SE]	Skills Training [ST]

Learning	Education	Training
Proficiency Learning [PL]	Proficiency Education [PE]	Proficiency Training [PT]
Accelerated Learning [AL]	Accelerated Education [AE]	Accelerated Training [AT]

3-Word Combinations		
Learning	Education	Training
Quick Proficiency Learning [QPL]	Quick Proficiency Education [QPE]	Quick Proficiency Training [QPT]
Rapid Proficiency Learning [RPL]	Rapid Proficiency Education [RPE]	Rapid Proficiency Training [RPT]
Immersive Proficiency Learning [IPL]	Immersive Proficiency Education [IPE]	Immersive Proficiency Training [IPT]
Immersive Skills Learning [ISL]	Immersive Skills Education [ISE]	Immersive Skills Training [IST]
Accelerated Proficiency Learning [APL]—"Apple"	Accelerated Proficiency Education [APE]	Accelerated Proficiency Training [APT]—"Apt"
Accelerated Skills Learning [ASL]	Accelerated Skills Education [ASE]	Accelerated Skills Training [AST]

I thought that both "Apple" and "APT" had some relevance to Education/Learning.

4-Word Combinations		
Learning	Education	Training
Quick Proficiency Skills Learning [QPSL]	Quick Proficiency Skills Education [QPSE]	Quick Proficiency Skills Training [QPST]

(continues)

Learning	Education	Training
Rapid Proficiency Skills Learning [RPSL]	Rapid Proficiency Skills Education [RPSE]	Rapid Proficiency Skills Training [RPST]
Immersive Proficiency Skills Learning [IPSL]	Immersive Proficiency Skills Education [IPSE]	Immersive Proficiency Skills Training [IPST]
Accelerated Proficiency Skills Learning [APSL]	Accelerated Proficiency Skills Education [APSE]	Accelerated Proficiency Skills Training [APST]

I then tested a combination of these terms with different people in different groups to get their unfiltered responses. I learned a lot from those interactions. And the result took me in a different direction.

In particular, I discovered an education category that had been defined but rarely used—and with no obvious market leader. The category was labeled "microeducation."

After doing some research and testing, I elected to adopt this terminology and to position GreenFig within this category.

Based on all of this work, how did I decide to describe the company and its product category? Here it is:

> **"GreenFig is a microeducation company offering microdegrees in applied business science."**

Let's deconstruct that mission statement:

Microeducation—a new type of education with a name that implies that it is shorter in duration (one semester/200 hours) than traditional forms of education.

Microdegrees—a "shorter" degree than that obtained from a regular university, but that still implies that the student has mastered some topic. In this case, the GreenFig microdegree has been designed to prepare its students to pass the certification exams demanded by companies such as Google, Marketo, Salesforce, and other business software providers.

Applied Business Science—the term "business science" is juxtapositioned with "computer science" and "data science." Computer and data scientists are technical; they use math and statistics to analyze transactions. Business scientists, by comparison, are not necessarily technical. In fact, we have found that the best ones possess liberal arts degrees. Business scientists are trained to set up and operate the business application software—which generates transactions—that powers each business function, including customer success, finance, marketing, sales, service, and support. The word "applied" refers to the hands-on training and integrated work experience the company offers.

You may be wondering how I came up with the company name "GreenFig." I didn't. My wife and daughters did.

First, I concluded that I wanted an abstract name. They came up with the word GreenFig after a bunch of brainstorming and suggested the name to me.

They liked the word "green" because it is a colloquialism for "beginner." And, based on traditional Jewish beliefs, the fig is the "tree of knowledge." So, they put the two words, green and fig, together to come up with GreenFig—beginning knowledge! We tested it with different groups, and it tested well. And, oh yeah, the most important thing . . . the URL for that name still was available.

[A last word of advice: once you've created your message, get it in the hands of a real writer—especially someone trained in advertising copy or captions—and have that person take out superfluous verbiage and make the statement as tight and precise as it can possibly be.]

GreenFig is just getting off the ground, but it is doing well as its message resonates with higher-ed and corporations. But, as with any startup, it will survive only if it can convert that awareness and interest into strong revenue growth—traction.

CONSUMER CATEGORIES

What if you have an idea for a consumer application or product—does "category creation" still apply?

Yes. And in some ways, even more so.

Consider Apple, a company with products for both consumers and businesses.

Did Apple create the PC category? Did Apple create the phone category? Did Apple create the tablet category? Did Apple create the camera category? The watch category? Or put another way, did Steve Jobs create any of these categories?

Clearly, no. All of these are consumer categories—even personal computers (a fact often forgotten)—that existed before Steve Jobs decided to enter them.

Instead, what Steve and Apple did was to reimagine—redefine—existing categories to create an entirely different consumer experience and expectation. In fact, as the company's fame grew, the mere addition of the name "Apple" or the prefix "i" instantly created a de facto new category.

Today, with rare exception, most consumer categories are simply established categories that have been redefined by amazing new companies with amazing new products.

That isn't always the case, though. A recent exception, for example, is Uber, which defines its category as a peer-to-peer ridesharing, food delivery, and transportation network company—*not* a taxi company.

• • •

> " Uber is a $3.5 billion lesson in building for how the world
> 'should' work instead of optimizing for how the world
> 'does' work."

AARON LEVIE, CEO, Box

The biggest categorization challenge for consumer startups is overcoming the signal-to-noise ratio. That is, there are so many consumer products in the market, and so many new products continuously coming on line, that consumers are overwhelmed by the noise—mostly via advertising—of companies, new and old, competing for our attention.

For a new consumer company, simply creating a new category or redefining an existing category is typically insufficient nowadays for it to gain attention. It is also, in most cases, extraordinarily expensive to rise above that noise.

In the face of that, consumer startups must focus on the category they believe they want to compete in, promote the key new and innovative features they provide, and, most of all, use nontraditional marketing tools—including social "amplification"—to tell their story.

Deciding which consumer category you want to create or redefine up front is particularly critical in this competitive environment. Unlike business customers, who think about "return on investment" (the main criterion for a B2B product or service), consumers in many cases are more concerned with what a product says about their "social status."

Think about it. If I want personal transportation, I have a variety of choices. I could decide to use varying types of demand car services (e.g., taxis, Uber, Lyft, Wingz, or ZipCar), drive an environmentally low-impact car (e.g., Prius, Leaf, Tesla), or purchase a luxury automobile (e.g., Bentley, Rolls Royce) or a high-performance sports car (e.g., Ferrari, Aston Martin). Any one of these will get me from point A to point B. But they each make a statement about who I am as a person, while telling others something about me. My transportation choice communicates my social status.

> " A brand is no longer what we tell consumers it is, it is what consumers tell each other it is."
>
> —
> **SCOTT DAVID COOK**, Founder, Intuit

This is why consumer startups must decide—from the very beginning—what they want their "brand" to stand for as a social signifier and in what category they intend to compete. This very strategic Minimum Viable Category decision will determine to whom and where you will begin to market and sell your products. Remember, you will be signaling this decision to customers from the very first moment—and if your aim is wrong, there will be hell to pay repositioning yourself on the right track. You must get it right the first time.

Since "social status" is so important for consumer startups, developing brand credibility quickly is critical. This is why consumer companies (early-stage and otherwise) like to "borrow the brand" of well-known consumers (e.g., athletes and celebrities) who have already earned the trust of consumers. (Whether that trust is warranted is a different topic.)

However, only a few lucky consumer startups—usually with celebrities or athletes as members of their investor group—have the financial wherewithal or relationships to use celebrity or athlete endorsements or to get noticed.

So the lowest-cost and most readily accessible way for a consumer startup to gain category awareness and interest is via word of mouth from friends. Friends trust friends. And friends recommend products they like to their friends.

Today, thanks to social networks, it has never been easier to leverage this behavior. Of course, we all recognize that this is the power of Facebook and other social networks.

Facebook enables new consumer startups to quickly and cost-effectively reach "friends." Friends recommend consumer products they like to their friends. And on it goes. A truly innovative product that is "friend-recommended" can quickly go viral.

Category ownership for consumer startups (and incumbents) must have a solid customer awareness and acquisition strategy that employs the use of Facebook, Instagram, Pinterest, Snapchat, Twitter, and other social networks. Otherwise, you will be competing with one hand tied behind your back. Being an entrepreneur is hard enough without that.

Conversely, the tactic B2C companies can best employ to generate initial awareness and interest, and to confirm a strong MVC, is conducting "Smoke Tests." The nature of this method is something I will discuss in the next chapter, "Getting to IPR."

KEY TAKEAWAYS

The Minimum Viable Category value inflection point is closely linked to the Ideation value inflection point. As the concept of your product comes together, you should perform significant market-engineering—market research to validate the opportunity—and begin to formulate features and feature prioritization.

Before moving beyond MVC, you must have a well-formed thesis regarding the category you intend to define/redefine and formalize a well-thought-out messaging matrix.

The following are the key milestones you should have reached before moving on to your Initial Product Release.

PRODUCT

Product—Prototyping and UX/UI work, along with certain feature prioritization, should be explored. Thorough market-validated and prospect feedback should begin and be captured leading to a quan-

(continues)

titatively verified product and feature list. Objective analysis of the feedback should be used to determine whether to continue as planned, iterate, or shut down. Beta customers should be identified and lined up for the Initial Product Release.

REVENUE

Revenue—To successfully reach and move beyond MVC, you need to understand and agree upon the category in which you intend to compete. If it's an existing category, you need to redefine it in your terms. If it's a new category, you need to name the category and define it. You should have a list of From/Tos, that is, how the world will change due to your new product/service. After coming up with the category, you must develop a comprehensive messaging matrix that explains what the company is, what it does, how it compares with potential competitors, initial pricing ideas, boilerplate messaging, etc.

I highly recommend that all team members read the book *Play Bigger* to understand the category-definition process.

TEAM

Team—Few changes beyond the Ideation value inflection point, unless you have been able to raise some or additional capital based upon your concept. Most likely, any team changes at this point will involve a few engineers or product managers who elect to join.

SYSTEMS

Systems—As with the Ideation stage, at MVC systems do not yet play a significant role. You should have some basic tools that enable your team to communicate and collaborate effectively and share information easily. You only need basic applications, such as email, spreadsheets, collaboration software, word-processing and engineering applications (e.g., build/QA system, bug database, user stories). You should have established processes and systems so you can easily track expenses, make payments, and manage equity, hiring, payroll, and benefits.

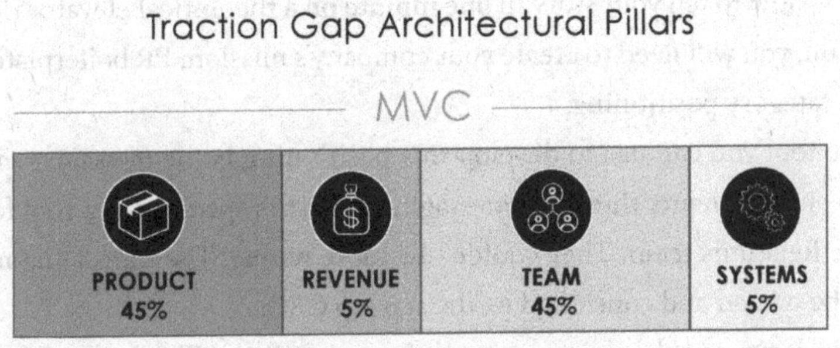

FIGURE 13

Percentage of emphasis during this stage.

The following are the key principles Wildcat Venture Partners looks for at MVC:

■ Traction Gap Principles ■
MVC

Product	Capture statistically valid market feedback to produce a verified product and feature list.
Revenue	Define or redefine the category you intend to build/compete in; lock in your initial value propositions, pricing models, and positioning.
Team	Do not hire anyone who cannot accelerate initial product release.
Systems	Establish your startup's initial governance and core values.

TRACTION GAP HACKS ► MVC

When you are first beginning your startup, one of the more challenging issues you may face is how to explain your concept and product to people who are hearing about it for the first time. After all, if it is truly disruptive, then, by definition, it will be radically new to the listener. He or she will likely need to take time and think about what it means and determine how it fits into the world they already know.

It may be a cliché, but you really are going to need to develop your "elevator pitch"—how to tell your story in one minute on a theoretical elevator ride. In addition, you will need to create your company's mission, PR boilerplate, and other category positioning.

The tool you can use to develop this positioning is the *messaging matrix*. Some entrepreneurs think the messaging matrix is specifically a tool for the Public Relations team. They couldn't be more wrong. The messaging matrix must be owned and controlled by the startup CEO.

This document should represent the startup CEO's official point of view, a formal "message of record" that everyone in the company should rely on for any and all communications.

It should capture the way in which the CEO wants everyone in the company to explain:

- ► What the company does,
- ► How the products fit in and stand out,
- ► The From/To definitions (as defined above and in the book *Play Bigger*),
- ► The approved mission statement, and
- ► Competitive positioning.

In other words, the messaging matrix must be the official "go to" document that defines and describes your startup. If you choose to add new positioning, language, etc., the messaging matrix must be revised to reflect those changes and rolled out across the company.

The fastest way to wreck—or never create—your brand is to allow everyone in your startup to invent their own idea of what your brand is, and to use their own language to explain who you are and what you do.

One of the things I like to do during due diligence when I first meet members of a startup team is to ask each individual to tell me what the company's mission statement is and what category they are in. Their responses tell me a lot about whether the CEO and team understand the importance of category design and brand—and whether they are all working to accomplish the same thing.

The messaging matrix plays a pivotal role toward ensuring that everyone in the startup understands the mission they are on and why. Once hardened, like the US Constitution, it should be difficult to change and should only be revised when the CEO approves a revision.

In the Appendix, I provide you with a comprehensive messaging matrix I developed for GreenFig. It took me more than three months and countless hours to develop and finalize this document. During that period, I tested and iterated upon the category name, definitions, and positioning with a variety of groups, including companies, students, and universities.

I was careful not to engage the venture community—even my own firm—until I had finalized this important work and was confident I had adequately defined a new category and positioned GreenFig satisfactorily within that category. The result was a successful seed financing of $1M that gave me and the GreenFig team the opportunity to explore pricing and business models and to deliver their first courses.

(Again, while you are investing significant resources and effort in "product-engineering" in the go-to-product phase, you must concurrently invest an equal—perhaps even greater—effort in "market-engineering" by defining/redefining the category and validating the market in which you want to compete. These are as critical to the success of your startup as your product is.)

Category and brand creation begin by developing your "messaging matrix" as the foundational category and brand document. Once finalized, every employee in your company must internalize—and memorize—key positioning statements established within your messaging matrix.

You should digitally post your final "branding document," developed from your messaging matrix, so that everyone in the company has access to it. As part of the onboarding process for new employees, you would be well served to require them to read the document and take—and even pass—a test, to ensure that they have mastered and can effectively communicate your positioning. And, if you have employees on board who haven't read the brand document and taken the test, you should demand that they do so as a condition of ongoing employment.

The fact is that anyone in your company can Tweet or make posts to many social media sites; therefore, every one of your employees is a potential brand ambassador. You want to be sure that if they mention or discuss your company in those forums, they can accurately position who you are and what you do. And, if you modify your positioning, you must update your messaging matrix and bring the entire company up to speed with your new positioning—and the rationale for the changes.

Your instructions to your employees should be something like: "You can position us any way you'd like, as long as the words you use are the exact words from our approved messaging matrix and brand document. Our brand—and ultimately our valuation as a company—depends on all of us to do this effectively." If you elect not to formalize and emphasize this process, you will diminish and compromise your ability to create and sustain a category and a brand.

4

GETTING TO INITIAL PRODUCT RELEASE

THE TRACTION GAP

| GO-TO-PRODUCT ❯ | GO-TO-MARKET ❯ | GO-TO-SCALE ❯ |

IDEATION   MVC   IPR   MVP   MVR   MVT   SCALE

The next challenge you face before reaching the Traction Gap is the jump from Minimum Viable Category to the critical value inflection point of Initial Product Release, or IPR. In this chapter, I am going to cover:

- ▶ What it means to be a "market-first" startup and why this is critically important—in fact, mission critical,
- ▶ Why you need to develop a complete view of the market through "market signals," and
- ▶ Why you need to develop Market IQ.
- ▶ Then, in the Hacks section at the end of this chapter, I will discuss *how* you can capture some of the market signals you need to be a market-first company.

If you adopt the methods I describe, you will be able to engage with prospective customers or users to generate statistically relevant data that your team can use to help confirm ideas, determine key product features, and secure early-stage financing.

During this phase, you and your company team members should be focused on verifying that your product or service concept does indeed have merit in the marketplace—and, further, that it can be developed and brought to market cost-effectively and with relative certainty.

Getting Market Input

At this point, you have your idea; you believe you've got a candidate for your Minimum Viable Category; and you are ready to get on the path to Initial Product Release.

The first order of business is to engage prospective customers/users to determine whether your instincts and hunches are right. In other words, you need to talk to some of the people to whom you will eventually be selling your product or service.

Steve Blank, successful technology entrepreneur and now iconic author and professor, emphatically encourages teams to "get outside the four walls": engage with potential customers and get their feedback before spending time writing code or any other development program.

Frank Robinson, with SyncDev (who told me that Steve Blank credits him with coining the term "Minimum Viable Product"), says this is the moment to meet with people and "sell them" the product—even though it doesn't yet exist. The idea is to pitch your product as though it were already available (so the feedback you receive is specific, rather than speculative), see what resonates and what does not, and develop demand for your product as "back-ordered inventory."

As we've noted, market research shows that, in fact, most products fail (70 percent or more), eventually dying or becoming "zombies."[1]

This research further determined that the primary causes of this 70 percent failure rate are:

- weak market input
- inconsistent methodology
- poor product analytics

And *CB Insights* found that the No. 1 cause cited by entrepreneurs was . . . no market need.

Top 5 Reasons Startups Fail

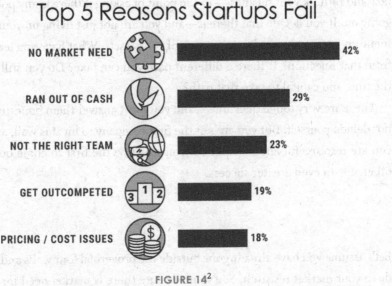

NO MARKET NEED	42%
RAN OUT OF CASH	29%
NOT THE RIGHT TEAM	23%
GET OUTCOMPETED	19%
PRICING / COST ISSUES	18%

FIGURE 14[2]

In other words, you may think you have a vital and irresistible product. But the market may see it as ultimately unnecessary.

The *CB Insights* research further found that "Tackling problems that are interesting to solve rather than those that serve a market need was cited as the No. 1 reason for failure." Indeed, this was noted by 42 percent of respondents.

An excerpt from an executive at Patient Communicator Inc. shared "I realized, essentially, that we had no customers because no one was really interested in the model we were pitching. Doctors want more patients, not an efficient office."

Treehouse Logic Inc. expressed: "Startups fail when they are not solving a market problem. We were not solving a large enough problem that we could universally serve with a scalable solution. We had great technology, great data on shopping behavior, great reputation as a thought leader, great expertise, great advisers, etc., but what we didn't have was technology or a business model that solved a pain point in a scalable way."

With this type of insight, of course, your startup is a nonstarter. If you discover that there is no potential demand for your product, you need to stop *now* and rethink your business—to the point of asking if there is any point in going on. If you decide that there is—and you are not just living on your momentum—then you need to take stock of your assets. What have you learned from that rejection? Is there a different path you can take? Do you still have the time and capital to take that path?

These are very tough questions—and you must answer them honestly and not delude yourself. But you are not the first company to hit this wall, and, if you are resourceful and disciplined, you won't be the first to come out the other side to even greater success.

———

Let's assume you have already gone outside the proverbial four walls and have done your market research. You've made sure there is market need for your product. At that point, you will believe you have established *product/market fit* for your product offering.

Let's say that you reached out to your friend working at Acme Corp. in the finance department and showed her some concepts for your finance application. You used slide mockups in your presentation and explained some cool new features you have in mind.

She gushed effusively about your great idea and encouraged you to continue. You asked her for intros to other people in finance groups at her company and she made them. You met with those people, and they too said nice things. You asked for feedback on certain key features you are contemplating. You asked them to rate and rank them. They did. You asked for more intros. They obliged.

Or, maybe, you invented a cool mobile app that (you hope) will eventually be distributed via the Apple Store or the Android App Store. You and your best friend coded up a prototype in a few months working in your college dorm. You shared what you're doing with your friends, family, schoolmates. Wow, they all said. You're stoked.

This took some time. But now you believe you are on to something.

After all, you spoke with a lot of people. You are confident that you have great market feedback and that if you build that business or consumer app with the features you've described, you are guaranteed to have a hit on your hands.

Really?

In the companies you spoke and met with, did you interview people with different titles—individual contributors, managers, and executives? Did you speak with potential users *and* economic buyers, recognizing that they are distinct constituencies? Did you speak with companies of all sizes in multiple different geographical locations?

If your product is a mobile app for consumers, did you speak with more than just your friends and family?

The problem with most startups and—with few exceptions—large incumbent companies, is that most do not conduct sufficiently statistically valid market research before moving into "build mode." Rather, they limit their research, often unconsciously selecting for positive response rather than going out of their comfort zone and looking expressly for critical comments.

The truth is that the amount of time and expertise required to conduct valid market research is usually beyond the internal skill sets of most established companies, let alone startups. Most don't have the capital, or don't feel they can afford the time, to invest in hiring an outside market research firm with the requisite skills to perform it.

Even with established companies, the pressure to bring new or updated products to market quickly can be intense. And besides, they tell themselves, why do they need broad market research? After all, they already know what customers or consumers want because . . . they're a market leader!

This attitude is a major factor for the enormous product failure rate. Think about what this means in terms of GDP!

So, you think your team is building the right product?

Patrick Campbell from *ProfitWell* produced a blog post about customer research. This research was sponsored by Adam Blake, CMO of ThriveHive. The survey included more than 3,000 companies using a subscription model and 1.2M subscription users.

The results from this survey were remarkable; I provide them here:

> Subscription and SaaS executives love to tell me they don't do customer research but by God, they love to A/B and multivariate test their way to success. Hill-climbing problems aside, in reality, we're not doing tests either. Nearly half of us are not even conducting 1 test per month and this includes marketing tests.
>
> We asked just over 2,500 product leaders to plot the last N features they built on a value matrix—which cross-references how much companies care about a particular feature compared to other features with how much they're willing to pay for features. In turn, this shows us what types of features we're putting out—be it core features, add-ons, or just plain trash.
>
> This is what your product leaders indicated they're building for the last five thousand features they built. A lot of differentiable and valuable features.

• • •

What We Think We're Building

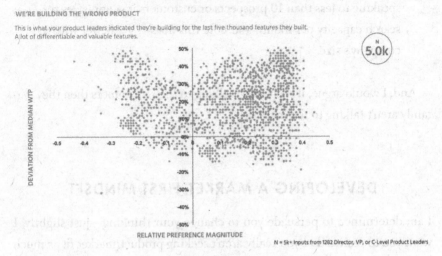

WE'RE BUILDING THE WRONG PRODUCT

This is what your product leaders indicated they're building for the last five thousand features they built. A lot of differentiable and valuable features.

N = 5k+ Inputs from 1282 Director, VP, or C-Level Product Leaders

FIGURE 15

We then went out and asked 1.2 million different customers about their actual willingness to pay and their actual preference for features using our statistical models, and this is what they indicated you're actually building.

What We're Actually Building

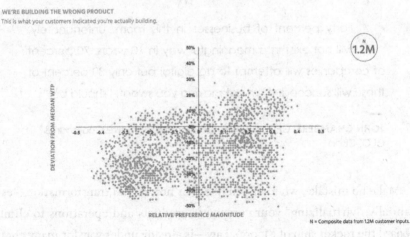

WE'RE BUILDING THE WRONG PRODUCT

This is what your customers indicated you're actually building.

N = Composite data from 1.2M customer inputs.

FIGURE 16

Executives indicated that 7 out of 10 of their organizations are speaking to less than 10 prospects or customers in a non-sales research capacity per month and note this doesn't get better with a company's size.[3]

And, I would argue, if they aren't talking to their customers then they certainly aren't talking to the market.

DEVELOPING A MARKET-FIRST MINDSET

I am determined to persuade you to change your thinking—just slightly. I want you to realize that you really aren't seeking product/market fit as much as you are looking for *market/product fit*. The difference may seem subtle, but it is, in fact, profound. Without a market, there is no need for your product.

You can only get market/product fit by adopting a market-first mindset and by using techniques that provide you with statistically valid market input. And it all has to be done quickly, because markets change rapidly.

In the digital economy, speed matters. Speed to market. Speed to decisions. Most people agree that digital transformation is what will enable companies to increase their velocity of new products and revenue.

> " Forty percent of businesses in this room, unfortunately, will not exist in a meaningful way in 10 years. 70 percent of companies will attempt to go digital but only 30 percent of those will succeed. If I'm not making you sweat, I should be."
>
> **JOHN CHAMBERS**, CEO, JC2 Ventures; former Executive Chairman & CEO, Cisco

Make no mistake, whether you like it or not, digital transformation—essentially, "virtualizing" your company's products and operations to climb aboard the rocket ship of Moore's Law—is already under way for many companies. This transformation will affect every company—B2C, B2B, B2B2C—and organization, of any size, in any industry, globally.

AI and machine-learning software that can operate on the "digital exhaust" of consumer and business transactions and signals in real time will provide companies with the ability to "think" smarter, act faster.

According to McKinsey and technology titans such as Tom Siebel, formerly CEO of Siebel Systems and now CEO of C3, a leading AI/ML company, the companies that don't get on the digital transformation train now are not likely to survive. More than 50 percent of the Fortune 500 companies that existed in 2000 are no longer around, gone due to acquisition or bankruptcy. And, the devastation isn't over. The companies that replaced them? Alphabet, Amazon, Salesforce, etc. These are companies that used digital transformation as a competitive weapon and won market leadership and category positions.

Over the next few years, digital transformation will compel all companies to retool their infrastructure and processes to secure and increase the top and bottom line.

In the 21st century, the top and bottom line begins with the product line.

- Product obsolescence will happen faster.
- Competitive advantages will disappear rapidly.
- Cash cows will be gored in months, not years.
- Internal product innovation and delivery skills will be an imperative, not just "nice to have."

Year after year, products will need to be designed and delivered faster than ever before. Mistakes will be more commonly fatal for companies of any size, not just startups.

In response, your product processes will need to adapt to become market-first and optimized to quickly provide you with the data you need to make accurate, fact-based—not opinion-based—product decisions.

If you are a startup leveraging digital transformation, this is great news; digital transformation is your tailwind. If you are an incumbent, this should serve as a warning.

THE MARKET-FIRST PRODUCT PROCESS

> " A great product manager has the brain of an engineer, the heart of a designer, and the speech of a diplomat."
>
> **DEEP NISHAR,** Senior Managing Partner, SoftBank Investment Advisers, former SVP, Products & User Experience at LinkedIn

I can't give you the Next Big Idea, but I will endeavor to show you how you can develop and leverage a market-first mindset and then manifest that mindset through the application of appropriate processes.

Those of us who have been involved in the product process—engineering, product marketing, UX design, and product management—have all learned, sometimes too late, about Lean startup methodologies and product/market fit.

Today, in our ever-faster-moving economy, if you want your product to succeed, you need to start thinking about *market/product fit* from the *moment* you begin the Ideation process. You must learn to become a *market-first company*. And to do that, you need to begin with a commitment to capture statistically valid market data.

Without accurate market data—delivered quickly—you are likely to fail. It is that simple. Thus, it is incumbent on you to get that data any way you can, as fast as you can.

Market research shows that for every three products that succeed, another seven fall short. For every three flashes of brilliance and intuition, there are another seven wrong guesses. For every three startups that actually do know best how to serve the market, there are seven startups or venture capitalists who think they know best, and don't.

The reality is that we live in a world that is overflowing with products and services. Today, more options than ever are flooding the market and all are competing for attention, excitement, and a finite pool of money.

There are some remarkable startups with amazing teams out there. But when the data shows that just 30 percent of products succeed (and that's the *best* case), everyone benefits from an approach that captures more useful information, not less.

You need *more than* a product-first approach, *more than* a customer-first approach, *more than* customer obsession. You need an approach that looks at future customers, potential customers, would-be customers, and, if you're an existing company with current customers, beyond them to engage the total market. You need to discover what drives your potential customers, what bugs them, and what motivates them to adopt new products and services. You need new kinds of data, and in this 21st century digital economy, you need all that data faster than ever before.

That is what I mean by market-first.

MARKET-FIRST DEFINED

The market-first product process demands that companies collect and interpret market signals from customers and noncustomers to identify existing and potential problems to be solved.

A strong "market signal" is generated by the combination of what the market *says* (captured via surveys, focus groups, social media, etc.) and what the market *does* (what people and businesses actually do). Acting on weak market signals (e.g., a small survey or focus group) instead of strong market signals (e.g., a broad market survey + product download and usage data) can, and often does, cause product failure.

Where do all of these market signals come from? The extent of this list may surprise you:

- ► Current customers
- ► Prospective customers

- Noncustomers
- Nonprospective customers
- Ecosystem
- Competition
- Influencers
- Partners
- Employees
- Vendors

How can you collect these market signals? This, too, is a list so extensive that it may surprise you:

- Discovery interviews
- Large-scale surveys
- Smoke tests
- Usability testing
- Usage monitoring
- A/B testing
- Engagement analysis
- Customer support
- NPS and customer experience data
- Social media sentiment
- Community feedback

Fortunately, there are now applications on the market that can help you collect market signals. But they work only if you acquire them and use the data they generate.

THE THREE PRINCIPLES OF MARKET-FIRST

To become a market-first startup, you must commit to adhering to three fundamental principles:

PRINCIPLE 1: Capture & Monitor Market Signals

A startup that embraces a market-first product process must incorporate a rigorous method for capturing and monitoring market signals—and doing so continuously over the life cycle of any product or service it brings to market.

PRINCIPLE 2: Continuously Measure & Test

A commitment to a market-first process requires your team to check its intuition with data. That means collecting and interpreting the market signals which, over time, include signals from your customers and, more importantly, *noncustomers*. It also means developing methods of *measuring and testing* your decision-making processes against facts, not opinions.

PRINCIPLE 3: Make Data-Driven Product Decisions

We are all inundated with calls for everyone and everything to be data-driven. So it is surprising how few startups—and their investors—have been willing to truly adopt a data-driven perspective before, during, and after product development. Instead, most simply pick selective data to support the same opinions they already hold. This becomes a self-fulfilling prophecy, producing the results you want rather than what you need. And those "wanted" results are the very ones that lead to large failure rates.

If you find yourself demanding that someone "show you the data" and yearning for real market signals before investing precious resources into a new product or feature, don't give up. Beware of moving forward without that empirical evidence from the market.

DEVELOPING MARKET IQ

Technical intelligence and market intelligence are not the same thing. Just because you are brilliant and capable of inventing new products or new features does not mean that you really have a data-driven understanding of the market for those products. Too often, just the opposite is true.

To become a market-first startup, you need to develop *Market IQ*.

How? You develop Market IQ by incorporating the principles of market-first processes and promulgating the adoption of a market-first mindset across the company. Startups with a strong Market IQ understand that they need to find a market/product fit before they begin to move forward with a new product design or upgrade.

Like all good measures of intelligence, Market IQ looks at multiple factors; in this case:

- what the market is concerned about,
- what causes those concerns, and, if possible,
- what potential solutions or products will ameliorate those concerns.

In life, being intelligent doesn't mean that every one of your ideas is correct. Nevertheless, the reason you want brilliant people working at your startup is that adopting a more intelligent approach to any problem increases the likelihood that you will succeed.

Market IQ is no different for a company. Being more intelligent in how you approach the product process makes it more likely that you will succeed in developing market/product fit for a new product design and upgrade.

> " Don't find customers for your products; find products for your customers."
>
> **SETH GODIN,** author; Founder & CEO, Do You Zoom

Many people find Seth Godin's statement obvious. They agree that you should always prioritize the market before focusing on product innovations. As we all know, however, agreeing to something in principle is easier than turning that principle into action.

In reality, very few companies use a market-first approach to product development. So what are they doing instead?

Startups, and even existing companies, tend to focus on products that they think represent solutions to big problems, and then find minimal selective data to support the investment.

Startups say they want to get market data, but it has always been so hard and expensive to get it quickly and accurately that they fall into the trap of finding selective data to support their preexisting perspectives. It is what statisticians call *confirmation bias*. And that is usually a very dangerous thing. However bad it is to realize your ignorance, it is infinitely worse to be confident in your inaccuracy. Bad questions inevitably lead to bad answers . . . and then to bad decisions.

Existing companies with customers are typically obsessed with focusing on current customers to the exclusion of the bigger picture—noncustomers—who often better represent the true overall market. These companies often also overemphasize certain parts of the market data when it is consistent with their world view and ignore or reject any data that challenges that image.

In short, startups—and companies in general—*say* they care about market input, but in practice reflect a method of decision making that prioritizes intuition and unrepresentative anecdotes about what their existing customers think.

The result? While everyone claims to care about the market, in reality most are simply "going through the motions" because they have already made up their minds regarding what they are going to do. This mindset and behavior are rampant among technology startups, ironically the very groups that should recognize what little they know about the marketplace.

Established companies often suffer from this disease as well. In their case it's usually disguised as "arrogance," and, if not attended to and addressed, it often can be a terminal disease.

My contention is simple: if everyone agrees that we should find products for a specific market or markets, then our practices should align with that and we should adhere to the three principles of being market-first.

OPINIONS VS. DATA

The problems that are outlined above don't stem from ill intentions or bad faith. All companies—startups or otherwise—want to do the right thing. But in the end, they almost always choose to implement the same set of practices over and over again because of time pressures, inertia and habit, and a lack of knowing a better way.

How do you prevent succumbing to the same deadly mistake?

What you need is a real framework, not just some nebulous concepts, along with real tools that make it easy to do the right thing and perform real market research. Only then can your startup focus on collecting and interpreting market signals rather than acting on intuition alone.

In short, your company must develop and work to cultivate its Market IQ.

By the way, intuition is inevitable. You can't escape it, even if you try. And just to be clear, you don't want to. You need it! Without intuition, you would have no starting point for collecting, interpreting, or acting on data. More importantly, you simply cannot collect data on everything. Intuition is critical to providing a place to start and focus as you learn more.

But you can't give intuition more respect than it is due. You can't be its slave. The problem is that for most startups, the big decisions related to product don't just use intuition to guide a data-driven process—intuition is the process. Worse yet, the team masquerades as being data-driven by finding only the selective data that support its preexisting plans. Now the company isn't just lying to the world, it is also lying to itself.

By comparison, a market-first product process harnesses the power of intuition to guide and discipline a subsequent intense data-driven process that can mean life or death for a new product.

_____

Here's an example of a big company that blew it. Apple.

Apple Newton

FIGURE 17

The Apple Newton is a classic case of the distinction between intelligence and Market IQ. After six years and $100 million in development, the Apple Newton was released in the early 1990s with a level of functionality that was mind-blowing for the era. The technology itself was impressive. I was at Apple at the time, running one of the company's engineering divisions, building object technology infrastructure, and I can assure you that some of Apple's best people were involved in this project. And why not? It was going to be the Next Big Thing.

Newton's new features included everything from constant Internet connectivity to touch screens to handwriting recognition. The product development team had truly created a disruptive and innovative technology.

The problem was that the intuition and brilliance that led the company to develop Newton was not combined with a Market IQ approach that might have revealed the limits of the market to support that innovation.

I'm not claiming that a market-first process would have saved the Apple Newton. Instead, I am suggesting that being market-first might have saved Apple the money that it invested in the Newton. Instead, prioritizing innovation and disruption over market assessment proved to be devastating. As Mat Honan noted in *Wired* magazine, *"The Newton wasn't just killed, it was violently murdered, dragged into a closet by its hair and kicked to death in its youth by one of technology's great men."*[4]

We now know that the intuition and intelligence that led to the advanced innovations found in the Apple Newton were in fact correct. Just look at your smartphone or tablet, both direct descendants of Newton, and both gigantic global markets. After his graphic description of the Newton's demise, Honan himself concedes: "And yet it was a remarkable device, one whose influence is still with us today. The tablet. The first computer designed to free us utterly from the desktop."

This comment raises an interesting question. Could a market-first process have saved Apple from making the investment in the Newton *at that particular moment?*

A market-first process would have required the intuition associated with the product to first be assessed based on the data. What types of data? Imagine if the Apple Newton had been the result of a series of Discovery Interviews where consumers had complained about being chained to their desktops. That would have set in motion the product development team with some great data that validated the intuition that this was a truly disruptive technology designed to help people overcome a basic problem. But that didn't happen. And I suspect that if this research had occurred, it would have found that the personal computer was still so young that this requisite frustration with desktops had not yet emerged.

That said, Discovery Interviews alone are not enough to satisfy the market-first process. Now imagine that the Apple Newton was also obsessed with usability testing to determine the basic functionality of the device in the various environments, such as coffee shops and conference rooms. Apple likely would have quickly discovered that the dearth of Internet availability in those locations at the time challenged their assumption of constant Internet connectivity.

Additional usability testing also would have revealed that their vaunted handwriting-recognition software was severely compromised—so much so, in fact, that cartoonist Garry Trudeau dedicated a week of *Doonesbury* to mocking its poor functionality. In Honan's view, "Handwriting recognition was supposed to be Newton's killer feature, and yet it was the feature that probably ultimately killed the product."

In the Hacks section of this chapter, I'll show you how to execute four collection processes to help you determine market signal: Discovery interviews, large-scale surveys, smoke tests, and A/B tests. I'm only covering this partial set—and even then, I'm just providing a cursory overview—because covering every market signal collection process in full detail would require an entire book dedicated to the topic. In fact, learning how to collect statistically valid market signals should be an integral part of a much longer, more formal product management course.

I hope you can see that a market-first process might have helped the product development team rely on more than the intuition that told them they were doing something truly innovative and disruptive. At a minimum, early usability testing in a Lean startup approach would have revealed that the market signals simply did not support the innovation.

The market-first process and mindset also would have revealed that, while there may have been a basic interest in moving beyond the confines of the desktop, releasing the Apple Newton into the world *before* it—and the world—had both full functionality and an adequate technology architecture would mean that the $100 million technology might literally become a laughing matter.

> " You've got to start with the customer experience and work back toward the technology—not the other way around."
>
> **STEVE JOBS**, Cofounder & CEO, Apple Inc.

So, why don't companies rely more on data for their product process? It is not because they don't want data. It is often because *they don't want to wait on the data*. They assume that it is too hard to get that data, especially from non-customers, in a timely fashion. So, instead, they "punt" and go with their gut.

Steve Capps was in charge of the Apple Newton's user interface and software development teams. In an interview with Honan, Capps admitted "We barely got it functioning by '93 when we started shipping it." His assessment on the failure of the Apple Newton was simple: "We were just way ahead of the technology."

The pressure to meet an external deadline is real. Everyone reading this book knows that. That's why a market-first approach is designed to install a process that enables you to harness the power of your intuition while simultaneously reducing the likelihood that a product fails because there is not enough data to support an intelligent decision. The most basic question that all products must face to be successful must always be: Is there a market for it right now?

CUSTOMER VS. MARKET

It sounds great to say that your company is customer-driven. After all, who can object to focusing on your customers? But, like everything in business, the question is: *At what expense?* If you are customer-driven at the expense of the market, then you can create huge issues for yourself in the long term.

A strong Market IQ that emanates from a market-driven mindset doesn't ignore customers. You can never stop listening to your customers. The key is to balance that feedback against other market participants, *especially non-customers*.

> " If I had asked people what they wanted, they would have said faster horses."
>
> **HENRY FORD,** Founder, Ford Motor Company

There are two risks associated with being too customer-driven.

1. **Feature Bloat**—As Clayton Christensen outlines in *The Innovator's Dilemma*, customers often provide feedback for incremental product improvement that can lead to feature bloat over time.
2. **Market Participation**—Focusing too much on customers means that you miss out on all the other market participants. While influencers and analysts can also be important constituents, the big-ticket groups are the noncustomers who may have never engaged with you or even visited your website.

Why pay so much attention to noncustomers? If you are wildly successful and have 20 percent of the market share, then that means you have four times as many noncustomers as customers. In truth, for most companies the ratio of noncustomers to customers is more like 10 to 30x.

In the long term, your noncustomers are a main source for growth. According to Clayton Christensen, they also help you generate ideas on breakthrough (instead of incremental) products and features.

This idea leads us to ask a very important set of questions:

- How well do you know your noncustomers? (As an early-stage startup, that might be your entire market.)
- If you're an existing company with existing products:
  - Why have they not heard of you?
  - If they have heard of you, why have they not visited your website?
  - If they did visit your website, why did they not engage?
  - If they did engage, why are they not converting?

Understanding the perspectives of your noncustomers—really, your potential customers—is an essential component of Market IQ, the market-first product process and mindset.

SEEING THE TREES AND THE FOREST

A critical component of developing your Market IQ is to be data-driven—*in practice*. Easy to say, but what does that really mean? Some of you may think you *are* data-driven. If you are part of a large incumbent company, you may have millions or tens of millions of users generating petabytes of data.

That sounds great. But, from the perspective of the market-first product process, it is not enough merely to have access to vast amounts of data. It is necessary, but not sufficient. The real question is: Do you have the right types of data? A market-first approach is designed to enhance the qualification funnel, which is essential for market fit.

Zynga knows this firsthand. Zynga is a master at A/B testing and click-stream analysis. The company has petabytes of data and can drill down to get a very precise understanding of what is happening.

What Zynga can't do well, however, is know *why* something is happening.

According to a former Zynga product executive, the data was so rich and so deep that the company was staring only into the bottom of the funnel. "It was like looking at your feet rather than looking at the horizon," this executive recalls. "From the perspective of Big Data, we weren't just focusing on the trees at the expense of the forest . . . we were analyzing the atoms that made up the bark of the trees."

Being truly data-driven still means acknowledging the need for the vast array of data that is now available to all of us, but also having a direction before diving in. This is a key distinction to avoid lapsing into an ad hoc product process where decisions are made based on an intense review of customer feedback without a vision for the overall market or the future of the product or its features. I will compare and contrast this ad hoc product process and the market-first product process later in this chapter.

For now, it is important to understand that this mistake is the embodiment of the concept of *shifting bottlenecks*. You can use the data to fix problems with execution by looking deep into the funnel, but at some point you get diminishing returns. At that key moment, you need to be able to look up, get a view of the horizon, and seek a new direction. Once you have identified this new direction, you can dig right back into the data to make the execution possible.

The key, then, to being data-driven is having the flexibility to shift your focus from the forest to the trees and back again as the situation requires. In doing so, you will use market and customer signals to guide your product development, rather than simply focusing on how much functionality you can achieve at the microscopic level.

PROBLEM SPACE VS. SOLUTION SPACE

> As a product manager at Intuit, I learned to write detailed product requirements that stayed in the problem space without getting into the solution space. We were trained to first focus on 'what' the product needed to accomplish for customers before getting into 'how' the product would accomplish it."

DAN OLSEN, Consultant, Olsen Solutions LLC; author, *The Lean Product Playbook*

What does Dan Olsen mean when he refers to a "problem space" versus a "solution space"?

A simple example can help illustrate both concepts.

Let's say you wake up one morning with a pain in your abdomen that is accompanied by nausea and fever. If you simply wanted fixes for each of these issues, you could reach for Pepto-Bismol for the stomach pain and the nausea, and ibuprofen for the fever. That approach, where you focus on treating the symptoms, is the solution space.

The problem space prompts you to ask why the symptoms are occurring in the first place. Could your symptoms represent the stomach flu, food poisoning, or something much worse—such as appendicitis—that might require an emergency response?

According to Olsen, you will eventually need to get to the solution space, but first you need to deal with the problem space. Not to do that would be like trying to cure appendicitis with Pepto-Bismol and ibuprofen—that solution can be extremely dangerous.

Why do companies fall for the solution space trap? Simple. Many market signals (e.g., customer complaints) come in the form of symptoms and even solutions (e.g., fix this or build this great new feature!). Your job is to interpret those signals, identify any root causes, brainstorm solutions, and then go back to the symptomatic customers to see if the root cause and solution are correct.

In other words, you allow the complaints to determine the boundaries of the problem—and from there, you choose the limit of the number of options for a solution. But what if the real problem is beyond those boundaries you've set for yourself? Then you will miss the problem completely; but worse, you will waste time and treasure in implementing the wrong solution.

When Oxo, a kitchen utensil company, asked customers what was wrong with its measuring cup, the customers talked about the cup's breaking when they dropped it or its having a slippery handle. But when Oxo watched people use the measuring cup, they saw people pour, then bend down to read the measurements, then pour, then bend, then pour, then bend. Nobody asked to be able to read the measurements while pouring, but Oxo was able to see the need. They now sell a measuring cup with the measurements at an angle so you can see the lines while pouring liquids into the cup.

Identifying and then operating within the problem space is, it almost goes without saying, a cornerstone of the market-first approach. And, in fact, it forms the basis of the definition of market-first.

The lesson is simple: start with the problem space, and you will end up with more effective solutions.

• • •

What Does the Market-First Product Process Look Like?

▪ From Product-First/To Market-First ▪

FROM	TO
Product-First	Market-First
Customer-driven focus	Market-driven focus (including noncustomers)
Making decisions based on opinions & anecdotes	Making decisions based on market facts & signals
Ad hoc product management	Data-driven product process
Focusing on the solution space	Focusing on the problem space

MARKET-FIRST BENEFITS

It is difficult to overestimate the benefits and importance of *knowing* the market to facilitate market/product fit. There are countless examples of product failures because companies assume that innovation and disruption are enough to guarantee demand. It isn't.

Companies that don't know the market can introduce products that go nowhere, because there's no market for them. Take Pepsi, for example. In the late 1980s, two trends collided. The cola wars were in full swing, with the two giants Coca-Cola and Pepsi routinely taking swings at each other, and the coffee market was shrinking. Coke and Pepsi left no market unexplored, trying to hijack each other's flavor profiles and making ill-fated brand partnerships and crossovers.

Looking for untapped markets, Pepsi zeroed in on the morning beverage market, which had been dominated by another caffeinated beverage, but of the hot variety: coffee. Given the coffee market's decline, Pepsi attempted to capture that market with a high-caffeine version of their soft drink, to kick-start a person's day. Pepsi A.M. was marketed toward the niche market of giving soda drinkers an alternative to coffee as their beverage of choice in the morning.

Needless to say, the demand for a morning soda had been grossly overestimated, and Pepsi A.M. was discontinued in 1990, just a year after being released into a couple of test markets.

If you are reading this book over a hot cup of coffee and not a cold can of Pepsi, it is because innovation and disruption alone do not generate market fit. Needless to say, Pepsi failed to take a market-first approach.

A market-first product approach helps increase the likelihood and speed of market/product fit by guiding the decision-making process with key data from market signals. If you are a startup with no prior product in a market, everyone is a noncustomer, and capturing accurate market signals from them is the only thing you have to rely on.

Armed with the data, startups can help facilitate market/product fit by:

- reducing pivots
- minimizing overbuilding or underbuilding MVP
- minimizing features that are not used

Once you cultivate a strong Market IQ, you begin to see that market/product fit is not a one-time event for a new product: the market continues to shift, and companies/products must constantly evolve as well.

MARKET-FIRST DEFINED BY OTHERS

I suspect many of you already intuitively recognize the benefits of a market-first product approach. In fact, there are lots of leaders across a variety of industries who have expressed the importance of considering the entire market. Here are some of my favorites:

> The key is to find your problem, understand your problem and only build something valuable if you're solving a problem you know better than anyone else. I knew exactly what problem I wanted to solve. Find a problem that you really are obsessed with and understand it better than anyone else, that's the only way to find a valuable answer. And do what you love, you'll do it and you'll love doing it and you'll be happy."

EMILY BROOKE, CEO & Founder, beryl.cc (formerly Blaze)

> We started by looking at the industry generally and found there was a gap in the market. We spent a lot of time researching the market, to understand what others were doing and where we could create value."

LUKE STATTER AND SAM DRIVER, Founders, Thousand Yard Films

> If you sit on your laurels, there's a risk your customers will move away from you. You could have a perfectly good product or service, but your customers may have become more demanding or there may be new, cheaper or more innovative competitors in the market."

JOHN FITZGERALD, Chief Executive, BRAVE

> Everybody always says that knowing your market is everything. Saying it is one thing, but understanding why it is so important will help you stay ahead of the pack."

JAMES CAAN, former Chairman, Startup Loans Company

I'M ALREADY MARKET-FIRST!

Excellent! That means you have already committed to using market signals from customers *and* noncustomers to help manage production.

In my experience, the people and startups who are committed to a market-first product approach ensure that they are committed to collecting and interpreting all the market signals, not just a select few.

Just to make sure that you are collecting and interpreting the best market signals, let's confirm that you collect data from current customers, prospective customers, noncustomers, nonprospective customers, ecosystem, competition, influencers, partners, and employees.

And that the data you are collecting involves the list I've provided previously: Discovery interviews, large-scale surveys, smoke tests, usability testing, usage data, A/B testing, engagement analysis, customer support, NPS and customer experience data, social media sentiment, and community feedback.

If you are missing any of these, you'd better make a convincing case to yourself that they aren't necessary. Until that occurs, you should be haunted by the possibility that you are missing a key source of valuable data.

THE TRANSITION TO MARKET-FIRST

One reason I am so passionate about the market-first product process is that I see the inevitability of its adoption. I am confident that you already know the old days of building products on a hunch are gone—or soon to be gone, because your competitors are ever more likely to pursue a market-first, data-driven approach.

You are a decision maker—and decision makers want to make decisions based on data. Decision makers have always longed for this, but getting salient data has previously been considered too difficult or time-consuming. And the introduction and widespread adoption of Agile software development methodologies, which advocate continuous releases of code into the market every three to four weeks rather than one or two releases a year, only exacerbates the market signal collection and market validation problem.

Making decisions without consulting data is simply not the world we live in anymore. According to the EMC Digital Universe 2014 report, "Like the physical universe, the digital universe is large—by 2020 containing nearly as many digital bits as there are stars in the universe. It is doubling in size every two years, and by 2020 the digital universe—the data we create and copy annually—will reach 44 zettabytes, or 44 trillion gigabytes."[5]

In the good old days, prior to, say, the 21st century, product teams could occasionally scrape by with intuition and selective data that supported their ideas. No longer. Now we can obtain mountains of useful data on every possible subject—all with the touch of a few keys. The challenge in the digital economy and the First Intelligence Age is no longer getting the right data. The challenge now is to ask the right questions.

The old excuses for not being market-first are vanishing by the second. The data is out there. The data is ready to be collected and interpreted. The market signals are ready to help fact-check, support, and expand the power of your intuition. The Golden Gut school of business strategy has been relegated to the dustbin of history.

> ❝ Startups don't fail because they lack a product; they fail because they lack customers and a profitable business model."
>
> —
>
> **STEVE BLANK**, Adjunct Professor, Stanford University; author, *The Startup Owner's Manual*

But how can you be market-first quickly and cost-effectively, especially when three resources you need as a startup—time, capital, and expertise—are in short supply?

Until recently, it has been extremely difficult unless you developed your own internal tools and expertise . . . and even then, it was challenging.

However, I am excited to share with you the fact that I decided to address this market-first problem head on. I personally founded—and Wildcat Venture Partners funded—a company called Obo (www.obo.pm), whose mission is to enable product teams to become market-first—make better, faster data-driven decisions so they can create products the market needs.

Obo executed a large market survey of more than 2,000 companies—half from the technology sector and the other half from all other industries—to identify key product challenges.

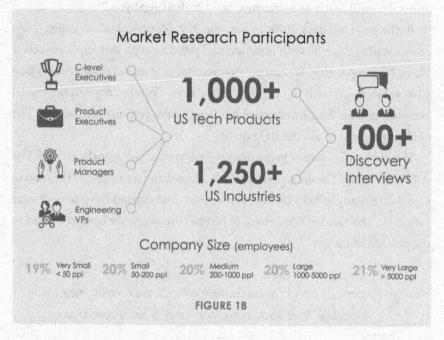

Market Research Participants

- C-level Executives
- Product Executives
- Product Managers
- Engineering VPs

1,000+ US Tech Products

1,250+ US Industries

100+ Discovery Interviews

Company Size (employees)

19% Very Small < 50 ppl   20% Small 50-200 ppl   20% Medium 200-1000 ppl   20% Large 1000-5000 ppl   21% Very Large > 5000 ppl

FIGURE 18

Here are some of the findings from the survey:

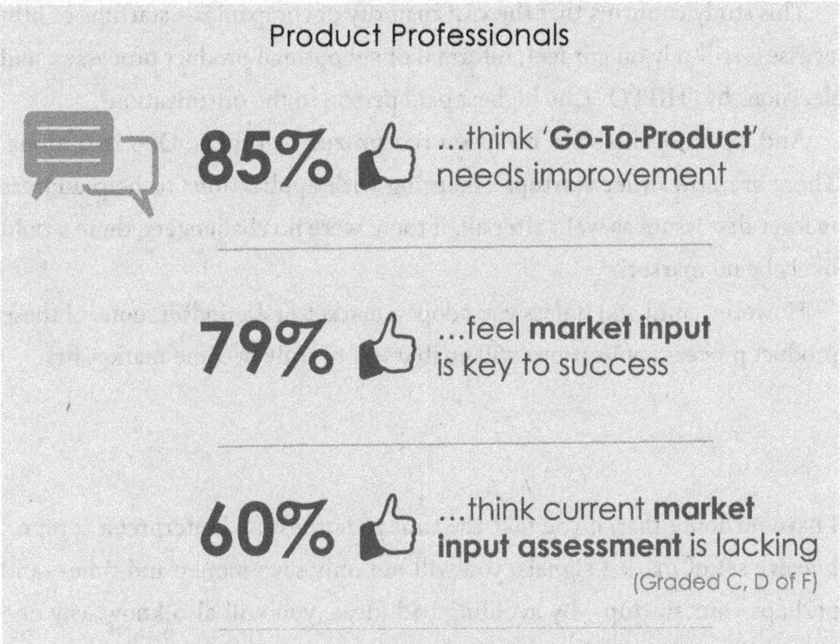

Product Professionals

 85% ...think '**Go-To-Product**' needs improvement

79% ...feel **market input** is key to success

60% ...think current **market input assessment** is lacking
(Graded C, D of F)

FIGURE 19

Leading Companies Aspire to Leverage

 66% ...**Best Practices,** but currently do not

★ Currently companies such as Nike, Google, Intuit, and P&G leverage best practices.

79% ...**Market Data,** but currently do not

★ Currently companies such as Chase, Toyota, Amazon, and Coca-Cola leverage market data.

FIGURE 20

This study confirms that the vast majority of companies—startups or otherwise—still rely on gut feel, informal or suboptimal product processes, and decisions by "HIPPO" (the highest paid person in the organization).

And, because this void has been recognized by others, Obo isn't alone. There are now other startups emerging with applications to help address market-first issues as well; after all, if there were no challengers, there would likely be no market!

However, until and unless you adopt a market-first mindset, none of these product process applications will enable you to truly become market-first.

———

I have no doubt that, if you take the time to harness and interpret a comprehensive set of market signals, you will not only save money and time—and perhaps your startup—by avoiding bad ideas, you will also know *why* one strategy is working and *why* another is not . . . which is the key information you need to really make a difference.

———

As part of the research for this book, I had a few members of our team interview Sean Ellis.[6] Sean is the CEO and founder of GrowthHackers.com. He is credited with coining the term "growth hacking" after using it to develop powerful growth strategies for Dropbox, Eventbrite, LogMeIn, and Lookout. Sean also founded and sold customer-insights company Qualaroo, growing it to millions of dollars in recurring revenue with customers such as Uber, Starbucks, and Amazon. Finally, he is the coauthor of *Hacking Growth*, a book which has received much attention since its initial publication in 2017.

Sean is considered by many to be the "guru" of growth marketing strategies—primarily for B2C companies—and his perspective is useful to this discussion. And many of these B2C marketing strategies also work for B2B marketing. B2B applications are now invited into companies through the "front door"—by individual employees and teams, not the IT department, who discover their initial utility and want to put them to use inside the company.

The discussion with Sean didn't focus exclusively on the go-to-market phase (in Chapter 6, "Getting to Minimum Viable Repeatability," I will share with you some of Sean's tips for customer acquisition); it also included his observations about reaching market/product fit and using data to confirm that companies actually had achieved this milestone. Sean said:

> I did a ton of surveying of companies when I worked with them, basically going in and asking "How would you feel if you could no longer use this product" and finding those people who say they'd be very disappointed without it and essentially trying to tap into the essence of what makes the product a must-have for people.
>
> Once I understand that, it starts to tell me who I should be targeting. Who are the people who say they'd be very disappointed without it? Then I can dig into how they discover products like this and start to give you more ideas about the channels to find them. But I can also figure out what is the main benefit that they get from the product and how can I set the right promise when new users are coming in based on what I know the product is great at already delivering.
>
> That might sound just like Marketing 101, but to give you an example, I ran a survey to the user base of one of my clients where I asked them "How would you feel if you could no longer use this product" and only 7 percent of the people came back and said they'd be very disappointed without the product. But they gave such a consistent signal of the benefit that they were getting that we were able to reposition the product on that benefit and then streamline the onboarding into just that part of the app. That only took a couple of weeks, but within two weeks we took the next cohort of people from 7 percent to 40 percent.

KEY TAKEAWAYS

Now let's put it all together, incorporating what we have just learned about the Initial Product Release, including a market-first approach.

If you have successfully reached IPR, your product should be quality-assured, with few critical bugs, and should be compelling visually and functionally to use. One of the biggest mistakes start-ups can make is to push their product out to consumers or business users before it is ready. That is especially tragic if that company *has* taken the time to understand what the market needs.

If the product is incomplete—if it still has a shoddy UX/UI or is filled with annoying bugs—it isn't ready for anyone to see or use. At IPR, your product should be ready for a full-fledged "Beta" program.

But that is only the beginning. Here is a closer look at the other milestones you will need to have reached to have a successful Initial Product Release:

PRODUCT

Product—Before a company reaches IPR, all team members should not just understand, but have internalized, what it means to be market-first. They should have met 1:1 with a statistically valid set of users and observe as they work with the product or service. Team members should have captured direct feedback and collectively documented and assessed what is and isn't working. This process can take anywhere from 3 to 6+ months, so you need to begin early. Meanwhile, the company should not declare that the product is in Beta or ready until all critical bugs or issues have been resolved, and until users rate the UX/UI at least an 8 on a scale of 10—and that it has a positive NPS score.

REVENUE

Revenue—Initial pricing models, marketing and sales waterfall conversion rate assumptions, and contract documents should be well-formed at this point. The company should have a good idea of how it intends to handle service-level agreements and reimbursements. It should also have a reasonable idea of how it intends to go to market: Field sales? Account-based marketing (ABM)? Self-serve? Inside sales? A combination of two or more? In parallel with product-engineering, the company should be doing in-depth market-engineering to determine the category you are defining/redefining, value propositions, pricing strategies, etc.

TEAM

Team—A few new team members should have been added in marketing to complete critical work such as the company's messaging matrix, positioning, naming, branding, and information architecture for the initial website, and to prepare content for the company's initial market launch. You will need to perform a significant amount of user/customer data analysis going forward. As a result, a key hire is a data analyst.

SYSTEMS

Systems—The company should have begun the process of formally evaluating systems that can automate various marketing and sales

(continues)

functions and support the initial revenue generation. The website should be well-architected to explain the company and the product, and, if appropriate, to enable onboarding and e-commerce functions; and it should be ready to go live.

You have now completed the Initial Product Release phase, a critical step toward traversing the Traction Gap. Now it is time to execute on that introduction. We'll investigate how that is done in the next chapters.

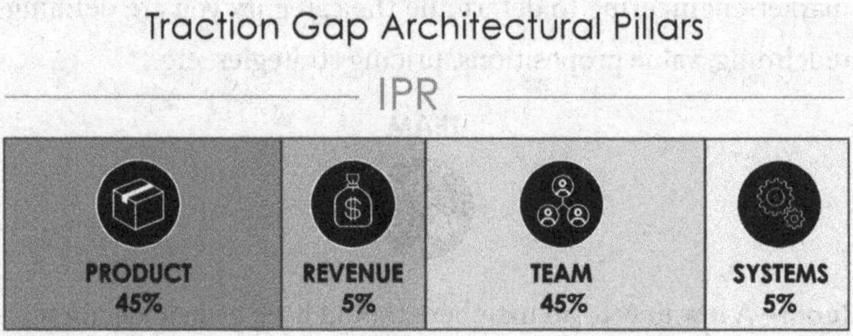

Traction Gap Architectural Pillars

IPR

| PRODUCT 45% | REVENUE 5% | TEAM 45% | SYSTEMS 5% |

FIGURE 21
Percentage of emphasis during this stage.

The following are the key principles Wildcat Venture Partners looks for at IPR:

■ Traction Gap Principles ■
IPR

Product	Don't build everything. Obsess about the things that users really rely on and actually use. Develop a market-first mindset and process.
Revenue	Focus on a subset of a market, then expand outward from there.
Team	Hire only the best people, preferably those you've worked with previously.
Systems	Keep your systems incredibly lightweight at this stage.

TRACTION GAP HACKS ▶ IPR

The following are four of several methods you can execute to capture market signals during the Ideation-to-IPR stage. They have been developed from some of the best product practices at companies in Silicon Valley.

Discovery Interviews

How do you generate ideas? If you are interested in finding problems to solve and features to build, I recommend you use Discovery Interviews. This is an in-depth interview technique designed to uncover new insights from stakeholders regarding:

- ▶ business strategy
- ▶ product strategy/product roadmaps
- ▶ visual brand strategy
- ▶ positioning and messaging
- ▶ website strategy and design
- ▶ marketing strategy and planning
- ▶ content strategy
- ▶ customer experience strategy[7]

Discovery Interviews are a great way of developing tens, if not hundreds, of new ideas. Additionally, Discovery Interviews can generate deeper insights with scale.

You typically should work with groups of 5, 10, or 20 if you are focusing on B2B. Why? If you are looking for a specific job title, you need a larger pool to have a better shot at tracking that person down. I recommend you use LinkedIn as a very effective way to reach out and find the right people with the right titles for your B2B interviews.

On the other hand, if you are focusing on B2C, then you may want to try a different tactic altogether. Why not try going to a coffee shop and offering to buy a coffee for the next person with a $5 gift card if they are up for answering questions for 10 minutes.

Which coffee shop? It depends. For example, you can use geography to pick a coffee shop near a college or a military base if that is who you are looking for.

What if you were looking for young mothers? Be creative and head to a park or neighborhood where you see lots of strollers in the middle of the day.

Once you have your subject locked in, you can start the interview process. Remember, this is a *Discovery* Interview, which means you must be careful not to bias the conversation.

Tips for conducting a Discovery Interview:

- ask open-ended questions first
- ask clarifying questions next
- ask to evaluate what others have said next
- ask them to make a choice (impose a cost)—what are your top 3 of these options I have here?

It is important to impose a cost, because people are full of ideas. Some of those ideas are good ideas. The problem is that customers are very smart about what they want, but they are not as smart about what it *costs* to make those dreams a reality.

It is critical then to determine just how badly customers really want a new feature or a new product. Imposing a cost means forcing them to confront an opportunity cost, such as "Would you give up two hours of battery life to make that happen?"

Ideally you can record audio of the interviews (video is too intimidating for many subjects), because people's notes are rarely accurate. In order to record, you will need permission—and sometimes gaining permission can be a bit of an impediment. But I have found that people become accustomed to the formal arrangement pretty quickly. It helps if you make sure that the microphone is small and unobtrusive. Even better, there are several phone and tablet applications that allow you to easily record interviews—no external microphone required.

Large-Scale Surveys

The beauty of Discovery Interviews is that they can generate lots of new ideas. Those ideas can translate into new proposals for features or products. What Discovery Interviews are *not* great at is giving you a real sense of what to prioritize at any given time.

Even in a large interview study of, say, twenty people you can end up concluding that you've uncovered a significant trend or preference . . . only to find out that instead you merely had twenty people with a particular bias, and that a larger pool of people would have shown otherwise.

That is why you should supplement your interviews with validation surveys. Validation surveys allow you to get a better sense of the overall market by tapping many more perspectives. You can take the 50 to 100 ideas that came out of a typical set of Discovery Interviews and ask people (especially noncustomers) what they think.

The key is to understand that you are using validation surveys to get a sense of preference. The instrument is not exhaustive, and that is intentional.

Greater depth is not always better if it means that people produce worse ideas. Asking someone to rank-order 10 things is reasonable, but asking them to rank-order 100 things produces junk data for anything beyond the first 10 items.

Some basic features of a good validation survey include:

► Questions that ask participants to rate all features on a scale from 1 to 5 or 1 to 7. There is lots of research out there on when you should prefer one of these scales to the other.

► Questions that include a stack rank feature. This gives better relative detail since the interview subjects are literally choosing how they would rank their preferences. As a helpful tip, any more than 10 items tends to become too difficult for participants.

► Questions that ask the participants to "pick the ones you like." This is great for usability studies, especially for a larger list of more than 15 items. As a helpful tip, limit the number of "picks" a person can make so you don't get the dreaded "they are all fine" response.

► Questions that are a simple thumbs-up or thumbs-down. Once again, this is great for usability studies when you have a larger list to work with.

► Questions that ask the audience to consider spending a specific amount of money, say $100. Ask the participant to allocate the funds across a list to determine what he or she would really be interested in buying.

The best survey is one that mixes all these question types, in order to approach the subject matter from multiple directions and modalities to triangulate in on the truth.

In addition to these types of questions, consider going a bit more advanced and employing some max differential and conjoint analysis instruments. Those can really provide some cool and insightful data.

Once you have your data, you will want to have some basic rules and tools for interpretation. You have probably taken several statistics courses over the years, so I won't regurgitate it all here, but suffice it to say that you want to make sure that you have a grasp of:

► confidence level and margin of error (confidence interval)
► directionality and statistical significance

- distribution type
- single vs. double-tailed
- Z-scores

Surveys are an important way to move from the ideas that are generated by Discovery Interviews toward an actual sense of the preferences of the market. Given the choice of using them or not, in most circumstances you should put them to work.

Companies such as Obo, which provide product teams with the ability to build market-first products, typically offer their own courses on how to do statistical validation and teach teams how to use their application suites.

Smoke Tests

Discovery Interviews generate ideas, and surveys help you take those ideas and discern a market preference. With luck, that will narrow your list to the top 10 ideas for features or products.

Now you need to know how many people would actually go beyond preference to *buy* the items in question.

One way to start getting a sense of real market demand is to run *smoke tests*. The goal here is to see how big the very top of the funnel is for each of the ideas we have generated and tested through surveys.

Each funnel typically has an outcome, such as increased revenue, virality, conversion rates, engagement rates, retention, etc.—but the critical question is how many people are at the very top and willing to try the product at all.

When I have seen a product or feature fail, it is often because of poor performance at the very top of the funnel. For these doomed products, there is only a small percent of users or target market that ever tries the product or feature. With such a small input, the number of potential customers that can be induced to buy becomes too small for profitability at the bottom of the funnel.

So if you believe that 25 percent of your target market is excited about your product and will try it right away . . . but only 2 percent actually *do* give it a try, then it doesn't matter that you have a 100 percent conversion rate for the rest of the funnel. The top of the funnel is simply too small to make that product a success.

How do you get a good sense of what percentage of users or target market will initially try a product or feature *before* you invest the time and money into writing a single line of code?

This is where smoke tests come in.

Smoke Test #1: Ad

Description: You show an ad for a prospective product or feature to a channel (e.g., LinkedIn, Facebook, or Google). A user clicks on the ad and ends up on a landing page. The page provides a short 2-to-4-sentence description of the product or feature.

After this description, the page says something like "Thank you for your interest. We are in the process of building this. If you would like to be notified when it is ready, please provide your email below."

The clicks on the ad will show you the reach for the concept. How many people are interested in the product or feature? The email addresses show how strong the interest really is because it imposes a cost—surrendering personal data—on the potential user. It is not as high a cost as a pre-order deposit; but it still shows interest, because no one wants to risk being "spammed" unless they are truly interested.

Smoke Test #2: Fake Door

Description: You use a widget that shows a pop-up or "toaster" ad in your website or app that describes the new concept or feature.

A toaster ad is an animated flash mini-commercial overlaid into a video. When a "toaster" ad appears onscreen, the viewer has the option to watch more about the commercial and is then taken to a "player within the player," where he or she is encouraged to interact with the advertiser's content. The video then continues to play after the user is finished viewing the ad.

After the short description, there is a "Try it now" button. When the user clicks the button, he or she sees a second pop-up that says "Thank you for your interest. We are in the process of building this. If you would like to be notified when it is ready, please provide your email below."

Once again, the clicks show reach and the email addresses show motivation.

These smoke tests can help you determine how large the top of the funnel is before you make a serious investment in your new product or feature.

With the mouth of the funnel secure, you can now focus on the throat of the funnel—the actual sales process—secure in the knowledge that you will have enough sales prospects with whom to work once the product is actually available.

A/B Testing

Once you are at the design stage and ready to proceed with specific decisions, you need to introduce *A/B testing*. A/B testing shows multiple variations concurrently.

The primary benefit of A/B testing is that you avoid the problems associated with traditional pre/post testing, in which a subject interacts with variations of the same product and is biased toward one simply because of the order in which they were presented.

There are times when you may not be able to perform concurrent operations. For example, you may not be in a position to run two databases from different vendors at the same time. So you have to be creative and do the best you can do within your constraints.

When A/B testing began to become more mainstream, there were two basic objections to this methodology.

First, there were no frameworks; it took a lot of custom coding and analysis to perform the testing properly.

Second, people argued that they did not have time to build a product more than once for testing.

In time, the first objection was remedied with technology; today there are lots of commercial products available to help with A/B testing. The second objection has been resolved through experience.

Invariably, when people release a new product or major feature, it performs at only about 30 to 40 percent of expectations in terms of revenue or conversion rates or engagement. That's bad enough; but if you release the product or feature without doing A/B testing, then you will have no real understanding *why* something is failing to perform up to expectations.

Many companies assume that the failure is due to those 3 or 4 sub-features that were left out. They then force the release of the new features . . . and the needle only moves a couple of points. That's when they panic.

Two things tend to happen next: companies either move on to other products or features in hopes that the next bright and shiny option will be more successful; or they simply load the current offering up with even more features. But, as often as not, this gesture fails as well, because they still don't understand the *why* of their depressed customer demand.

A/B testing breaks this vicious cycle because, when you release the 3 or 4 variants for testing, you get a comprehensive overview of what is and what is not working.

Experience suggests that if you release four variants, then one or two will work and one or two will not. You should update your A/B experiments every week, killing off the poorly performing variants and refining the ones that work.

A simple analogy helps reveal the power of good A/B testing. Imagine that you go to your car mechanic because you noticed an electrical issue. Perhaps the dashboard lights are going on and off. The mechanic does no troubleshooting and instead just starts replacing parts . . . on your dime. The mechanic may randomly end up actually fixing the problem; but without any troubleshooting, the mechanic can't inform you *what* the problem was in the first place—and you have spent a lot of money for that ignorance.

After 5 or 6 weeks of good usability testing, you can usually go from 40 percent of expectations to 80, 90, and sometimes even 120 percent of expectations. A/B testing ultimately is a methodical and data-driven approach to troubleshooting issues and isolating possible root causes. By comparison, nonsystematic testing ultimately may identify a problem, but provides no answers to prevent a similar problem from recurring.

When designing your A/B tests, here are several key principles you should follow:

- Typically limit to 2 to 4 variants for any given test.
- Keep the test population the same size for each variant. Thus, if 2 percent of population sees variant 1, then keep it to 2 percent for variants 2, 3, 4, etc. This makes it easier to compare results and avoid any scaling issues (sometimes when you double the population, the effect is nonlinear and may go up by only 50 percent instead of the expected 100 percent).
- You always need to have at least one control, so you have a benchmark to see how much each variant is better (or worse) than what you currently have.
- Testing in B2C is relatively easy—you may have millions of people and can get statistically relevant results (usually 1000s of clicks per metric) in a few days. Plus, if you upset anyone, the impact on your user base or revenues is likely very small.
- B2B has issues dealing with scale. It could take weeks or months to get to statistical significance. Plus, if you upset a customer, it could have a real impact on revenues and user base.
- If your testing population is not randomly distributed across the controls and variants, your results will not be valid and your testing must be restarted and old data thrown away.
- You should have more than one control. Why? You can compare results of two controls. If they are not fairly close, it highlights randomization issues and the need to restart the experiment. The downside is that it takes up samples, requiring more time to be statistically relevant.
- A/B tests are considered the gold standard for data on what works and what does not, but there are real limits on what you can test. Further, some B2C companies focus so much on A/B testing that they lose sight of the overall market.

PART

NAVIGATING THE GAP

Slide 29's "Go-to-Market"

5

GETTING TO
MINIMUM VIABLE
PRODUCT

THE
TRACTION GAP

Congratulations!

You've come a long way since Ideation. You are now formally in the early stages of the actual Traction Gap—it began when you reached your Initial Product Release (IPR)—although you are still in the middle of creating a product that your team can aggressively take to market. Everything you do at this point must be focused on reaching Minimum Viable Product (MVP) as quickly as you can—but not so quickly that you ignore this stage's essential building blocks that include determining product quality and product usage rates. You must also complete basic market-engineering tasks such as developing preliminary pricing models, value propositions, product demonstrations, and sales enablement content (e.g., white papers and video testimonials).

You should now have your initial team in place, defined (or redefined) your Minimum Viable Category, performed statistically valid market-first research, raised a seed or even a full round of financing, and placed the first version of your product (IPR) into the hands of consumers or business users.

Industry data—from startups that have successfully scaled—suggests that after reaching IPR, *you have only about six months to reach MVP.* Needless to say, you are already behind, even when you begin.

To achieve this growth objective, you must develop and implement a well-functioning Beta program so you can wring out the bugs, polish the user interface, and take care of some of that technical debt you've accumulated along the way.

At this point, everyone on your product team should be focused on the Beta program. Meanwhile, people with marketing, product marketing, and customer support skills should be preparing company launch plans (e.g., media strategy, initial revenue systems, and support systems) and tracking the metrics associated with reaching MVP.

To avoid those "Slide 29" issues I discussed in the first chapter, your initial product- and market-engineering tasks must be completed before you declare MVP. Trust me, no miracles are likely to occur, only results (traction) or the lack thereof based upon adequate preparation at this stage.

In this chapter, I share with you some of the key tasks you need to complete to generate traction and begin to scale, once you decide to declare MVP. These tasks include a discussion about pricing strategy (as mentioned above), measuring user engagement, the importance of implementing a customer experience function, capturing NPS scores and usage rates, the value of developing a community now versus later, and finalizing your category definition.

ESTABLISHING THE VALUE OF YOUR PRODUCT

MVP traditionally has been defined as the minimum number of features for which a customer will pay.

> "The minimum viable product is that version of a new product which allows a team to collect the maximum amount of validated learning about customers with the least effort."
>
> —
>
> **ERIC RIES**, CEO, Long-Term Stock Exchange

I take a slightly different view. I like what Bryan Stolle, my Wildcat partner, says of B2B applications and infrastructure: "I want to see companies pay to use Beta software."

A Beta product typically has not yet reached MVP. What Bryan means is that businesses will only pay for products from which they can derive value. And if they can be induced to pay you for Beta software, you can be sure early on that you are solving an important problem and delivering value. The fact is that until you can get a consumer or a business to fork over cash for your product or service, according to the IRS you're a hobby.

For consumers, the acid test is how often they use your product. This is why Daily Active Usage (DAU) rates are so important, especially for consumer applications, which generate revenue via advertising.

For business products, DAU rates matter, but revenue is the standard by which you will ultimately be evaluated. This implies that you should begin experimenting with your pricing model during the IPR-to-MVP phase. Don't worry, you don't have to have price locked in at this point, but now is the time to experiment with some "straw" pricing to test the market.

I recommend that you consider trying a smoke test (referred to below and an example of which is described at the end of Chapter 4, "Getting to Initial Product Release," in the Hacks section) to try out different offers and pricing before committing to them with formal public announcements. The same reasoning holds for customer proposals.

Pricing is a complex topic that involves many different factors, such as the market(s) you're competing in, competitive dynamics, and business model. I will make a few brief comments here about pricing a product or service.

I always encourage teams to focus on value-based pricing:

- How valuable is the product to a company or consumer?
- How much time does the product save, and what is that time worth?
- How much expense does it eliminate?
- How much revenue can it help generate?
- What does the product let you do that you can't live without, and what is that worth to the business or the consumer?

Many companies attempt to use return on investment (ROI) calculations for business products to develop their pricing and discount models. This approach is fine; however, it must be balanced against other products that may already exist in the market and the business models/pricing associated with those products. You can't determine price in a vacuum.

For example, let's say that through your ROI calculations you determine that your business application could save a company in your target market $1M per year. So you set your price to $250K, generating a strong ROI argument. But, if other companies are already in the market with similar products—even if those products aren't as good as yours—and they only charge $50K, then you will have a tough slog persuading prospective buyers to pay your price, no matter what your ROI calculations produce.

If you believe there are no competitors in your category, you are wrong. Trust me: if nothing else, you will be competing for part of a budget, and the end user's or company's decision to purchase or use a product or service will be based on the availability of time, cash, or both. If a consumer or business buys your product or service, they will have less to spend on another product. With businesses, there is typically not much, if any, unallocated budget just lying around. So a purchase decision for one solution always takes budget away from another group, product, project, or ability to hire the next employee.

In a market-first approach, you can evaluate your different price points using a smoke test to identify value propositions and potential pricing. A landing page attached to a digital ad in LinkedIn can act as a "one-question survey" that asks "What would you pay?" for this product.

Similarly, the other terms and conditions you attach to the purchase of your product (e.g., reimbursement policy or service levels) must be balanced against similar terms and conditions competitors may offer.

I remember suggesting to one of my B2B SaaS portfolio companies—which was wrestling with what terms it should offer in its first agreements—to initially adopt the same terms and conditions Salesforce used in its agreements. I happened to know that those terms had been well-vetted by Salesforce, accepted by the industry, and would establish a starting point that could be amended or revised later. This approach got the company off the ground and on the path to success.

Knowing what other companies in or near your category are offering with respect to their product capabilities, pricing, and other terms is a mandatory best practice if you intend to be a market-first company. Today, there are great products available, such as Skyword, AirPR, or even Google Alerts, that enable you to automatically track your competitors, and I highly recommend that you invest in one or more of them. The days of performing competitive research manually—or not at all—are long gone. Knowing what your competitors or potential competitors are doing at all times is not a "nice to have" business practice, it's mission-critical.

> ❝ It is not good enough anymore to use 'gut-feel' and best guesses to build and grow your sales team, especially when there are tools to help you make solid decisions based on predictable results."
>
> **LORI RICHARDSON**, Founding Member, Sales Enablement Society, B2B Sales Growth Strategist

Sean Ellis, CEO of Growthhacker.com, has a straightforward approach to pricing. In an interview, he told us:

So, finding the right price. This was something I did both with Dropbox and initially with LogMeIn, where I essentially tried to actually map a demand curve at different price points for a product.

I divided people [into groups] who were using the products. We took people who were on the free product and then laid out the benefit of what the paid product would be. We then told the first group that the cost of the product was going to be $50 a month. We told the next group the price was going to be $40 a month . . . all the way down. I don't remember exactly what the price differentials were, but basically I took ten groups and gave them ten different prices and then asked them what the likelihood was that they would buy a product that does X, Y, and Z and costs this price.

Then we gave each group a multiple choice: Definitely I'd buy it, maybe I'd buy it, I definitely wouldn't buy it, and then discounted each of those prices. If they said they'd definitely buy it, they might probably be a 50 percent conversion rate. If they said they'd probably buy it, maybe that would be a 20 percent conversion rate; and then we just discounted everybody else to zero. We were able to get a pretty smooth demand curve that helped us zoom in on a price where we could see what was the max yield price per 100 free users or 1000 free users; [we knew] this would be the price that was going to drive the most premium upgrades.

Dale Sakai, the cofounder of Obo and a thought leader in the product process, has stated: "Best-practice pricing requires conjoint, cluster analysis and market simulation. The simplified methods generally do not yield valid pricing levels." As with any relationship, with pricing "it's complicated."

Finally, when it comes to price, keep in mind that there is always a price the market will and won't bear. Determining what that price should be is considered an "art." It's something we work on at Wildcat with our early-stage portfolio companies. Each company is different, and therefore pricing is always a bespoke process.

USER FEEDBACK

You must design your Beta program so you can quickly and easily capture, process, and share data-driven feedback from customer and consumer product use.

The great news for software startups is that products on the market, such as MixPanel or Pendo, can give you daily product usage data and analytics that you can use to track user behavior.

During this phase, whatever usage/analytics application you choose, making sure you have your team focused on the quantitative *and* qualitative feedback is mission critical. You can't rely solely upon metrics; you also need qualitative feedback. Qualitative feedback comes only from meeting face-to-face with end-users and watching how they use the product and where they get stuck, and being ruthless about the user experience (UX).

> 66 That's actually one of the most disappointing things about doing user interviews and user feedback, which is why I think . . . people don't do it. You're going to get negative news about your favorite pet feature most of the time."
>
> —
> **EMMETT SHEAR,** CEO, Twitch

Investing in face-to-face time enables your customers and consumers to provide you with information not just about how often they use your product, but how they "feel" about using it. You need this feedback because *how* users feel will determine whether they will or will not recommend your product to other potential customers.

• • •

Engagement Analysis

We all know the excitement that comes from releasing a new product or feature. There is much celebration and many high-fives. But now you must ask the really important question: How are we doing?

During this phase, you need to have your *engagement analysis* strategy up and running.

> ❝ Get closer than ever to your customers. So close that you tell them what they need well before they realize it themselves."
>
> **STEVE JOBS,** Cofounder & CEO, Apple Inc.

Engagement is critical in the extreme: if no one uses your product or feature, then you don't have a successful product or feature regardless of how many people elected to try or purchase it at the start.

Industry-accepted metrics determine engagement for software applications. Venture investors will want you to apply them to know how your product stacks up in the real world. These metrics include:

- Monthly Active Users (MAU)
- Weekly Active Users (WAU)
- Daily Active Users (DAU)
- The ratio of DAU/MAU

For B2C software startups, Sequoia Ventures—a Silicon Valley venture capital icon for the past four decades—has stated that the standard DAU/MAU ratio is typically 10 to 20 percent, with only a handful of companies greater than 50 percent. According to Sequoia, Whatsapp has an astounding 70 percent DAU/MAU ratio!

For SaaS startups, the DAU/MAU ratio, according to MixPanel, is a proxy for *stickiness*; and the stickier your product, the more likely you'll generate a Customer Lifetime Value (CLTV) of more than 3x your Customer Acquisition Cost (CAC), the minimum multiple required to create a successful SaaS business.

According to a 2017 MixPanel Products Report, which studied more than 572 products, 1.3 billion unique users, and 50 billion transactional events, the median SaaS DAU/MAU ratio is 9.4 percent. This ratio suggests that the typical application is used only about three days per month per user. According to the same report, a SaaS DAU/MAU ratio of 20 percent is good, while 25 percent is exceptional.

That said, the type of SaaS product you offer will have a dramatic impact on your DAU/MAU ratio. A B2B collaboration application (e.g., Slack) should enjoy daily usage, while a back-office application may be used only occasionally.

All of this underscores the fact that not all users are the same. For example, execs may need only occasional access to your product, while the operations staff might use it steadily. So you may want to set separate DAU/MAU ratio targets based on user type.

Other metrics, used primarily by B2C software companies, help to determine higher-order levels of engagement. One of these is the *cohort retention curve*, which is the percentage of users that tries a product or feature on a given day, then visits or uses it one week, two weeks, three weeks, one month, two months, . . . later.

It is typical with this measure to see a plateau at some level (such as 20 percent) several months out. You can measure how the retention curves change (improve or worsen) as you add new features or go after different customer segments with the same product or feature. For example, you may want to experiment by adding a new level to a gaming application (new feature) or target women 45 and older in the UK (new customer segment) and then evaluate the response rates.

In my experience, the type of product you offer influences the type of engagement you need to analyze. I've also discovered, to my dismay, that some startups—typically B2Bs—don't gather any of this data at all. Not gathering data can be a deadly mistake.

On the other end of the spectrum, some startups generate cohort retention curves for entire products or features and gather a ridiculous amount of click-stream data, only some fraction of which is directly actionable. Too little data isn't good, and too much is simply overkill. It's up to you to decide the amount and type of data you need to base your product decisions on.

The two internal business functions that typically have direct contact with users are your customer experience and customer support teams. Let's take a closer look at both.

CUSTOMER EXPERIENCE VERSUS CUSTOMER SUPPORT

Customer Experience

We all know customer support is a key business function; it is critical to take care of your customers and keep them happy and loyal. But a relatively new function has emerged designated "customer experience" (CX), which is equally critical but with an entirely different set of objectives.

Customer experience is concerned with how your product and company are perceived by your customers or from the consumer's perspective. In other words, customer experience is all about how your users feel and what the market thinks about your startup and its products.

Customer experience management (CEM) should be staffed separately from your other business functions, so that these dedicated employees can focus exclusively on the interactions between a customer and the organization throughout the customer life cycle.

The CEM role is specifically different from customer support, because:

▶ It takes the customer's perspective and point of view;
▶ It forces the company to evaluate and respond to customer interactions;

▶ It is responsible for capturing customers' responses, expectations, and market signals and translating that data into actionable information.

Customer Support

Many startup teams assume, since their customers have an opportunity to express their opinions to the customer support group, that those customers represent the market and are a strong source of market signals. It's true that customer support is essential to provide customers with a channel through which to express frustrations—and sometimes even jubilation—about their experiences with a feature or product. And customer support is also excellent for helping to identify bugs and getting to an engineering fix.

However, customer support represents a very selective set of feedback from people with problems. And not just any people with problems, but the subset of those people who are motivated enough to reach out to express their frustrations.

> ❝ Your most unhappy customers are your greatest source of learning."
>
> **BILL GATES**, Cofounder, Microsoft

Finally, customer support is great at helping to identify the symptoms of a problem. There are plenty of metrics that can be used to figure out just how big a problem something is, based upon the quantity and types of customer responses.

The problem is that customer support is not chartered to generate and capture *new* ideas. This group only reflects the perspectives of your *current* customers, specifically only those current customers who are motivated enough to speak up. In practice, this can be as little as 1 to 5 percent of your overall customer base—and they may not share all the characteristics of the other 90+ percent of your customers.

Perhaps more importantly, this cohort does not include any of your *noncus-tomers*, the largest part of your potential market and a critical source of sig-nals. The feedback into your customer support group represents a very narrow and selective group of people, which, by definition, introduces bias into your metrics.

The market-first process requires you to find *all* the constituencies that make up the entire market, including your noncustomers, the largest part of the market.

It was precisely to fulfill this unmet need that the idea of customer experi-ence teams was born. Simply put, their job is to capture that valuable data (from both customers and noncustomers), data that customer support is not chartered to engage with.

Time for a reality check: let's say that you are a startup that is only at IPR and working your way to MVP. You are unlikely to have both a customer sup-port group and a customer experience team. In fact, you probably don't have either. Frankly, if you are like most startups at this stage, it is highly unlikely that you have the capital to staff these functions, or the bandwidth to manage them. Instead, you most likely will have your engineers and product managers doing double or triple duty. That's why the days and weeks are long and seem-ingly never-ending.

But even if you don't have the luxuries of a customer support group and customer experience teams, you still must assign specific customer support and customer experience objectives to members of your product team.

In other words, you can't ignore these duties just because you don't have the people power. After all, this is critical information you will need to make a market-first, data-driven, *and qualitative* decision to declare Minimum Via-ble Product.

I cannot stress enough that the market-first product process compels you to actively perform market research, and to capture market signals well be-yond the customer support call center log. And, during the Beta program, you must actively engage, human to human, with your end-users to truly under-stand what is and what isn't working with your product. This manual, hands-on exercise is time-intensive and requires the startup to commit significant amounts of its scarce human capital to the process.

NET PROMOTER SCORE (NPS)

Recently, there has been some controversy over the accuracy of the Net Promoter Score (NPS) as a metric to gauge the loyalty of a customer's relationship to a company. However, in spite of this current debate, for many companies the NPS remains the gold standard for measuring customer satisfaction.

> ❝ NPS creates a view of customer loyalty. The absolute score is less important than the trend. We learn from both promoters and detractors. Most importantly, we have been able to associate NPS improvement with growth."
>
> ── **JEFF IMMELT**, former CEO, General Electric

NPS is measured on a scale of –100 to 100. Anything greater than 0 is considered acceptable. 0 to 50 = good; 50 to 70 = excellent; 70+ = outstanding, you couldn't do anything better; and 100 is basically theoretical and not actually attainable.

Net Promoter Score (NPS)

PROMOTERS % - DETRACTORS % = NET PROMOTER SCORE

FIGURE 22

NPS tells you how your brand rates compared to those of a competitor, so you can use it only to determine if you are improving based on your own benchmark.

NPS is one of the best metrics you can use during the IPR-to-MVP phase. Because of its focus on loyalty, it is a good alternative to measuring customer satisfaction: Will customers continue to use your product?

NPS is also a component of customer experience management, but it is important to separate it out. NPS was developed by (and is a registered trademark of) Fred Reichheld, Bain & Company, and Satmetrix Systems.

The fact that it is used by more than two thirds of Fortune 100 companies shows just how powerful NPS has proven to be in helping companies understand what is really happening with their customers.

Some people object to such a focus on loyalty; but as Bruce Temkin from Temkin Group argues, that when NPS is used effectively "it has been enormously successful at catalyzing the attention of senior executives on the issue of customer experience; it's made customer experience relevant to the executive suite. And one of the best things about NPS, which doesn't get enough attention, is that it has introduced a common language around customer segments: Promoters, Passives, and Detractors."

When combined with DAU/MAU (Daily Active Users/Monthly Active Users) metrics, NPS can help you demonstrate to investors and your team that you have a product that is both sticky and beloved by companies and consumers. At this stage, even when you have little or no revenue, these metrics can be crucial in helping you show investors that you have continued to reduce risk and moved closer toward that elusive goal of Minimum Viable Traction.

But how do you capture the NPS when users are reticent to fill out long surveys? That is the beauty of the NPS; you need to ask and have your users answer just two questions:

1. How likely are you to recommend our product/service to a friend?
2. What is the most important reason for your score?

Since NPS relies upon only those two questions, the data is relatively easy to capture and the survey typically has a high response rate.

You can capture NPS data from within your application or via email. If you are not familiar with how to capture and use NPS data and want more information about how to set up an NPS survey, how the scoring works, and how to process and analyze a survey, a simple web search reveals many websites with the information you need, and those websites walk you through the process.

Some researchers recommend that companies ask the NPS questions immediately after some form of user engagement—for example, answering a support question—so that the experience is fresh. Other companies choose to use email to send out NPS surveys on a regular basis to all their customers.

At this stage, as you work toward MVP, and you deliver new releases regularly to your Beta customers, each new release is the perfect time to email an NPS survey, specifically shortly after the release after your users have had the chance to work with the new version of the product.

> ❝ NPS—always keep in mind that your customers always love you more at the beginning of your relationship. To maintain that engagement it is important to constantly refine your customer experience."
>
> —
>
> **KATHRYN PETRALIA**, Cofounder & President, Kabbage

CUSTOMER COMMUNITIES

More and more customers are turning away from 1-800 numbers and toward online communities of other customers when they want to express an opinion on a product or feature. There are countless online communities dedicated both to reviewing products and features and to giving other consumers advice about how to proceed with their purchases.

> " Feedback from our developer and customer communi-
> ties is essential to delivering compelling products. Adobe
> Labs fosters community involvement early in the product devel-
> opment cycle, enables access to emerging technologies, and
> ultimately helps to build better products."
>
> **KEVIN LYNCH**, VP, Technology, Apple; former CTO, Adobe

I recommend that you consider building a community earlier rather than later. Even though you will have relatively few users at this point, I would make the investment now. Community and customer advocacy software is relatively inexpensive and should be a key part of your website. This will be an invaluable resource for you over time as you move to the go-to-scale phase, and it can give you invaluable feedback during your Beta and future programs.

I was an investor in Get Satisfaction, which was acquired by Sprinklr. Get Satisfaction enables companies to easily set up and create a community. So I know the power of communities and can't recommend them enough.

That said, a word of caution with communities. You may experience a strong temptation to take over and influence your community in the name of protecting your brand reputation. Resist the temptation.

Based on my experience with Get Satisfaction, it is a big mistake for a company to try to influence its community. This behavior can result in a serious set of problems as employees end up wasting a significant amount of their time arguing with trolls. And, if your employees are discovered to be posing as a consumer or customer and making "fake" posts, you may have a PR disaster on your hands. At the very least, your customers will no longer trust your intentions.

The key is to accept communities for what they are. Some of the posters on the site will complain about problems that are clearly user error; others will have insightful comments that could help you proceed with your next evolution of a product or feature. Thus, just like customer experience management, you must always keep in mind that, while useful, such online communities are also composed of self-selecting groups of people who are enthusiastic for one reason or another—a characteristic that once again introduces bias.

The key is to try to create appropriate relationships with your community that enable you to give and take honest feedback without being so defensive that you try to control every post on every message board.

You will find that the best feedback will come from the communities you cannot control, so you have to make yourself a partner rather than a moderator, meaning you have to be willing to admit mistakes and ask for help in generating new ideas and new product features.

While these newer venues are a great source of information, don't assume that any post on any random discussion board represents the perspective of *all* your customers and noncustomers. Don't panic at every post. Take a breath and acknowledge it for what it is—feedback.

I would resist putting someone who is inexperienced in charge of building and managing your community. I believe it's better to put an employee with product marketing or product management experience in charge. An engaging personality and a little life experience will be an asset in this role.

Early in your startup's journey, when you have scarce resources, you can rotate people through this role on a daily or weekly basis, though you risk some loss of continuity in your relationship with your users.

Your community will quickly become one of your most important assets—and a very special insurance policy. For example, they will come to your defense if someone unfairly accuses your startup of nefarious behavior. Most importantly, your community can and will serve as a valuable reference source for noncustomers who are searching for users like themselves—and who are unwilling to invest and use your products until they find them.

• • •

CAPTURING AND OPERATING ON FEEDBACK

" There is no failure. Only feedback."

ROBERT G. ALLEN, author, *The One Minute Millionaire*

As you have probably experienced, once you have a product in the market, it is very easy to receive some initial customer feedback—and then turn to your team and ask: "Is it possible for us to do that?" That is understandable. We all want to satisfy our customers, especially early on.

The problem, which many of you have also doubtless experienced, is that when a company—especially startups with few customers—gets this focused on a customer-driven approach, it ends up adding features without any data about whether or not the new feature or new product is something the broader market needs.

" I think we over-invested in personalization before it had product/market fit. Looking back, what I wished I had done differently is have a small team of folks working on getting six reference customers who are using the product, paying for the product and are willing to be public spokespeople for the product as a way to really define the SLA between our product-engineering efforts and the go-to-market."

DAN SIROKER, Founder & CEO, Optimizely

Furthermore, few companies think about *usability*. A new feature or product may be deemed valuable by a few customers, but could actually *destroy* value for many others by adding too much complexity. In other words, before asking "Can we do this?" you should ask "*Should* we do this?"

For example, if you add a special feature that applies only to a few customers or prospective customers that results in a few extra clicks for everyone to reach a popular feature, that could be a poor tradeoff.

By comparison, a market-first product approach uses data to determine whether it is worth the effort, time, and money to develop a new feature or product simply because a portion of the existing customer base would like it. Thus, a market-first approach disciplines your product development decision making.

Anyone who has been involved in the product process has had to deal with the real risk of feature bloat due to one-off customer requests. How do you resolve it? I suspect you, like many others, asked the consumer or customer whether or not they *really* needed the additional feature or product. Or you attempted an indirect approach to gauge their true need, rather than their whim or a fad.

So how does a product manager determine whether a feature or new product is worth pursuing? How does she prioritize features?

In truth, some product managers do use opinions or anecdotes. Others use survey data from existing customers. And, honestly, many simply go with their gut, calling it "intuition." This is a very risky way to do business. Sometimes you'll get lucky and be called a genius; but the next time, your luck will run out and you'll flop—and your startup could be left on the rocks of your mistake in judgment.

By comparison, a market-first product approach encourages everyone involved in the product process to examine market signals from both customers *and* noncustomers. When the product team does this, it is likely to enhance product and feature success by:

- ▸ Avoiding costly R&D on features and products that won't actually sell or be used by customers;
- ▸ Developing a method for managing customer satisfaction without becoming so customer-driven that the company loses its overall vision for the market.

NEW CAPABILITIES AND FEATURES

Now that you are beyond Initial Product Release, at some point you will ask yourself: "What's next?"

The key to answering that question is understanding more than just the market for your existing product. You must also know how to refine and iterate that market over time. The great product managers are naturally drawn to the data to make such decisions.

Imagine that you could easily, quickly, and cost-effectively go beyond simply surveying your existing customers, that you could access the entire market for input. Further imagine that you had fast, easy, and inexpensive access to:

- ▶ Discovery Interviews,
- ▶ Large-scale surveys,
- ▶ Smoke tests,
- ▶ Usability testing,
- ▶ A/B testing,
- ▶ Engagement analysis,
- ▶ Customer support data,
- ▶ NPS and customer experience data,
- ▶ Social media sentiment, and
- ▶ Community feedback data.

How much better would your product decisions be with all that data?

I know what you could—and would—do: you would innovate with confidence because your product team's intuition could be quickly and statistically validated or refuted. In fact, new software applications from companies such as Obo and others already exist to do just that. They enable product teams and companies of any size to become market-first and data-driven.

FINALIZING YOUR CATEGORY

I already wrote about category creation and its importance in Chapter 3—"The Road to Category King." Since this is such a critical factor in your ultimate success, I now want to make a few additional comments. Market-engineering is an iterative process, as is product-engineering. If you want to maximize your probability of success to generate traction, you need to continuously test your assumptions. Category creation is a critical component of the market-engineering process and therefore deserves special attention.

I bring up the topic of category creation again because this is a pivotal moment when you should assess your MVC and either validate or revise your category positioning. This is a crucial task to accomplish before you are completely engulfed in the treacherous go-to-market phase and launch your company and product offerings fully into the market.

In the book *Play Bigger*, first referred to in chapter 3, Christopher Lochhead and his coauthors make the case that winning isn't defined as beating the competition at the old game. Rather, their book suggests, you have to invent a whole new game, by defining, developing, and (over time) dominating a whole new market category.

As simple as this premise may seem, creating real value through market creation rather than simply trying to win in existing markets is not so simple. The key is focusing on solving real market needs in a different way—and making sure that you position the market instead of being positioned by it.

As I stated in Chapter 3, the data on the power of this approach is overwhelming. Consider research that suggests that the Category King consistently captures as much as 76 percent of *all* market profits.[1]

How is that possible?

The critical distinction is that the Category Kings sell the problem and not the "better" solution to an existing problem. Further, they are the thought leaders that *define* the problem, which means they become the default choice for customers looking to solve that problem.

The reason category creation is so vital to a market-first product approach is that category creation packages what has been learned from market signals and communicates those signals back to the market in a way that helps everyone recognize the importance of focusing on the problem space rather than the solution space.

That's one reason why a market-first product approach can be so vital to any business, whether it points to an immediate solution or not. If you can identify a true market problem and then use the market signals to communicate that problem, you can become a Category King whether or not you have the immediate or even best solution available.

At this point, your company should have worked with many users/companies and you should be confident—from data and feedback—that you have the right value propositions, initial pricing and terms, and category positioning to begin marketing and selling your product in earnest.

You are—or are rapidly becoming—a truly market-first team. You listen to market signals. And you have proven that you have the right *market/product* fit because companies have indicated that they are willing to pay—or have already paid—to use your product. Or, in the case of consumers, they are actively using your product, and downloads and DAUs are increasing due to word-of-mouth and other virality programs you've developed.

Now, here is a very important point you must internalize:

You have complete control over when you declare MVP, and the decision to do so is a vitally critical decision point for you and your startup. For example, few investors will fault you if you decide to take an extra six months to make that user experience really shine.

Once you do formally declare MVP, investors will scrutinize and compare your growth (traction) with similar early-stage companies using a similar business model. Investors will measure how fast you are acquiring revenue, users, usage—or all three. If you fail to scale at the same or better pace as other startups in a comparable market using a similar business model, investors will lose interest and you may find that you become yet another failed startup statistic. For example, as I explained in Chapter 2, "Applying the Traction Gap Framework," to equal the best B2B SaaS companies, you must reach $1M ARR within one year of reaching MVP, $3M ARR by the end of the second year, and at least $10M ARR by the end of year three.

Thus, the moment you declare MVP is an incredibly important turning point for your startup.

KEY TAKEAWAYS

Here are some milestones to help you determine when it's time to declare MVP:

PRODUCT

Product—You know you can declare MVP when user and customer feedback suggest that at least 80 percent of those polled actively use and endorse your offering and are willing to promote it to other people and companies: in other words, when you receive a positive NPS score. Key product and feature assumptions—especially usage and churn (loss of customers, covered later) rates—also need to have been verified by data.

REVENUE

Revenue—The management team should still be largely responsible and actively engaged in all the marketing and sales processes.

(continues)

The company should be focused on refining positioning, marketing, and sales campaigns, and it should identify any points of friction so that it can smoothly move to Minimum Viable Repeatability. The period between MVP and MVR should be used to confirm or iterate the initial assumptions regarding market, category, customer/consumer acquisition techniques, pricing models, customer/consumer acquisition costs, sales cycles, etc. This is the time to begin planning a full company and product launch.

TEAM

Team—The team should now be expanded to include a few members who can help with support, customer success, and revenue creation and processing.

SYSTEMS

Systems—The company should be able to easily construct agreements, take payments of multiple kinds (e.g., e-commerce, purchase orders), and provide remuneration. The company should be preparing for the first scaling phase—MVR—by ensuring that its systems are capable of quickly and cost-effectively adding people, customers, and partners; processing invoices and internal expenses; and generating analytical insights into the key operating metrics of the business.

• • •

Mark Organ is the founder and former CEO of Eloqua and currently the founder and CEO of Influitive. Eloqua, founded in 2000, was one of the first marketing automation companies and was purchased by Oracle in 2012 for around $800M. In getting to MVP, Mark counsels companies as follows:

Product—"Fall in love with your customers. Spend time with your end-users."

Revenue—"Don't hire a VP Sales yet—you don't need it."

Team—"Don't over-title people at this stage. And only hire top talent. At Eloqua, only 1 out of 9 remained on the senior leadership team post-IPO."

Systems—"You don't need much. We used Salesforce. We focused on pipeline snapshots—from the last week to the next. We used email and chat and had a website."

Now is the moment to begin in earnest the exhilarating ride of the go-to-market phase, and getting to Minimum Viable Repeatability (MVR). We'll look at that in-depth in the next chapter.

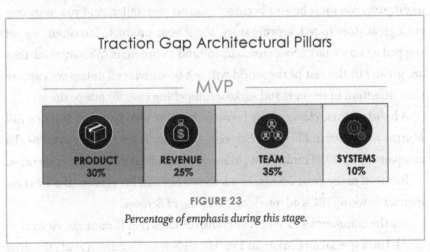

FIGURE 23

Percentage of emphasis during this stage.

The following are the key principles Wildcat Venture Partners looks for at MVP:

■ Traction Gap Principles ■
MVP

Product	Measure your customer engagement and usage rates, not just the number of customers.
Revenue	Select revenue metrics carefully and maintain a disciplined focus around them.
Team	Hire slow, fire fast—quickly remove toxic team members.
Systems	Keep your burn low—too much funding can cause bad behavior.

TRACTION GAP HACKS ► MVP

Storytelling

If you are the CEO of a startup, the leader of a division, or a spokesperson for a company, you must be—or become—a great storyteller. And you must create a great story to tell, an epic story, about your product. Too often, we get trapped when we talk about our company and its products. We may think they are great, but the rest of the world will not be convinced unless we capture their attention in seconds and make a compelling case for our position.

A holiday movie classic at my house is the 1988 film *Scrooged*. Starring Bill Murray as a modern Ebenezer Scrooge, the story is set in a powerful media company, IBC, with Frank Cross (Murray) as an advertising agency executive.

In one of many great scenes, Frank shows his staff his version of a TV commercial hawking IBC's adapted-for-TV airing of *Scrooge*.

For the commercial to succeed, Frank declares that it must get viewers to watch IBC's special on Christmas Eve. His ad features scenes of acid rain, drug addiction, a freeway killer firing a shotgun, and an airplane being blown up by terrorists. Frank states that the purpose of the ad is to remind people of how terrifying the world can be—is—and that Christmas is needed now more than ever. The narrator then delivers the pitch with: "Don't miss Charles Dickens's immortal classic, *Scrooge*. Your life might just depend on it." With gasps and frightened looks, Frank's staff is appalled over the commercial, but Frank confidently says,

"Not bad, huh?"

The point is that while Frank Cross's commercial may be just slightly off base, his message isn't. Especially so in today's world, where everyone is constantly bombarded with messaging. Your message—your point of view—needs to be strong enough to cause people to stop what they are doing and pay attention to what you have to say.

To accomplish this, you must begin with *a story of epic change* with an equally epic hero (your company/your products). If you can find that epic story, and tell it in a cogent and powerful way, your prospects, your customers, and your investors will listen to what you have to say.

One of the best storytellers in technology was Steve Jobs. He always began his presentations by introducing his audience to a new reality and inviting us to "think different" about what the benefits of that new reality might be. When he introduced a product, it was always "insanely great," designed to enable us to think *and act* differently.

Marc Benioff, CEO of Salesforce, is another great storyteller. In fact, his annual user event, Dreamforce, which attracts 100,000 people or more each year to San Francisco and online via real-time streaming, is a giant one-week "storytelling" event.

Every year, Marc uses Dreamforce to introduce his latest vision, combined with celebrity entertainment and parties. Marc is always front and center, the ringleader of the show.

Is this about fun and games? Absolutely not. Marc knows this is his annual opportunity to educate, while entertaining the vast numbers of people and companies to whom he markets and sells. Everyone who attends Dreamforce—physically or virtually—comes away knowing precisely what Marc's and Salesforce's priorities are for at least the next year.

Marc leads off by introducing and discussing a key problem the world is facing—and always ends with his announcement and demonstration of his newest product that will solve that big problem, usually accompanied and endorsed by a big-name Hollywood performer, professional athlete, or tech celebrity to make sure you are paying attention. For example, in 2017 Marc made "trailblazers" the main theme. He claimed: "Everyone has the power to be a Trailblazer and make the world a better place." Using this theme, he introduced the notion of a Salesforce Economy, driven by developers, CEOs, administrators, and anyone who is part of the Salesforce ecosystem. Marc went on to state that this ecosystem would provide more than 3 million new jobs and nearly $900B in new revenue by 2022. Then, he followed up this inspirational message by introducing a slew of new products designed to make Salesforce trailblazers even more successful.

This way, when a Salesforce account rep meets with a customer or prospect after the event, the "target" has already been softened and is open to hearing about the new Salesforce offering.

Dreamforce is a full out-of-body experience designed to tell you a story—several, actually—and to reinforce that new reality by enabling you to interact with 100,000+ of your new best friends through the experience.

———

In the chapter about Minimum Viable Category, I shared with you how GreenFig, an EdTech company, arrived at its MVC as a microeducation company offering microdegrees in applied business science.

Now, let me share with you how GreenFig's CEO tells the same story.

The story doesn't begin with GreenFig; it begins with a *big problem* we all face, in this case, the prospect and fear of machines taking over human jobs, potentially relegating millions of people to the unemployment line.

It begins. . . .

> The 21st century, a digital economy, and digital transformation are currently affecting every company, globally.
>
> Digital transformation won't just affect technology.
>
> It will transform the global workforce as we currently know it.

- Many of the jobs currently filled by humans will disappear, just as manual-labor jobs were replaced by machines during the Industrial Age.
- In the 21st century, the First Intelligence Age, machine learning will replace as many—if not most—traditional roles held by humans.

How will we as a society prepare ourselves?

- Universities are still teaching primarily the same content in the same way they always have.
- And core subjects in English, history, etc. are still highly relevant to ensure that we all have a basic understanding of who we are, where we fit in, and how to communicate and work with each other.
- But unless you are studying for a career in STEM, you will likely not graduate with the skills that will result in immediate employment after graduation.
- That said, were you aware that only 6.5% of all US jobs are STEM-related? Did you know that only 24% of all high school seniors score 650 or more on the math section of their SATs, the minimum required to get into a good STEM program?
- The fact is that 40% of US companies require workers skilled in operating the 21st-century "soft machinery"— business application software.
- These are jobs in sales operations, marketing operations, demand generation, service, support, customer success, etc. These roles require people who are trained business scientists, not computer or data scientists.
- More than STEM, industry needs workers who understand the "science" of a business function and who are certified in how to operate—not code—the

business application software that powers those
functions.

- Application software from industry leaders such as
  Google, Salesforce, Marketo, Oracle, SAP, and many
  others.
- Business scientists must be critical thinkers,
  collaborators, and creative thinkers. This is what liberal
  arts programs foster. As a result, people with liberal arts
  degrees are ideally suited to become business scientists.

Who is solving this problem?

GreenFig—a microeducation company offering microdegrees in
applied business science. GreenFig's mission is to train business
scientists.

The remaining "actors" of GreenFig's "story"—its offerings, its format,
etc.—are all just the supporting cast in the story. And, as you no doubt noticed, GreenFig presents itself as the hero that saves the day.

By connecting with a global issue that everyone knows is happening, and
is equally concerned about—and then offering a potential solution to the
problem—GreenFig is able to rise above the noise. In the story's setup, its
offerings, its business model, and its competitors weren't mentioned.

GreenFig also knows that it needs to earn permission to tell you those
things. Before you will listen, it needs to tap in to your emotions. Once it accomplishes that, you are prepared to actively listen to how GreenFig fits in
and stands out in the education market.

So, what is your "epic story"?

- What is the big problem you have identified and are solving?
- Does it tap into a movement or issue featured in the media or the
  global markets?
- Is it something people are already familiar with or recognize as an
  issue?

▶ Can you quantify the problem in terms of its magnitude—that is, the cost in human or financial capital?

The more you can accomplish each of these things, the more likely it is that you will capture your audience's undivided attention.

PARTNERING FOR SUCCESS

Early-adopter customers are different from early-market customers, and the former can't serve as references to reassure the latter. Use partners (established companies or other, more advanced startups) to overcome this problem (chasm).

What is one factor *all* business software startups—at any stage—need to succeed?

Partners.

You can't go it alone. You don't have enough capital or brand power.

Sure, you will start out on your own. But by the time you reach MVT, you will need to have cultivated a few partners you can work with to help you overcome many of the key issues you will face beyond MVT.

And although you may only be at Minimum Viable Product, it's not too soon to determine which companies would make good partners for you to reach MVR, MVT, and beyond, and to develop a strategy to work with them.

As a startup, you are most likely to market and sell to the Early Adopters and Innovators, as described in Geoffrey Moore's book *Crossing the Chasm*. To find your way onto the proverbial "Main Street" requires reference selling—and not just any old references. Those references must come from companies similar to the prospects with whom you are speaking. Early Adopters want to see others like themselves using your products before they will buy.

The problem is circular. So, in *Crossing the Chasm* terms, you must begin to scale and move from Early Adopters to companies that are part of the Early Majority, a much larger market. How do you secure those first wins?

One way to solve this problem is to identify and work with a company that has already established credibility with the Early Majority to *"borrow their brand."* That is, by partnering with you they are implicitly endorsing you with prospective customers and can give you the needed brand power you don't currently possess.

By partnering with a startup, an incumbent can bring new capabilities to its customers and prospects and fill in gaps in its current product offerings. In return, the startup, of course, gains access to companies it would not ordinarily be able to reach on its own.

Another approach is to join forces with other startups with complementary products and services. By jointly participating in events and other demand-generation programs, you can dramatically reduce the cost of customer acquisition and brand awareness.

In the process, you will also create a symbiotic ecosystem that is reliant upon your success for its own. This ecosystem will serve as an effective barrier to help you thwart emerging competitors.

I know a little about this topic because I was responsible for creating and expanding the Siebel Systems partnering program from its inception. Siebel made partnering a core competency and used it as a competitive weapon. In just four years, we grew from our first partner (Accenture) and little revenue to more than 750 partners—consisting of systems integrators, hardware companies, software companies, and others, and nearly $2B in annual revenue. These weren't "resellers"; these partners jointly went to market with us via events, email campaigns, advertising, and sales calls. We worked together, but we sold our products/solutions and they sold theirs. Over time, much of our partners' lead generation and revenue was dependent upon Siebel Systems, thereby keeping them close and potential competitors at bay.

At its peak, Siebel had more than 200 Alliance Managers working in its Alliance organization, managing relationships with consulting, hardware, software, and other partners important to its mission.

This effort was a significant investment, especially compared with how most companies staff and manage their partnerships. Why did Tom Siebel make this investment? One word: revenue. Our alliance team helped to drive nearly $1B in annual Siebel revenue via these partnerships. We won awards from *Forbes* and IDC for our innovative approach. As the head of the Alliance organization, I reported directly to Tom because of the importance of this function in revenue generation.

Unfortunately, most startups and large companies only pay "lip service" to their partner programs, if they have one at all. Few, if any, invest any significant effort and offer "toothless" programs—no commitments by either side—by hiring a few people, placing them under the Sales, Marketing, or Products organizations, and then expecting the group to work with dozens, even hundreds, of companies. And they wonder why their partner programs produce very little in terms of tangible business results.

If you want real partners and a partner program that delivers results—revenue and market share—here are some basic principles you should follow:

- The partnership must be sponsored and supported by the CEO.
- Both companies must assign and hold accountable at least one person from each company to achieve the objectives of the partnership.
- The people assigned to the partnership must develop a joint business plan that describes the objectives of the partnership, including revenue targets, key accounts, technical integrations, comarketing activities, etc.
- Both companies must commit to invest in an agreed amount of comarketing activities to create brand and demand awareness.
- The CEOs and those responsible for the success of the partnership must agree to meet quarterly to review accomplishments and any issues associated with the partnership.

If you want to learn more about how to build a successful partnering program, I encourage you to read the Harvard Business School case study titled *Siebel Systems: Partnering to Scale*. You can do a simple search: "partnering to scale Harvard Siebel" and find the study. Download a copy; it provides a prescriptive, detailed framework and overview of how to build and staff a partner program that can help you successfully scale.

6

GETTING TO MINIMUM VIABLE REPEATABILITY

R eaching the next value inflection point, Minimum Viable Repeatability (MVR), is the most challenging phase you and your startup team will face in traversing the Traction Gap.

Not to be overly dramatic, but, as far as the venture investment community is concerned, your ability to achieve MVR from MVP over the subsequent year-and-a-half—in what will be a shockingly short 18 months—will determine whether your startup lives or dies. Remember: the Traction Gap Framework is as much about creating a financial product for venture investors as anything else.

Making this challenge infinitely worse is that now, in this phase of your startup, you essentially are no longer in control of your fate. In the go-to-product phase, from Ideation through MVP, you were in charge of your destiny. You decided which features to build and which initial consumers/companies to work with. During that phase, you were principally concerned with creating a product that worked and that companies or consumers would use.

Unfortunately, this business-building process is about to get a whole lot tougher. As you leave the go-to-product phase, you are at the mercy of the unforgiving market—potential consumers or customers—as you attempt to efficiently and cost-effectively make those businesses and consumers aware of your offerings and persuade them to purchase your product or service.

The market will either judge your product and business model worthy or it will relegate it to the startup scrap heap. This is capitalism at its most brutal—and best.

The clock is now ticking mercilessly. After you declare MVP, savvy investors expect to see healthy growth metrics—downloads, conversion rates, usage rates, and revenues—that suit your business, and no amount of hand waving on your part will save you. A fancy slideshow or prototype describing "how great it will be" will no longer cut it. You will be evaluated on hard, empirical metrics, notably how quickly and efficiently you can generate awareness and interest, thereby acquiring users of your product.

From Ideation to IPR to MVP, a lot of your attention was focused on Product Architecture. Now the constraint on your growth shifts from the product process to Revenue Architecture and executing the plans you developed as an outcome of your market-engineering process. Now you must concentrate on, and invest in, programs that generate market awareness and demand for your product—scaling the company and identifying and resolving all the attendant issues. And you don't have much time to do it.

You must begin the extremely challenging process of expanding your team beyond just people with specific product skills. Now you need to add team members with a mix of revenue and system architecture skills. But only a few; true scaling of your revenue engine must wait until you actually reach the MVR value inflection point.

Further, you must find people with a combination of strategy and execution skills—a rare breed. And you can't afford to hire the wrong people, because mis-hires at this stage cost time, a resource that is in short supply.

No wonder this phase is so challenging.

This is also the point in your company's life cycle when a few members of your team, possibly some of your closest friends and those who began with the company, may not be well-suited to continue. These partings are sometimes neither voluntary nor happy. The worst can end friendships and even lead to litigation.

> ❝ Most of our mistakes were within the Team Architecture. The team you start with will not be the team you need to grow with, and that team will not be the team you need to scale."
>
> ▬
>
> **KATHRYN PETRALIA,** Cofounder & President, Kabbage

Most early-stage startup CEOs and their teams have experience building products, either through school or prior work engagements. Unfortunately, I have found that most do not have the equivalent experience in building a category, architecting a team skilled across all functions, or developing Revenue Architecture. In other words, you will be leaving your safe zone to operate in a foreign environment with few guideposts.

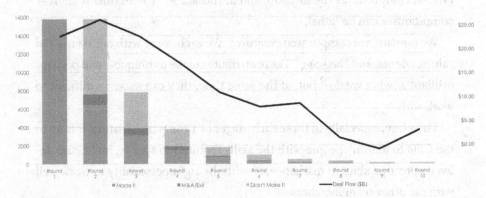

Startup Failure Rate

FIGURE 24

We are mindful of the 80 percent failure rate for startups, and we don't want you to fail. This chapter is devoted to helping you avoid the many pitfalls of this stage of your business's journey.

As I mentioned, Product Architecture was the key Traction Gap Framework pillar in the prior stages. Now, as you move from MVP to MVR, the other three pillars begin to play a more prominent role. So I am going to focus on them in this chapter to help guide you through this stage—from MVP to MVR. I'll begin with Team Architecture.

TEAM ARCHITECTURE

> " Coming together is a beginning. Keeping together is progress. Working together is success."
>
> **HENRY FORD**, Founder, Ford Motor Company

The universal feedback from every CEO interview I have ever conducted is that Team is by far the most important of the four Traction Gap Architecture Pillars.

That makes sense. Startups, after all, are composed of human beings who must work together to accomplish a goal. Anything that gets in the way of that process compromises the mission, and at this stage—where time is short—compromises can be lethal.

We humans are complicated creatures. We each come with our own set of values, talents, and "baggage." Those attributes make us unique—and perhaps brilliant at what we do—but, at the same time, they can make us difficult to work with.

Therefore, especially in these early stages of a company's history, it is up to the CEO to identify people with the skills required to specify, build, and deliver a great product to market—*and* with the right personality to work well with the other team members.

Unfortunately, some people with the most gifted product talents do not make great team members. Or, as the company grows, those with otherwise remarkable individual skills are not capable of scaling with the company, nor do they necessarily want to move from an individual contribution role to that of a leader of people and teams.

The 50 or so CEOs and founders we interviewed for this book all provided similar advice: "Hire slowly, fire fast." It's hard, but if the people you started with aren't cutting it, you must transition them out of the company or move them into roles better suited for their skill sets.

You may ask "How do I find the right people with the right skills, personality, and the ability to scale?" I don't have a ready answer to that, but I can give you a process you can use to avoid mis-hires in whom you select to bring onto the team.

ORGANIZING FOR SUCCESS

Here are some hard lessons I've learned in my 25+ years working on the operating side of startups and corporate life, combined with my experience working with early and mid-stage companies as an investor.

> *Direct Reports*—The people the CEO appoints as direct reports signal to customers, employees, business partners, and investors what matters to the CEO and what he or she believes is critical to the company's success. So choose your direct reports carefully, as you are telling a lot of people what is important to you.

> *Decision Making*—Adding layers of management between the CEO and the people who are executing the business model can slow down decision making and reduce the speed of decision execution. I have found that lackluster or tardy execution can kill a startup. CEOs are usually CEOs because they have excellent intuition and the ability to analyze data and make good decisions quickly. Thus, relying upon others to "interpret" data, market signals, and employee issues may actually slow that interpretation and introduce suboptimal decision making. The best startup organization is usually the flattest one.

▸ *Visibility*—The CEO must have fast and accurate visibility into what is going on in his or her business. Therefore, the CEO should have the people responsible for executing key elements of the business model installed as direct reports. Here is a list of likely candidates for direct reporting, along with the scope of their responsibilities:

VP Marketing—responsible for the initial creation of revenue through demand generation (top of the funnel) and "future" revenue (revenue from future sales periods).

VP Sales—responsible for delivering "in period" revenue—inside and field sales, for example.

VP Support—responsible for assuring that the product works as marketed/sold.

VP Service—responsible for implementing a service and support apparatus (if this is a part of your business model).

VP Products—responsible for capturing and specifying a complete product that meets market demand; includes product marketing and product management.

VP Engineering—responsible for building and delivering a complete product.

VP Customer Success—responsible for making sure your customers are happy and using the product every day. One customer success rep for every $1M ARR is generally considered best practice, but this varies based upon the Average Contract Value (ACV) of your product or service.

VP Finance—among many things, responsible for internal systems, as well as the accounting and collecting of revenue.

VP HR—responsible for vetting and recruiting key employees along with managing employee benefits, etc. Although HR is a critical function, few startups at this early stage are in a financial position to invest in a fulltime HR professional. At this stage, I recommend using a trusted third party on a contract basis until post MVT.

VP Alliances/BD—responsible for the interface with many different corporate partners that enables the startup to go to market more effectively and to deliver a complete solution.

VP Channels—responsible for managing indirect sales (if they are a key part of the company's business model).

VP Customer Experience—responsible for capturing and reporting market signals via a variety of channels, including communities, market surveys, etc.

In my experience, a CEO and/or a GM should be able to handle between 7 and 10 direct reports if each of those reports is an A player and runs his/her organization effectively. This recommendation fits with the findings of anthropologists (and experts on military leadership) that the most effective span of control for leaders is about a half-dozen subordinates.

At this stage—any stage, really, but especially now—the fewer the layers between the CEO and the front-line team, the better the access and visibility that CEO has to the unvarnished truth of the business. You may not have the financial resources to hire all these functional leads at this stage, but the functions I've described *must* be covered by the people you do have on board.

HIRING—THE INTERVIEW PROCESS

> ❝ I am convinced that nothing we do is more important than hiring and developing people. At the end of the day, you bet on people, not on strategies."
>
> —
>
> **LARRY BOSSIDY,** former CEO, Allied Signal Corporation; Chairman, Honeywell Corporation

If you sit down with a number of HR executives and ask each of them which questions companies should ask candidates during the interview process to ensure they select the "best fit" person, you will likely hear a wide range of answers, some of them even contradictory.

Over time, larger companies develop their own processes and techniques (e.g., psychographic testing) to uncover whether or not a candidate will succeed in their organization and integrate into their culture.

And technology is playing an ever greater role in this process. For example, one new company has emerged—Aingel, spun out of NYU—that is using AI to assess candidates, even entire management teams, based upon their social media posts, LinkedIn profiles, and other digital "exhaust," to predict their ultimate success. This is public data so no permission is required from the candidates. They don't even need to know they are being profiled. Aingel uses its machine learning-based algorithms to compare an individual's traits with others known to be successful in similar roles to determine that candidate's likelihood of success. And Aingel accomplishes this feat with surprising accuracy.

Beyond assurances that no employment laws are violated, companies of any size must develop a talent recruitment and hiring process that enables them to quickly and accurately identify which candidates are the most likely to be successful in their organizations.

The dilemma is that most interviewers are typically asked to reach an accurate judgment of this complexity in just the 60- to 90-minute time span of a typical interview. Making these judgments is truly one of the most difficult tasks in all business. Not surprisingly, industry statistics suggest that many don't get it right.

Glassdoor.com commissioned research with Brandon-Hall that discovered that 95 percent of employers surveyed admitted to making hiring mistakes each year. Meanwhile, Dice Inc., a talent company, reports that "a study by the Society for Human Resources Management (SHRM), [determined that a bad hire] could cost up to five times a bad hire's annual salary." According to the *Harvard Business Review*, as much as 80 percent of employee turnover stems from bad hiring decisions.

The mistakes are hugely costly for larger companies, but devastating for early-stage startups that teeter on the brink of viability from quarter to quarter.

So what can a startup do to enjoy a relatively straightforward and accurate way of determining whether a candidate will be successful?

In my experience, you can reliably pursue only two lines of questioning to determine whether someone is the right choice:

1. Is the person truly skilled in the function for which he/she is interviewing?
2. Will this person fit into the culture of the company?

Other questions are "nice," but in my experience they are superfluous to predicting the success of a particular candidate.

I suggest that you develop a set of questions that will test the candidate for expertise in the slot for which he or she is interviewing, whether in engineering, sales, marketing, finance, etc. Those skills-based questions should be created by your best employees in similar roles, or by people who you consider to be skilled subject-matter experts and willing to advise you. These people should also conduct that portion of the interview; after all, only they are qualified to ask those skills-based questions and ascertain the accuracy of the answers.

For example, if you are trying to fill a technical role, the candidate should be required to perform a "code test." If the role is in product marketing, the candidate should be required to write a positioning document.

Beyond being competent in his or her field, in order for a candidate to remain with the company as a long-term employee, he/she also must fit in culturally and adopt and adhere to your Core Values. More about Core Values, which are important, is covered in the next section of this chapter.

For example, if the team believes coming in early and working late is a Core Value, then the interviewers should ask whether the candidate is willing to do this. The candidate's attitude needn't be completely congruent with the company's culture, but it should be very close. The candidate also should meet with a number of members of the group, and company, to test for personality fit, as opposed to job competence (the candidate should have already passed the latter by this point).

Assuming the candidate successfully crosses this hurdle, the company should then conduct follow-on reference checks that are designed to substantiate or refute the competence claims of the candidate.

Three of those checks should be references the candidate provides. Another three should be conducted with people *not* on the candidate's reference list, but suggested by the references provided by the candidate.

No reference can tell you whether the candidate will be a cultural fit; only the members of the hiring company can get a feel for this, because only they know the culture of their company.

> " Attracting quality engineering talent when we were competing against prominent Silicon Valley companies was difficult. While we could have gone the route of lower-cost engineering, quality engineer talent was critical. We ended up targeting geographies/countries that we were familiar with outside the Valley and building out the engineering team where they could be the core engineering team, just in a remote location."
>
> **AMY PRESSMAN,** Cofounder, Medallia

The company should also include at least two people in the interview process who are not there acting as official interviewers. Instead, they are there to sell the candidate on why that person should join the company. These people might be senior executives, board members, or other company employees (typically industry veterans, though you might mix in newly hired contemporaries of the candidate), who are good at face-to-face communications.

I don't believe this approach is a perfect solution, but if you follow its simple process, I believe it will help you to reduce the percentage of your "bad" hires.

WHO SHOULD *NOT* INTERVIEW CANDIDATES

If you have not personally held the role for which you are interviewing a candidate—at the stage the startup is currently operating—do the company a favor and be a "cheerleader" only. Do not pretend to be a role-based interviewer.

Instead, recruit two or three people who have successfully held those positions at the stage the company is in, and have them perform a skills-based interview to determine if the candidate's skills are sufficient.

When you or other members of your startup's management team meet with the candidate, you all should evaluate the candidate for cultural fit, not job competence.

> " Hiring people is an art, not a science, and resumes can't tell you whether someone will fit into a company's culture."
>
> **HOWARD SHULTZ,** Executive Chairman, Starbucks

Any board members/investors involved in the hiring process should express to the candidate the reasons they made the investment in the company and why they are excited about its prospects.

Too many times I have seen startup executives and venture investors allow their egos to get in the way and want to "interview" candidates for positions they have never personally held. That is almost always a mistake. If you aren't a skilled auto mechanic, would you work on your own car? Wouldn't you prefer that professionals perform the task on your behalf?

So please recruit a "skilled mechanic"—someone with the specific skills for the roles you need filled—to do the interviewing. Otherwise, don't be surprised if you have an employment misfire. And remember, prior to MVR, mis-hires can be fatal.

CORE VALUES

> " The CEO is not in charge of the company. The values are.
> If, at the end of our careers, we have not passed along positive values, we have abdicated our leadership role to build organizations that thrive."
>
> — **DAVE LOGAN,** author, *Tribal Leadership: Leveraging Natural Groups to Build a Thriving Organization*

I mentioned "Core Values"; now let's look at this concept more closely.

Core Values are specifically and inextricably tied to the culture of the company. And culture, like a product, is not something that should be built ad hoc. Its features must be chiseled in from the beginning.

Whether or not he or she likes it, the CEO is also the "Chief Culture Officer." The culture of any organization always starts at—and if poorly designed and implemented, rots from—the top.

It has become popular for startups to create Core Value statements, typically something that's rolled out in the form of a nicely printed document that employees are expected to pin to their cubicle walls and pay fealty to an obligatory slide presented at company All Hands meetings.

It's not that these statements are all bad; in fact, your Core Values *should* be written down and shared with everyone in the company. It is only when stated Core Values deviate from reality—the day-to-day actions performed by the CEO, executives, and managers—that employees begin to seriously question the integrity of the company. Hypocrisy is not conducive to employee morale. And, in today's world of social media, this discord can easily and quickly show up in public forums, such as Glassdoor.com, as anonymous posts reviling the company and management. This discord can make it challenging to hire top talent as they perform their own due diligence on the startup and its practices.

The key to success with Core Values that work to create a great culture is to ensure that the values are developed jointly with members of the rank and file, as well as with the management team. If these values are ever violated, the CEO and management team must take swift and decisive action to demonstrate that they support the Core Values with more than lip service.

Finally, a good statement of Core Values needs to be sufficiently precise and concrete and regularly evaluated against the real behavior of the company. A nebulous statement—Google's "Do No Evil"—is open to an almost infinite number of interpretations and can come back to bite you. And a statement that is lofty but essentially meaningless—"We cherish our customers"—might as well never be written at all.

Siebel Systems produced a Core Values book that was the output of the Siebel Founder's Circle (a group of people Tom Siebel hand-picked representing all levels and functions of the company). "Professionalism" was one of the Core Values described in the book. All Siebel employees who were customer-facing or in management and executive roles were required to wear suits and ties, even engineers. No eating was allowed at your desk—to encourage employees to talk to each other at lunch, etc. Every Siebel employee knew that professionalism was one of the Siebel Core Values and what it meant; they lived these Core Values every day.

THE STARTUP GOVERNANCE PROCESS

When you are an early-stage startup, every waking hour is an opportunity to move your company forward. Devoting anything that isn't related to product or market momentum is wasted effort.

Naturally, the last thing startup teams want to do is invest time and energy into superfluous meetings, especially when those meetings are not directly related to building or selling the product.

Many startups use collaboration technologies, such as Slack, Confluence, and Google Docs, as a way to keep people informed on project status. These technologies enable the team to dispense with too many wasteful meetings. That's great. However, now that you are beyond MVP, you are likely to begin bringing on people not directly involved in day-to-day product decisions. These folks are likely to work in finance, marketing, and sales. They are often also relatively recent additions, who do not yet have the benefit of knowing the company decision-making process or who to go to, to get things done.

While collaboration software is useful to communicate among functional team members, it is insufficient to effectively communicate all that is happening across the company. For now, at least, virtual communication isn't able to adequately articulate the "nuances" that people must hear directly by interacting face to face with each other.

To avoid communication issues, I suggest that startups consider holding at least two regular meetings. These are, first, the weekly executive staff meeting; and, second, the executive quarterly planning meeting followed quickly by an All Hands meeting, referred to earlier, that communicates the objectives and decisions made during the executive quarterly planning meeting.

THE WEEKLY EXECUTIVE STAFF MEETING

I joined Siebel Systems as a member of the executive team when the company was a small startup, with just a few million in revenues and fewer than fifty employees. I held a variety of roles in the company that ranged from the head of marketing, to the head of alliances, to running the company's "on demand" division (its SaaS products). Ultimately, I ran the product division, where I was responsible for defining and delivering all the products in the company catalog. So I personally went through many stages of growth in a variety of different positions.

From that experience, I came to believe that the weekly executive staff meeting process enabled Siebel to manage its phenomenal growth, from a handful to 8,000 employees and $2 billion in revenues in just five years. The weekly executive staff meeting played a key role in ensuring effective communication and collaboration across our team and company.

That is also why I recommend that the executive staff meeting should be a mandatory, standing meeting held by the CEO every week at the same time.

The time that seems to work best for most startups is from 10 A.M. to noon on Mondays. This is before the work week kicks off in earnest—and it's late enough that most of the executive team members can attend either physically or virtually. This timing is especially true for the engineering lead, whose team always seems to want to start late and work late. That said, you can of course set up this meeting to be any time that works best; as long as it is held every week, at the same time, everyone knows it is mandatory, and it takes precedence over anything and everything else. No exceptions.

In the early stages of your startup, most of the agenda will be driven by engineering and product management issues. But, by MVP, other issues (e.g., sales, marketing, and HR) will begin to surface and should be placed on the agenda.

Over the twelve years that Siebel Systems was an independent entity (until it was purchased by Oracle in late 2005), the executive staff meeting format never much varied. Each week, Tom's direct reports provided a summary of:

- ▶ What our functions and teams accomplished in the prior week,
- ▶ What we expected to accomplish in the coming week,
- ▶ Any key issues we needed to share and solicit input on or that required a decision by Tom or others on the executive staff.

Also, at these meetings, the head of Sales provided an update on the sales forecast for the quarter, using a "worst, expect, best" format.

Worst—if everything fell apart
Expect—the most likely case
Best—if everything came together

We called this sales forecast the "WEB report," and it was shared with everyone on the team. Why? Because each of us, typically, had something to do with getting a new customer over the line.

As Siebel became larger, each of Tom's direct reports would hold their own staff meeting immediately after Tom's exec staff meeting. This way, we could quickly convey important information to our direct reports. They, in turn, would hold a staff meeting with their direct reports.

In this way, critical information, vital to the company's scaling, was easily and quickly conveyed every week—human to human, throughout the company—even when, in time, we had thousands of employees scattered around the globe.

Today, even with significant advances in collaboration technology, nothing can replace human-to-human, two-way, real-time communication and interaction to ensure that information is accurately exchanged.

THE EXECUTIVE QUARTERLY PLANNING MEETING

> You have a meeting to make a decision, not to decide on the question."
>
> **BILL GATES,** Cofounder, Microsoft

At this stage, your startup is rapidly going through many changes. You are adding new people, new users, and new processes. You are quickly learning from market and user feedback what is and what isn't working regarding your product. You also are discovering how effective you are at reaching out and persuading companies and new users to try your product or service. And, not least, you are learning what they like and don't like once they do.

Due to this rapid change, whatever annual plan, processes, or Management by Objectives (MBOs)—Google uses the term Objectives and Key Results (OKRs)—you set at the beginning of the year are likely to be obsolete by midyear, perhaps even sooner.

Setting annual goals and metrics is fine, and this should be done. But I have found that startups also need to constantly be on the lookout for emerging constraints on growth, identify their root causes, and remove them.

I recommend using a quarterly planning offsite meeting that begins on a

Friday afternoon and runs through Sunday—so it provides less interference with the work week—as a way to address constraints on growth.

Each member of the senior executive team should come prepared to discuss the quarterly objectives their organization accomplished, objectives that were unfulfilled, and their plans and targets for the subsequent quarter.

At these meetings, the CEO should kick off the discussion by summarizing the last quarter's accomplishments and introducing whatever issues are gating the company's ability to grow. These issues can and do vary widely. For example, one quarter the snag may be product issues, the next it may be hiring, demand generation, or competition. The entire management team should engage, determine, and activate solutions to solve those problems. The offsite should not end until each identified problem has been assigned a specific owner, key measurable objectives have been set, and a due date is assigned for its resolution.

By having someone who represents each business function in the room at the same time, everyone hears the problems and is on board with the decisions made to solve them by the time the team leaves for home on Sunday afternoon.

The CEO should then report the outcome of the planning offsite to all employees the following week, in an All Hands meeting. This procedure keeps everyone in the company up to speed with the overall status of the business and key issues that management is focused on solving, and ensures that everyone knows the CEO's priorities for the upcoming quarter.

With the right team and processes in place, we will now turn our attention to the next Traction Gap architectural pillar: Revenue. Your ability to quickly develop your Revenue Architecture is fundamental to your success. Scaling can't begin in earnest unless and until you complete this foundational work.

REVENUE ARCHITECTURE

> " Our goal is long-term growth in revenue and absolute prof-
> it . . . so we invest aggressively in future innovation while
> tightly managing our short-term costs."
>
> **LARRY PAGE,** Cofounder, Google

As noted, once you declare MVP, you are formally on the hook to start growing your customer or user base. And investors will expect you to grow at least
as fast as comparable startups using a similar business model.

If you are a SaaS company, for example, once you reach MVP you must
grow your revenue at least to $1M (ending ARR) within one year and add
another $1M ARR (a total of $2M ending ARR) in the following six months
to reach MVR. These aren't my metrics, they are the metrics B2B companies
such as Salesforce, Marketo, Workday, and many other successful SaaS companies achieved when they were at this stage of growth.

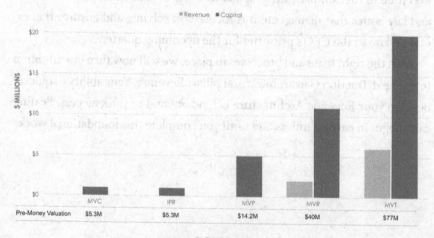

FIGURE 25

B2C STARTUPS

If you are a B2C startup, you differ slightly from your B2B brethren, in that reaching MVR is not typically linked to revenue. Instead, investors will judge your success on other factors such as downloads, daily active usage rates, and churn.

After interviewing many successful B2C investors, we were surprised to learn that most don't use hard-and-fast metrics to determine MVR, the earliest point in time where good venture investors are willing to make a serious investment in a B2C startup.

Instead, these investors rely on a number of factors, including the velocity of growth (such as month-over-month percentage increases in downloads), decreasing user acquisition costs and churn rates, strong virality coefficients, significant daily active usage rates, and DAU/MAU ratios.

Since most B2C startups use a revenue model supported by advertising or data monetization, the size of the overall user base and the frequency at which the application or marketplace is accessed determine its ultimate value. So it makes sense that investors look for similar metrics that advertisers will value.

We asked Sean Ellis, CEO of Growthhacker.com, about B2C customer acquisition. Sean advises that it's all about identifying the optimal channel to reach and convert users:

> "For me, the most important growth channel tends to be organic growth—and it needs to be fed by the channels that you can invest into. So, the first thing that I'm really doing is just making sure that I can take someone from consideration to activation inside the product."

To substantially improve customer acquisition and conversion rates, Sean suggests, start by buying keywords related to your offerings. At this point, you aren't really trying to do demand generation. He describes this initial process as "harvesting"—significant testing of landing pages and keywords—to see what works in getting people to sign up—register—and use your product.

The next challenge is to ensure that they aren't just registering, that they actually use the product. With one of the companies he worked with, Sean was able to get a lot of registrations through the channels he selected, but "*the majority of them, or 90 percent of them, were not using the products. Never used them, not even once.*"

This finding was a company-threatening issue. Sean admitted that his "comfort zone" is channel building. But he knew that if he didn't resolve this conversion issue, the company would have even bigger problems downstream. He took his findings to the CEO and explained the issue, that 90 percent or more of the people who registered to use the product never used it. He suggested that the management team needed to switch strategies from pure acquisition to focusing on activation: getting people to use the product. But this would require some product changes, specifically during the onboarding process. Based on the data, the CEO agreed.

This change in strategy meant the company had to put the current product roadmap on hold while everyone then focused on solving the issue of how to effectively onboard initial customers. The results? After four months of performing numerous experiments and iterations, they were able to get about a 10x improvement in the signup-to-actual-usage rate. After that, they went back and tested the channels where they had been struggling with registration-to-activation conversions. To their relief, those channels now scaled.

During our team's interview with Sean, we wanted to find out some of the specific tactics he'd used to drive these highly improved conversion rates. He said that they went to the worst-performing channels, the ones with a 90 percent dropoff after the signup stage. They inserted A/B testing at this point, with different offers, etc. But that didn't really change the dropoff rates. They didn't find out until they decided to ask the consumers who made it through this step why they'd signed up but hadn't downloaded the product; they had captured the user's email address during the registration process so they could send a follow-up email to ask this question. The reason for the dropoff, they discovered, was that consumers were skeptical whether or not the product was really free. With that information in hand, they were able to resolve the problem.

Sean commented on this finding:

> "So, we changed the onboarding to give them a choice, download the free version or download the paid version. We put a big graphical check mark in the free version so it wasn't like we were trying to push them to download the paid version, but because they saw that a paid version existed, suddenly the free was more credible and so we got about a 300 percent improvement in downloads just from that one experiment."

Intrigued by these techniques, my team asked Sean if he'd be willing to share some other techniques he used to improve purchase conversion rates. Here is one example:

> "One experiment was when they signed up for the free product we actually gave them, we'd give them a message that said for the first 30 days you get full premium functionality and it will automatically change to the free version after those 30 days. Then they would discover one premium feature during the 30-day trial that they really liked and that was enough to double the upgrade rate."

STRIVING FOR *MARKETING/PRODUCT* FIT

An important comment about MVR here for B2B startups. Although revenue is certainly an important metric, so is the number of customers/users you've acquired. Investors want to see "repeatability," and that means obtaining a good number of logos (customers) or users who are deriving value from your product. So, if you have a complex enterprise application with an ACV of $500K, then four customers—or less—might generate $2M ARR. That isn't MVR. Investors will likely want to see that you have at least 20 customers, maybe more, before feeling confident that there is a "real" market and giving you credit for reaching MVR.

No matter what market you serve or your business model, after you reach MVP the pressure is now on to grow. In spite of all that pressure, now is *not* the time to add significant marketing and sales resources and begin outbound advertising and other marketing campaigns.

Why? Because while you may have established market/product fit at this point, you do not yet have *marketing/product* fit.

> " Startups are inherently chaotic. The rapid shift in the business model is what differentiates a startup from an established company. Pivots are the essence of entrepreneurship and the key to startup success. If you can't pivot or pivot quickly, chances are you will fail."
>
> **STEVE BLANK,** Adjunct Professor, Stanford University; author, *The Startup Owner's Manual*

What Steve Blank's comment means is that while you may have a market-first offering determined by statistically valid market research, and while you also may have confidence in the product you've built from your Beta program feedback, you still as yet do not have valid proof that you have the right value propositions and processes to convert awareness and interest from the market into actual revenue.

In fact, you will only know you have marketing/product fit once you have complete confidence that you understand the entire buyer's journey, that is, how to engage companies/users, create interest, and convert that interest into revenue. And that you are increasingly able to predict how long that journey will take and what percentage of the time a prospect will become first a customer and then a repeat user.

Until you know for certain you have marketing/product fit, you must limit your investment in your revenue engine: marketing and sales teams coupled with brand and demand-generation programs.

During this precarious stage, the members of your management team must serve as a proxy for the company's revenue engine. They must go on sales calls or engage with businesses or consumers. They must listen and learn from user engagements and develop a sense of what to say, what to demonstrate, and what must be done consistently to get a sale over the line.

Then the management team needs to document the process and the content using messaging frameworks, scripted demos, videos, sales training and enablement tools, white papers, etc., so they can use them in corporate marketing and sales programs.

If your average contract value is $60K, then you will need 33 companies to reach $2M ARR and the MVR value inflection point. My point here is that you do not need a big sales or marketing team to accomplish this objective.

The key takeaway I want to emphasize is that during the MVP-to-MVR stage, the startup's management team should by and large "own sales and marketing." This is the only way to ensure that teams across your startup are learning what it will really take to begin to scale.

If you scale marketing and sales immediately after MVP, you will create two problems. First, you will have put layers (people) between yourself and the market. Doing so costs valuable capital.

Second, you will introduce *filtering*. In the absence of tried, tested, and proven value propositions and sales processes, the people you've brought in to marketing and sales roles will simply invent those propositions. They will experiment and then provide you with their filtered point of view with respect to what is and isn't working.

You do *not* want to do this. If you do, you are putting the fate of your startup into the hands of people who most likely do not have as much experience as the management team. And they may not have the ability to accurately tell you what is and isn't working during the buying process.

Meanwhile, as you are running these unstructured experiments, you will continue to burn valuable capital without making significant progress toward your one-year, $1M ARR goal and, subsequently, $2M ARR, which is the approximate revenue you should have achieved at the MVR value inflection point.

You may find yourself with dwindling capital at the worst possible time. You may not be able to go back to your original investors and say "We need more capital to figure out why we aren't seeing any traction yet." If they are early-stage investors, they may be relying on you to prove traction so your next group of investors—those who want and need to see real market metrics, not a PowerPoint slide show—can make an investment decision. But . . . you don't have those metrics for those investors—or those metrics are questionable—because you don't have traction! You are now trapped in the very definition of a "vicious cycle."

This "vicious cycle" is the trap into which a sizable percentage of startups fall. And they did it to themselves, because they mistook MVP as the time when they needed to lock in that revenue engine.

Don't do it. Save that step for when you reach MVR.

_____

During the interviews for this book, we discovered several valuable lessons that startups would be wise to consider as they move from MVP to MVR:

- While there were many naysayers about Marketo initially, Phil Fernandez, founder and CEO, said the company was able to rise above the skepticism by working with a core group of customers to build a product they wanted. This method of working sometimes meant slowing down on sales to focus on teaching existing customers how to use and get the most out of the product.

- Marketo developed five years of revenue projections at the start, and while it didn't always go as planned, the company hit its numbers every single quarter. A key to that was working closely with the head of sales, who each month was asked "What is our goal for next month?" By doing that month after month and quarter after quarter, Marketo was able to stay on the right path.

- Eighty percent of the CEOs we interviewed had a clear plan for profit, revenue, and growth by the Minimum Viable Repeatability (MVR) stage. Executives said they worked closely with the first few customers to ensure their success with the product before expanding to a broader customer base in the early stages. Another important success factor was developing a clear financial and pricing model early on.

These findings are monumental. Think about it: 80 percent of successful startup teams had a clear plan for profit, revenue, and growth by the MVR stage. If a startup is focused entirely on product and not on revenue, the path through the Traction Gap could be elusive, if not impossible.

SYSTEMS ARCHITECTURE

When you are initially advancing from MVP to MVR, you do not need many more systems beyond the ones you set up at the beginning of your startup. And most of those should be primarily back office-oriented for the finance (e.g., payroll, A/P, A/R), engineering, and product teams.

However, as you move further away from MVP and closer to MVR, you will need to investigate specific front-office marketing and sales technologies that you will want to use to power your business model from MVR to MVT.

At that point, the typical challenge becomes selecting from the more than 7,000 marketing and sales technologies available in the marketplace. It can be an overwhelming, paralyzing experience.

I suggest keeping the process as simple as possible and using industry-leading software, for no other reason than when you hire marketing and sales personnel, they are likely to know how to set up, run, and maintain your selected applications.

The tools/applications you use also will be determined by the go-to-market business model you choose. If you have products that target B2B and use a direct sales model, those factors will dictate the use of one set of tools; if you use an e-commerce model, you will have to use a different set.

I really liked what one of our portfolio companies did when it finalized its "RevTech" (i.e., marketing tech + sales tech) stack. It has a high ACV, nearly

$400K, and primarily uses a direct sales model. So the tools its management selected were chosen to specifically fit that purpose.

More important than the specific tools they chose, I liked the way they showed the board the tools they use for demand generation that differ from sales pipeline development.

I recommend that your go-to-market team pursue a similar strategy and develop a "lead to cash" RevTech Systems Architecture that fits the demands and enables the growth of your business.

■ **Tools by Sales Stage and Use**[1] ■

Stages	FULL COVERAGE WITH TOOLS & DATA						
	DEMAND				**SALES PIPELINE**		
	Targeted	**Aware**	**Qualified**	**Engage**	**Discover**	**Manage**	**Proposal**
Conversion Goals	Leads to Qualified Accounts	MQA to Opp	Opp to Customer	Customer to Advocate	New Business	More Business	Top of Mind
Web Forms/ CTAs	SUMO (in Production)						
Targeted Display Ads	TERMINUS (in Production)						
Account-Based Tracking/ Analytics	ENGAGIO (in Production – Except PlayMaker)						
ADR Email & VOIP	OUTREACH (in Production)						
Contact Data Hygiene	DISCOVERorg (in Production)						
Prospecting	DISCOVERorg/Data.com (in Production)						
Marketing Automation	MARKETO (in Production)						
CRM	SALESFORCE (in Production)						

CAPITAL, PERFORMANCE METRICS, AND FALSE POSITIVES

I began this chapter by saying that getting from MVP to MVR will be your toughest challenge. By now, you probably agree.

During this time, not only will you need to demonstrate that you can grow your business, but you may also be faced with having to raise your next round of capital, especially if you didn't plan your prior raise carefully.

As I said in the Introduction, more than anything, the Traction Gap Framework is a way for you to understand how to plan for and engineer your financing.

In particular, you should attempt to raise sufficient capital to get from just before MVP all the way to MVR. To do that, you will need proof that you were able both to build a product and then carry it through a Beta program, demonstrating that you can build your product and get customers to use it, repeatedly. And you've developed all the metrics to show a prospective early-stage investor.

The MVP-to-MVR stage will be the last time you can raise capital without having to show growth data: new customers, users, usage rates, etc. This also is the last time that you will still be mostly a slide deck company as opposed to a spreadsheet company; as the latter, investors will demand that you show them your month-over-month growth rates, churn, downloads, DAU rates, CAC, CAC ratios, and the like.

You will need to engineer your financing round coming off of IPR and just before declaring MVP, and you will require enough capital so that you are confident you can make it all the way to MVR, and slightly beyond.

How much capital is "enough" capital? You need to reach at least $2M ending ARR. If you use the calculations I showed you in Chapter 2, you'll need at least $4M to do that, more likely $5M to $6M.

Warning: if you fail to make it to MVR on this capital, you will find raising new capital to be exceedingly difficult, perhaps impossible. So don't worry about giving up too much ownership in your company at this stage; give up enough to get to MVR, because getting there is all that matters right now. After you reach MVR, you will find it a lot easier to raise capital at higher valuations that are less dilutive to your ownership in your startup.

———

I want to caution you from declaring MVR too early. You can be fooled into believing it's time to move to the next phase by a "false positive," revenue growth, that is, using revenue growth as the sole metric to base your decision to begin the scaling process—adding significant marketing and sales re-sources—to get to Minimum Viable Traction.

Mark Organ is the founder and CEO of Influitive and former founder and CEO of Eloqua. He is an experienced, successful entrepreneur.

Here is his story about prematurely scaling Influitive:

"We grew from $1M to $4M to $8M ARR so it looked solid but there were actually some things we didn't figure out. Some of the traction was an illusion, fueled by curious marketers who wanted to give our ideas a try but weren't truly committed to them.

"Now after a lot of hard work we have figured it out, dramati-cally improved churn while cutting burn by 70%, and are growing again.

"Unfortunately, our premature scaling has cost us valuable time and money, and possibly ownership as well if we raise another round.

"We still have a good shot at building a big category again, like marketing automation. We could have had less risk and dilution if we'd had a more accurate mental model for what was really happen-ing with our customer installations. If we were being truly honest with ourselves, we would have admitted that for some of our cus-tomer segments and use cases, the required level of engagement and value was insufficient for us to push the pedal to the metal.

"Another nuance here that may be specific for category creators is that the first MVP is really not enough to achieve category dominance—or even viability.

"This was true at Eloqua and at Influitive as well. Eloqua didn't really take off until we created the automation layer, more than 4 years after founding, which allowed multiple marketing functions to migrate onto it from other platforms.

"At Influitive, our first product is pretty good but I think what will make us go supernova is the beefing up of our community functionality, which will allow multiple functions in marketing and customer success to migrate onto it from other platforms, like Marketo for example."

One of the ways you can avoid false positives and mistakenly declare MVR (even MVT) too early is by closely monitoring your usage ratios (DAU/MAU or WAU/MAU) for each customer.

Poor usage ratios indicate that your product hasn't yet crossed over from "nice to have" to "must have." Ignore these warning signs at your peril; you will be sorely surprised by excessive churn rates later on, even though you experienced early wins. You must ruthlessly focus on your usage ratios, which is how your customers/users will tell you that you are really ready for scaling.

To make this last point abundantly clear, listen to Mark Organ:

"We didn't start tracking WAU/MAU for both advocate and admin users until our churn started to get into uncomfortable territory. And when it did, instead of pulling back on the burn, we kept it high and assumed we would figure it out like we always had before, in a few months. It took us a couple of years to figure it out and we burned too much cash."

You *must* avoid being part of the 80 percent to 90+ percent failure rate. You must reach the next value inflection point, Minimum Viable Traction, on this capital, and you have little more than a year to do it. And that is the topic of the next chapter.

The following table provides a set of key B2B and B2C metrics that you should target and attain by the time you reach the MVR value inflection point:

Key Minimum Viable Repeatability Target Metrics

	B2B	B2C
Stage Duration	1.5 years	1–1.5 years
Revenue	$2M ARR	N/A
Downloads	N/A	Depends
DAU/MAU	25%	25% Minimum
Churn	< 10% (Enterprise) < 30% (SMB)	< 30%
CAC Ratio	< 2.0	< 1.0
CLTV	>= 3x	>= 3x

KEY TAKEAWAYS

Minimum Viable Repeatability is the smallest level of repeatability a startup can execute to demonstrate the feasibility of its business model, market/product fit, and marketing/product fit. MVR is one of the most challenging value inflection points for most startups to achieve.

At MVR, a startup has demonstrated that it has some understanding of "how" and "why" customers are acquired. It now knows a significant amount about its target market, has semi-effective product positioning, has developed a reasonable sales pitch, and enjoys a handle on the primary sales objections and rational responses to them. It also has a few reference customers. And it should be generating about $2M ARR.

Before moving on to the MVT, you should have reached the following Traction Gap architecture milestones.

PRODUCT

Product—A company at MVR has proven that it can successfully develop and deliver multiple versions of its product into the market. It has shown that it can reliably make product and feature trade-off decisions and can accurately predict when those products and features will be delivered to customers and the market at large. At this stage, the company should have a well-formed and well-documented product roadmap and have obtained quantitative market evidence to support why certain products and features should be developed. Finally, it has developed the ability to bring new products and features to market by working closely with marketing, sales, customer success, and support teams.

REVENUE

Revenue—At MVR, a company has established processes and patterns that suggest it has a viable business model. It understands how much capital is required to acquire customers/users and the amount of investment required to retain them. By this time, the company should have captured and documented its Customer Acquisition Costs (CAC), CAC ratios, Customer Lifetime Value (CLTV), marketing and sales waterfalls with conversion rates that lead to revenue, and Customer Retention Costs (CRC) and CRC ratios. In addition, the company must have gathered enough statistical evidence to show that if it invests a certain amount of

(continues)

capital on sales and marketing, it can reliably convert those investments into recognized revenue.

TEAM

Team—It is at MVR, and only at MVR, that a company should begin to invest substantially in marketing and sales personnel and programs. Every member of the company should be trained and certified on the startup's messaging matrix, so that everyone correctly positions the company and its offerings via corporate presentations and demonstrations.

SYSTEMS

Systems—The company should have implemented systems of record, engagement, and intelligence for each key business function, including customer success, engineering, finance, marketing, product management, sales, service, and support.

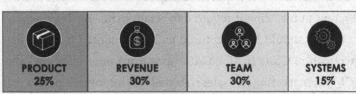

FIGURE 26

Percentage of emphasis during this stage.

The following are the key principles Wildcat Venture Partners looks for at MVR:

■ Traction Gap Principles ■
MVR

Product	Measure your product's success and communicate those metrics with customers to influence retention.
Revenue	Leverage reference selling to fuel a repeatable sales engine.
Team	Not everyone is good at every stage of the company. Remove anyone who isn't consistently producing.
Systems	Spend more time on finance than you think you should; make sure the math works.

TRACTION GAP HACKS ► MVR

Generating Investor Interest: Using a Smoke Test

I invest primarily in B2B startups, and one of the things I counsel them to do is to design their product for *two* primary cohorts. One cohort is the group of people who will use their product to perform operational tasks. The other cohort is the group of people who are the economic buyers, those executives who won't be using the product regularly but will be required to approve the ongoing use of the application.

The feature set for the executives usually consists of a report or set of reports that showcase key business operating metrics. These reports should contain valuable, usable content, and be designed so they can be automatically distributed daily, weekly, etc. and, if they were to stop coming, would be sorely missed.

At this stage of your startup, these executive reports can serve another very useful purpose. The following is a real-world example of how they can help you generate awareness and interest from potential investors.

I was fortunate to have been the first investor in Marketo, when it was just an idea and three people: Phil Fernandez, Jon Miller, and Dave Morandi. The company at this early stage had neither code nor customers.

After we sold Siebel to Oracle, I elected to join a venture firm to learn venture investing. One of the first ideas I brought with me was to create, or find and invest in, a startup that would transform the role of B2B marketing from what I affectionately called "party planning" into a critical revenue-generating function.

At the time, marketing was viewed by almost every company as a cost center. When I ran marketing for Siebel, marketing was indeed a cost center, but we also used Wharton "quant jocks"—Wharton is well known for its quantitative analysis curriculum and its students who excel in this area—to build models to predict—and generate—future period revenue. We didn't always like the predictions, but we became uncannily accurate at making them. I had long thought that we could convert what we did manually into an application-software offering.

In the summer of 2006, I was introduced to the founding Marketo team, with an even better vision than mine—and experience building successful marketing applications at E.piphany; that's why I elected to invest in them. Jon Miller told me a few years later that when they met with me, they were about two weeks from disbanding after being rejected by every other venture capital firm on Sand Hill Road. [By the way, every VC firm has its secret "anti-portfolio": all the startups they passed on that went on to become phenomenal successes. I have mine, too: Box and Veeva come to mind.]

I remember saying to Phil Fernandez, Marketo's CEO, at the time, "If you can make the CMO (Chief Marketing Officer) role as critical as the CSO (Chief Sales Officer), you will create a $1B company." As it turned out, Phil, Jon, Dave, and the Marketo team did a lot better than that. Marketo executed its IPO in 2013 and, in 2016, Vista Equity purchased Marketo for $1.8B. And, the company was recently acquired by Adobe for $4.75B.

But it wasn't all roses with Marketo. Marketo had a very difficult time attracting venture investors for its Series A. At the time, B2B marketing was considered a cost center, an expense, and B2B marketers were eminently expendable. They were always one of the first groups to be downsized or eliminated during any company downturn. And marketers didn't have the authority to purchase technology. I know it sounds crazy today, with more than 7,000 products featured on the MarTech "Lumascape" and CMOs enjoying among the largest budgets in technology. But, at the time Marketo entered the market, marketers were typically only provided a budget at the beginning of a current quarter—and expenses were usually limited to activities such as events, PR, collateral, web design, and email campaigns.

Even after Marketo began to do well, other venture firms and most industry executives were skeptical of the marketing automation market. I remember meeting with Marc Benioff at the time to see what he thought about marketing automation. I told him what Marketo was doing, and he said something like "Why would you build a marketing automation company? Those are the first people we fire, and there are only a couple of them anyway. You can't make any money from marketing." He didn't say those exact words, but this is the essence of what he said.

I didn't share with Marc that Marketo's pricing model wasn't based purely on seats, that they were also going to charge based on opportunities processed. Marc's pretty smart, so I didn't feel compelled to let him in on everything.

We were eventually able to persuade two other venture firms to invest in Marketo. I believe they invested because the partners at those firms had some operational background and could see the potential for Marketo and its offerings.

It wasn't until three or four years later that the tables turned and the company began to be deluged with interested investors. Why?

Growth hackers employed by venture firms? No. That was a little-known concept at the time, and Marketo was a B2B startup, not B2C. So it had very little "digital exhaust" to hack.

Curious as to why Marketo had suddenly become so interesting to the venture community when it had been a virtual pariah, I did some investigating. I spoke with a few of the partners from the venture firms that had expressed interest in Marketo.

Interestingly, each said they had recently attended several of their portfolio board meetings, and at each of them they were presented with a new type of report showcasing leads, lead conversion rates, customer acquisition costs, etc. And these reports had all been produced by Marketo. When they saw the Marketo logo at the bottom of every page, they decided they needed to check out the company.

Marketo may not have intentionally engineered this outcome—but you can. If you are selling into other startups, you too can develop one or more reports featuring key business metrics that are easy for your customers—startups—to put into their board decks. By doing so, like a billboard on the freeway, you can capture the attention of venture investors "driving by." If they see these reports and your logo often enough, they will reach out to you.

7

THE FINAL SPRINT TO MINIMUM VIABLE TRACTION

THE
TRACTION GAP

s I have shown at the end of prior chapters, different Traction Gap architectural pillars come into prominence at different stages.

For example, Product Architecture is paramount through the go-to-product phase and will determine whether you reach Minimum Viable Product.

Beginning with MVP, Revenue Architecture takes a critical and central position. Until Minimum Viable Repeatability, Systems Architecture does not play a significant role. Now, however, as you move from MVR to MVT, Systems Architecture comes to the forefront because it is time to scale the processes you've put in place at all levels.

Industry data suggests that once you reach MVR, you have about 12 to 18 months to reach MVT, demonstrating month over month/quarter over quarter incremental growth. Your business model—B2B, B2C, or B2B2C—will determine what that growth velocity needs to be to generate interest from the investment community; I've outlined and discussed these metrics in prior chapters, although there are no absolutes.

By now, you should have released several versions of your product. You have marketed and sold your offerings multiple times to companies or consumers. You are beginning to get a sense of what it takes internally to make that happen. You have hired more people into the organization. Your value propositions are working and your business model is hardening. You have proof that you have reached *market/product fit* and, more importantly, as I explained previously, *marketing/product fit*. You are beginning to be able to reliably predict prospect conversion rates because you are building a historical track record of your startup's pipeline and team's performance.

You have quantitative and qualitative proof that it is time to "power up" and scale. But scaling will require more capital, people, and technology (systems).

Yes, that's right. It's time to raise capital. Joy. Not.

Once again, you find yourself having to "get outside the four walls," but not for market or user feedback. Now it's all about visiting the investor community to raise capital. And it definitely comes at an inconvenient time, because you must also manage your ever-growing business. And you can't miss a beat: hitting monthly and quarterly growth targets is mission critical.

You can't "stay inside" with your current investors because in most cases it is unlikely that they will lead this next investment round. They may participate in the financing, but most assuredly they expect you to reach out to the next group in the venture ecosystem: mid-stage investors. And, these mid-stage investors are a different type of "hunter"; they seek startups that show early signs of market momentum, and they use facts—performance metrics—to confirm that you are the game they seek.

RAISING CAPITAL

Very few startups can get from MVR to MVT without a fresh round of capital. For example, if you are a B2B SaaS company, at MVR you will be generating about $2M ARR. To reach MVT, you must get to $6M ARR ($500K MRR) within the next 12 to 18 months. That's an incremental $4M ARR, not accounting for any churn—that is, loss of customers. I have more detail about churn later in this chapter.

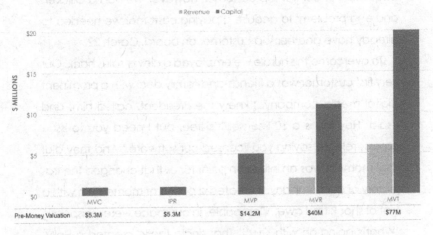

FIGURE 27

As I outlined in Chapter 3, for every $1 of new bookings, you will need at least $1 for sales and marketing and another $1 for R&D and GA. So, to add $4M of additional ARR, you will typically need to raise and invest at least $8M of capital.

This monetary need suggests raising a new round of $10M or more just after reaching MVR, to give you the resources and time to reach MVT—and a little beyond—before you need to raise later-stage capital. Refer to the chart at the end of Chapter 2; there you can see that the median capital raise for startups at MVR is about $11M.

Unlike your last capital raise prior to MVP, which was based upon team, market opportunity, and some early customer/consumer wins and adoption, you will raise this round (or not) based on your business performance. Your valuation will be a function of your growth velocity (how fast revenues and/ or usage rates are growing over what period of time), CAC, CAC ratio, gross margins, new logo attainment, churn rates, etc.

> " I've found that success in an enterprise software company
> can rely so heavily on the acquisition of certain clients. For
> example, at Salesforce, customers become emblematic of prog-
> ress and tipping points. At Krux, we were an early stage company
> with great ambition trying to get our legs under us through the
> acquisition of our first top customer. However, we had a chicken
> and egg problem; to acquire a paying customer we needed to
> already have another top customer on board. Catch 22.
>
> To overcome this hurdle we employed a clever sales hack. Our
> very first customer was a friends-and-family deal with a prominent
> digital media company. I knew the President, called him, and
> I said 'Hey this is a $0 license. It's free, but I need you to issue
> a press release saying you licensed our software.' And they did.
> That moment was an inflection point for us that changed the tra-
> jectory of our company. It created a patina of momentum with a
> hint of shock and awe. Companies in our space were whispering
> 'What's going on with Krux?' That single tactic created a Holly-
> wood façade of pure demand-gen. It was never a rampage, but
> customers started coming to us like moths to a flame after that."

TOM CHAVEZ, CEO & Cofounder, Krux

Whereas your last investor deck led with an overview that featured the
market opportunity and your product and a few customer/consumer testimonials, your new investor deck must begin with and feature the performance
of the business. Mid-to-later-stage investors get excited about performance
first; everything else is secondary. They want to see evidence that the proverbial dogs are eating the dog food.

I find that most entrepreneurs, even at this stage, make the mistake of featuring their product first in their investor decks. It's understandable, because

they are proud of their innovation and that is what works with prospective customers and consumers. But that isn't necessarily what savvy early-stage investors are evaluating. If they are experienced, they look for teams who have identified a big problem or opportunity with a large and addressable market ripe for disruptive innovation. This interest is why early-stage entrepreneurs in the go-to-product phase should lead with a story about "epic change" in a large market and how they intend to disrupt it before diving into their innovation's product features and a demo.

A mid-stage investor deck, which still requires an epic story up front, must quickly move into an overview of the startup's performance featuring the quantitative over the qualitative. You must lead with "here is how we are doing," not "here is how great it will be." The product overview and demo should come *after* your epic story and performance discussion, not before.

I know some venture investors will disagree with me about what elements an investor deck should prioritize first, second . . . but I'm basing my comments on watching the reactions and comments from my partners and other investors over hundreds, if not thousands, of early-stage startup presentations.

The vast majority of startups that reach this point have raised venture capital previously. The process of raising capital this time is virtually the same; identify firms and GPs in those firms who have demonstrated an interest in startups at your stage and have made investments in the market(s) where you participate. This time, you will be walking in with actual performance metrics that demonstrate that you can build a product and acquire users cost-effectively. Feature your metrics. Then show them how big the market opportunity is and how you will become the category leader in it.

So, what are investors looking for to ensure you're ready to begin the scaling process? My Wildcat partner Bryan Stolle breaks it down as follows:

Planning and Achieving the Plan—Investors want to know whether the startup can make a plan and execute it. This may sound obvious, but it's surprising how many would-be entrepreneurs fail at this. We have found that there is a high correlation between startup teams that consistently meet or exceed their plans, and successful venture returns for investors and significant wealth-creation for the founders and employees. The key parts of the plan and performance to plan that will be most scrutinized include the product delivery plan, the hiring plan, and the sales or user adoption plan.

Attract and Build a Team—No one can go it alone. Nothing has a bigger impact on eventual success than the quality of the team. Great entrepreneurs build great teams. Great teams produce great results. During the MVR stage, investors will be more interested in a team with great multi-role players that are getting it done, than in an executive team built for the future.

User Adoption/Sales Execution—Investors will focus hardest on the level of repeatability demonstrated in user adoption or customer acquisition. Is there some rhyme and reason to "how" and "why" customers are acquired? The company should now have a decent grip on: a) who the target user or customer is; b) what an effective product positioning and sales pitch looks like; c) the primary sales objections; and d) what causes churn, user abandonment, or low engagement. It should have solid use cases with demonstrable ROI, and the ever-critical success stories and reference customers. The company should be ready now to hire real salespeople, or invest marketing dollars in user acquisition, and expect the investment to be reasonably effective and efficient.

For investors, the most compelling metric will be rapid period-over-period (week, month, quarter) growth rates, but only as long as the customers or users meet some of the following criteria:

- *Average Annual Contract Value (ACV) or Annual Revenue Per User (ARPU)*—The size of the average transaction, usually measured in terms of ACV or ARPU, tells an investor a lot about the viability of the chosen business model. In an enterprise SaaS company, for example, ACV usually needs to be north of $75K to produce enough margin to fund a direct sales team. In a self-serve model, ACV will typically be much lower. For ARPU-driven models, there isn't a hard target number or range, because the viability of the model at any given ARPU is so dependent on customer acquisition cost (CAC), but as a data point, Facebook's North American ARPU at the end of 2017 was over $13.00/user. Investors will want to know not just what those metrics are today, but what the trend looks like. What do the trends suggest about long-term steady state, and achieving a profitable business model?

Revenue expansion/Engagement extension–For B2B, will the customer be buying more (more users, more apps or modules, etc.), and how often? For B2C, is the user engaging more frequently (or at least holding steady), and is there any evidence of a viral effect?

If the company has a land-and-expand business model, is there consistent proof that the "expand" part is taking place? How large have the initial purchases (land) been and the next follow-on purchase (expand)? How quickly does the customer come back for more, and how often? Because the data set is still lean leading up to MVR, it's very common for investors to call customers and ask them specifically about their expansion plans regarding the product, and not just their satisfaction with the current state of the product. They will also delve into whether expansion is contingent on new features or other changes or improvements to the product.

Note, at MVR, CAC is typically still much higher than long-term projections, so it's not a key decision criterion, as long as it's not crazy high or way out of balance with revenue or user acquisition: if you are buying customers at any cost, that will be apparent, and usually a big negative. On the other hand, a declining CAC trend is certainly encouraging to investors. For B2C companies, the scrutiny may be higher even at this early stage.

Stable churn—In most business models, keeping current customers is just as important as adding new customers. Prior to MVR, since there is typically a limited number of customers, there won't be a lot of churn (loss of customers) data. As a result, any churn is concerning, especially for B2B companies. Expect potential investors to dig into the causes behind churn, which customers are churning, and how much the churned-out customers were contributing to revenue.

Market size validation—Market size determines the ultimate value of the business being created. Investors will look for signals in the previous metrics to help them understand how large the market can be, and/or to validate your assessment of the market size. These clues can include types and distribution of customers (industry, size, etc.); initial, current, and estimated future account value (percentage of account penetration); or the Lifetime Value (LTV) of a business or consumer.

One last and often-discussed point: at MVR, you have likely only penetrated one market, geography, or user segment. At this point, you've been focused on proving that you can successfully acquire target customers or users. If you can do it once, it's reasonably likely you can do it again (but certainly not guaranteed). Initial forays into a new market area aren't the worst idea, as long as these ventures are not at the expense of success in your primary focus area. Focus, based on a strong fact-based view on which markets to develop when, is also often an investment criterion!

Many VCs won't invest at MVR, and in fact won't invest until you reach the MVT stage or later, partly because of a lack of early-stage expertise, and partly because a number often have to put larger sums of capital to work, which is easier to justify as the risks decrease and the valuations increase. Fortunately, a group of true early-stage investors are still looking for opportunities, and if you nail the points above and prove you have reached MVR, you should be in a good position to raise the necessary capital to reach MVT.

SYSTEMS ARCHITECTURE

Systems Architecture has not played a pivotal role in your journey across the Traction Gap—until now. From MVR to MVT, however, Systems Architecture takes a more prominent role. And Systems Architecture involves more than just technology, although technology is a key factor. It includes the business processes you establish and will affect every functional area of your startup.

Through MVR, your startup has remained "lean" in terms of the number of people it employs. Now, however, you must bring new people into the company to support newly required functions, including sales operations and customer support.

Your new folks, by definition, weren't there in the beginning with you. They don't know why certain decisions were made before they became team members. They don't know how those decisions were made. They bring their prior work experience into your startup in the form of opinions and bias of "what works best." These opinions can create friction and discord.

Your challenge is to quickly harness your new workforce to accomplish your startup's mission to reach MVT in 12 to 18 months. You don't have time for miscommunication, poor collaboration, suboptimal data capturing and mining processes, or adjudicating squabbles related to differing opinions about what is "best" for the startup.

Therefore, you must set up systems and processes that enable you to hire the right people, communicate and coordinate effectively with them, and implement solutions that enable you to capture and retain users as fast as possible at the lowest possible cost.

From Ideation to MVR, you were primarily focused on creating a market-first product with enough users to validate a market.

Now you must turn your attention to building a scaling machine. Your scaling machine must be optimized to produce your product, customers/users, and revenue. This machine consists of humans, technology, and process—and the systems to power and empower them.

At this point, you don't need more strategists, you need what I call "executionists." And you need to put processes in place across the company so that your executionists can collaborate and operate as fast and effectively as possible without "the wheels coming off."

For many early-stage CEOs, building a scaling machine is not their forte. Many—most—are typically great product and market visionaries. Operations? Not as much. If operations isn't their specialty, now is the time to invest in a few people who are great operators and can help to build the scaling machine.

These are people who have experience setting up and running business application software and the processes to drive them. They need to understand how marketing and sales and back-office operations work together and how to connect and integrate your website, marketing automation, CRM, and back-office systems, such as order management, billing, customer success, and support. They have demonstrated excellence in setting up and helping other startups at your stage. This is no time for on-the-job training. You need people who know what to do and how to do it.

Before reaching MVR, these people were unnecessary overhead. Now they are essential. Without them, you will fail to reach MVT.

REVENUE ARCHITECTURE

> " Don't be desperate for revenue. Focus on adding value to the customer and the revenue will follow."

AMY PRESSMAN, Cofounder, Medallia

Through this point in the book, I have been focused on showing you what it will take for your startup to make it from Ideation to MVT. Now it is time to discuss how this process fits into an overall strategy to become a category king.

The metrics vary depending on the type of business model, but since this book is focused on early-stage B2B software startups, I'm going to show you the growth rates you must attain if you hope to become a market leader.

Several years ago, Neeraj Agrawal, a GP with Battery Ventures and many successful SaaS investments to his credit, released an analysis of eight of the top SaaS companies and the ARR growth they achieved over their first five years. He began with a uniform starting point, which was when each company was generating about $2M ARR, not Day 0 or company formation.

Neeraj stresses how important it is to get to $2M ARR and that the management team should be the primary "revenue engine" to get there. This is consistent with the information I gave you in Chapter 6 regarding the initial marketing and sales processes.

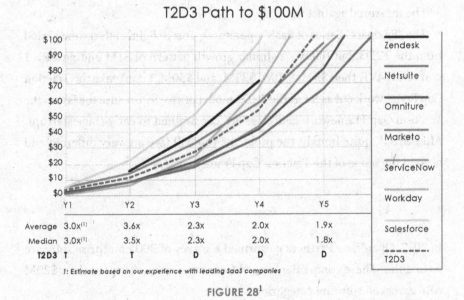

FIGURE 28[1]

Neeraj created the above chart, which shows how seven public SaaS companies—Marketo [which was taken private and acquired by Adobe since this chart was created], NetSuite, Omniture, Salesforce, ServiceNow, Workday, and Zendesk—each managed to triple revenue twice and double three times after reaching $2M ARR.

The challenge is to triple from $2M ARR to $6M ARR within 1 year, then triple again to $18M ARR, and then double to $36M ARR, $72M ARR, and $144M ARR.

I didn't know Neeraj was putting this data together as I was independently working on Traction Gap Framework metrics. We came to similar conclusions because we were working from a similar set of data. He has a much tidier name—T2D3—where I had been calling this particular revenue growth model the "Fibonacci Series of SaaS," a reflection of my science training in college.

Although Neeraj and I arrived at our conclusions independently, my findings and advice to early-stage teams are consistent with his. The T2D3 model correlates with the Traction Gap Framework value inflection points; this is why reaching these points in the time I've outlined in the Traction Gap Framework is so important. All investors know about the T2D3 model, so you will be measured against it.

The "Fibonacci Series of SaaS" operates against a slightly offset time period from the T2D3, but follows a similar growth pattern of $1M ending ARR 1 year after MVP, then $3M, $10M, $25M, and $50M. I don't take the Traction Gap Framework out as far as the T2D3 model primarily because the issues the Traction Gap Framework addresses are constrained to early-stage startups. After $10M, quite frankly, the problems you will face are very different and beyond the scope of the Traction Gap Framework.

In 2017, OpenView Partners performed a survey of 300 enterprise software companies. These companies ranged from pre-revenue to more than $20M ARR across all software categories.

From their survey and from the data of all venture-backed SaaS companies, they determined that the likelihood of your SaaS startup achieving $100M ARR in 5 years is about 0.1 percent.

From their report, *"In the boardroom, you've probably been told that after you hit your first $1M in ARR, you should triple twice, then double three times (known popularly as T2D3), ultimately reaching $100M ARR about 5 years later. But, of the ten most recent enterprise SaaS IPOs, only two—Nutanix and Cloudera (they collectively burned about $1.4 billion)—managed to actually grow at this break-neck speed. A handful of others were close behind, but half of them took eight or more years."* [Note from Bruce—Battery actually states that the T2D3 model begins around $2M ARR.]

So, what are the actual median growth rates of all venture-backed SaaS companies? OpenView Partners produced this great chart:

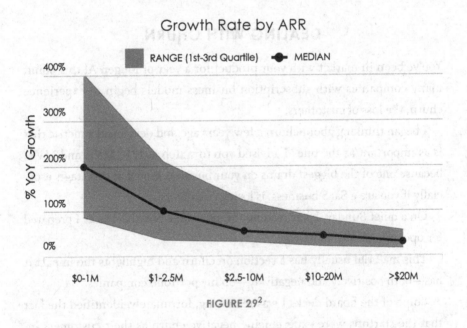

FIGURE 29[2]

How do the findings of the OpenView Partners survey reconcile with the T2D3 model, the Traction Gap Framework, and their associated growth rates? Simple. The achievements of the companies in the T2D3 model represent some of the "very best-in-class" SaaS companies. I believe these are the growth rates you should aim for if you want to maximize the likelihood and the amount of financing you need with the minimum amount of equity dilution. It doesn't mean you can't secure financing from the venture community if you don't hit T2D3 metrics, but you may not be able to raise as much as you'd like or you may have to give up more equity ownership for any given investment.

Finally, a personal observation: The data in the OpenView Partners survey comes from the entire market of venture-backed SaaS companies. And, as I stated in the beginning of this book, the facts show that more than 80 percent of all startups fail, which means that many of the companies that make up the OpenView Partners survey dataset, statistically, will fail as well. So you may grow slower than T2D3, but you may not survive if you do.

DEALING WITH CHURN

You've been in market with your product for a year or longer. At this point, many companies with subscription business models begin to experience churn, the loss of customers.

I began thinking about churn a few years ago and developed a metric that is as important as the ones I advised you to watch at IPR, MVP, and MVR, because one of the biggest drains on your business model at this stage, especially if you are a SaaS business, is losing customers.

On a quiet Sunday, I was reading through some board decks as I prepared for upcoming board meetings.

This material usually has a section on churn and highlights the impact it has—both positively and negatively—on my portfolio companies.

Some of the board decks I was reviewing, fortunately, identified the fact that the startups were experiencing negative churn as their customers increased the footprint of the portfolio company's technology.

I got to thinking about this issue.

You have a significant number of metrics you can use to measure top-of-the-funnel health for companies that use a SaaS business model: Customer Acquisition Cost Ratio (CAC Ratio), Customer Lifetime Value (CLTV), etc.; Bessemer Ventures did a great job introducing these concepts and terms to the market more than a decade ago.

These are tried, tested, and proven metrics that management teams and investors use to evaluate how well a company with a recurring revenue model is performing.

However, churn is also a critical component of the SaaS model. I asked myself, "Why don't we have a common metric to measure the health of the bottom of the funnel?"

Key questions are:

▸ Shouldn't we know how much we are spending to retain a customer?
▸ At what point should we "fire" a customer, if ever?
▸ Should that point vary by industry or type of customer?
▸ When should we parachute in our "customer success" teams to prevent loss of a customer?

It seemed to me that if we have a Customer Acquisition Cost metric, shouldn't we have a Customer Retention Cost (CRC) metric—the cost to "save" a customer—and what elements we would use to measure the CRC and CRC ratio?

So I put together a bunch of thoughts on what should go into the calculation of such a metric and sent that over to Totango, one of my portfolio companies.

Totango provides a customer success platform. Software companies and others use Totango's platform to help determine whether or not a customer is deriving value from a software product. This information enables customer success teams to "parachute in" and help a customer derive value from their software product, thereby mitigating a key issue associated with churn.

Given that Totango is "in the business of reducing churn," it seemed to me only natural that they would take these initial concepts and launch the CRC and CRC ratio metrics into the industry as a whole.

They did this with a fantastic white paper on CRC, titled *The Missing SaaS Metric—Customer Retention Cost.*[3] Here is an excerpt that shows you how to calculate this metric:

CUSTOMER RETENTION COST (CRC) PER CUSTOMER

To calculate the average annual cost to retain a customer, divide annualized customer retention cost (e.g., CRC for the last quarter x 4) by the total number of active customers.

$$\text{Annual CRC per Customer} = \text{Annualized CRC} / \text{\# Active Customers}$$

CRC Ratio

The CRC ratio should attempt to answer the question: how much are we investing to make sure we can retain and renew every dollar of revenue from our existing customers? The point is that in a SaaS business, you are always trying to protect all of your revenue, not just the revenue that is up for renewal in the next month or quarter. In its simplest form, the CRC ratio can be calculated as follows:

$$\text{CRC Ratio} = \text{Annual CRC} / \text{Annual Revenue or ARR}$$

I would encourage anyone dealing with churn/retention to do a simple web search and read the entire white paper.

SOCIAL PROOFING THROUGH ADVOCACY MARKETING

Once upon a time, we learned that to successfully scale a business we needed reference customers and consumers. Geoffrey Moore taught us that the majority of any given market didn't want to be the first to try a new product; they wanted to be sure that others had tried it first and had success with it.

Today, that is still very much the case, perhaps even more so. Why? We are so heavily bombarded with advertising from every corner that it's hard to wade through the cacophony. More than ever, perhaps, we rely on what our friends and peers have to say regarding business or consumer products; most of us simply don't have the time to sort out every option and claim. In the last century, we called it "word of mouth" and considered it an important, if imprecise, selling tool. Today we've got social media to help us through the noise. The terms you need to keep in mind are referral marketing, or social proofing. It can be managed more skillfully than "word of mouth" and can make or break your product and your company.

"I'll just buy from a brand I already know and trust." This attitude may not be stated verbally, but it is very much the behavior businesses and consumers exhibit when faced with too many choices and too little time/too many facts to sort through. This attitude can kill your startup; you're not a trusted brand, you're just another screaming voice adding to the noise. You're part of the problem, not the cure.

Who can help you break through the noise so you can tell your story or, more importantly, get the market to listen? That would be trusted advisers, respected industry experts, other professionals in companies admired by your prospects, or, in the case of consumer products, friends and known celebrities.

This is what social proofing is all about: acquiring and using references in digital form—using advocacy marketing technology—so your message and your brand are easily accessible anywhere, anytime, and your customers can access these references as needed and at their convenience.

Greg Ciotti, in a Neil Patel Digital blog post, wrote that there are seven concepts you must understand about social proofing in order for it to be successful.[4] In summary:

1. Don't use negative social proofing: that is, don't suggest that "bad things will happen" if someone doesn't use your product. This tactic has been shown to turn people off and is not effective.
2. Do use positive social proofing. Refer to the benefits other notable companies or people are getting from your products, rather than your product's potential cost savings to the customer. Use this benefits language on your home and landing pages.

3. Use pictures with all your social proofing. Photos of smiling people are the most successful kind. Humans relate to happy humans.

4. As we learned from Geoffrey Moore's *Crossing the Chasm* years ago, people are influenced by other people like themselves. It is critically important to understand the personas of your buyers: you need to use people with a particular persona to market to others with similar personas.

5. Anecdotes—customer stories—are by far the best social proofing tactics. But be careful that your legal and marketing departments don't sterilize these testaments. They need to be authentic and in the voice of your customers.

6. The most powerful voices are those of "influencers"—people who have "street cred" with the target personas you want to reach. These voices are worth their weight in gold. Use whatever legal means you can to get them.

7. It's better to have no social proof than low social proof. For example, if you have blog content on your website with very few likes or shares, eliminate it. Like a bar with few patrons, people look in but then leave. You will see it in your bounce rates. The interpretation is that your content and products are not trustworthy.

There are several advocacy marketing applications on the market, such as Influitive, and I would encourage you to review several and select at least one.

The journey between Minimum Viable Repeatability to Minimum Viable Traction must, by definition, be fast and furious. As we've discussed, to be on model with the growth rates of the successful startups that came before you, you must roughly triple your customers and your revenue from MVR and reach MVT in about one year.

To do that, you will need to enlist the help of your best customers using social proofing. Find a way to remind them that it's in their best interests to help you so that you stay in existence and they can continue to use your products. Don't be shy about pushing through big-company legal teams, who always want to say no to these requests. Remember, every company, no matter how large today, was a small company at one point, albeit perhaps long ago. Push for the social proofing you need through your internal sponsors! It's mission critical.

According to Sean Ellis, CEO of Growthhacker.com, referral marketing, a component of social proofing, is critical:

> "The most important thing about the referral is that no one is going to refer their friends to a product if they don't actually use it, so make sure [your customers] have a good experience inside the product."

One of Sean's clients was Dropbox. Referral marketing plays a significant role at Dropbox for dramatically increasing growth and revenue:

> "[Dropbox] actually has a kind of popover to sign up for Dropbox or sign in. You can dismiss it and then just access the file, but I know that there's a large enough percentage of people [who] I'm sure fill out that form that they're getting a bunch of sign-ups that way. If you refer someone else, you get 250 megabytes and they get 250 additional free megabytes in a free subscription on Dropbox. That's a kind of double-sided referral program."

USING SOCIAL MEDIA

Many business people look to Sun Tzu to see potential applications from his theory of war to the business world. And when it comes to social media, we find lots of companies that treat business like a war.

They think of social media as a cauldron of controversy waiting to bubble over with a negative post that goes viral and sinks the stock of the company overnight.

Although I certainly understand that sentiment, I think social media is better viewed as customer communities on steroids. That means, once again, this is a select group of people and therefore there is bias, but it also means that key feedback can be gleaned from these groups as well.

Think of social media as a welcome source of feedback rather than something to be censored or controlled; it can be invaluable for gathering data and sentiments about your product or feature.

Be ready to acknowledge mistakes, but to also correct misconceptions. Doing both builds trust.

After all, you must be completely self-aware if you plan to compete and win in the market.

The following table provides a set of key B2B and B2C metrics that you should target and attain by the time you reach the MVT value inflection point:

■ Key Minimum Viable Traction Target Metrics ■

	B2B	B2C
Stage Duration	1 year	1 year
Revenue	$6M ARR	N/A
DAU/MAU	25%	25%
CAC Ratio	< 1.0	N/A
Viral Coefficient*	> .2	> 1.0

*For a B2C company, a viral coefficient of less than 1.0 implies no growth and a company destined for failure. However, for a B2B company, viral growth is only one growth source; other sources include traditional marketing programs and techniques.

KEY TAKEAWAYS

■

Reaching Minimum Viable Traction signals a company's exit from the Traction Gap. To get there, your team had to rely on the lessons it learned along the way to reach MVR—what worked and what didn't. After MVT, a startup must be prepared to triple, then double year over year for at least the next 3 years on its way toward a liquidity event, either an IPO or an acquisition.

Lack of liquidity can significantly impair your ability to hire and retain key personnel so you can continue to grow. The business challenges after MVT are beyond the scope of the Traction Gap Framework, but are well codified in Geoffrey Moore's classic book, *Crossing the Chasm*, to which I've referred many times and which I highly recommend if you are not familiar with it.

Upon reaching Minimum Viable Traction, your team should have accomplished the following milestones:

PRODUCT

Product—The product has matured significantly since MVP. It no longer has significant performance or functional deficiencies. All product efforts can be focused on achieving more revenue per account or expanding into new market segments to secure additional market share. The company may elect to acquire, or partner with, a product or team that can complement its offerings.

REVENUE

Revenue—You've had 12 to 18 months of successive quarter-over-quarter growth. If you are a B2B startup, you are generating, based on industry averages, around $6M ARR. The data shows that the company knows what it is doing. You are beginning to explore new markets with new marketing and sales approaches. You may

(continues)

be expanding into new geographies. You are dealing with more sophisticated territories and compensation plans. The company is about to become a lot more complicated to run as it prepares for large-scale growth. You must build a revenue plan—and corresponding operating and financial plans—that ensure that you can continue to scale at the same rate as other comparable companies did at your stage. You probably raised capital at the beginning or just prior to MVR to finance you through to MVT. Now, after this 12- to 18-month period, you are ready to create a new financing, based upon performance, that will compel growth investors to invest in your company.

TEAM

Team—At this point, the majority of your management team should be complete, but some team members may be showing signs that they are not able to scale with the company. They may have been great early-stage contributors; but as the complexities of the business amplify, others from outside the company may be more suitable to take on leadership roles. Recognizing this earlier rather than later and taking action is critical to the growth and long-term survival of the company.

SYSTEMS

Systems—The systems evaluated and implemented after reaching MVR should be sufficient to power the startup to MVT. (It will take a few more years before the company will need to also set up processes that prepare it to operate as a public entity.) As the company contemplates moving into new geographies or other market segments (e.g., large enterprises), it will need to implement additional accounting, security, and financial controls along with 24/7 service and support systems.

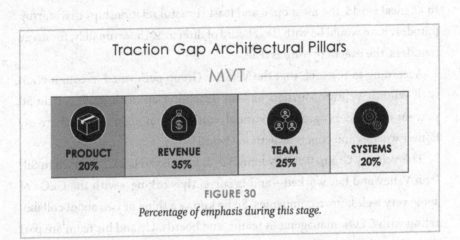

FIGURE 30

Percentage of emphasis during this stage.

The following are the key principles Wildcat Venture Partners looks for at MVT:

■ Traction Gap Principles ■
MVT

Product	Prioritize removing technical debt over new features.
Revenue	Refine pricing models, customer acquisition strategies, hire sales resources slightly ahead of demand.
Team	Deliberately construct a high-quality board—and advisers.
Systems	Implement advanced front and back office systems.

• • •

TRACTION GAP HACKS ▶ MVT

Working with Your Board

In an ideal world, the most open and least stressful relationships that startup founders have would be with their board of directors. Unfortunately, for many founders, the exact opposite is true.

According to research that the Velocity Group performed in conjunction with Wildcat Venture Partners and the Traction Gap Institute, less than 50 percent of founders agree very strongly with the statement "I can share my honest worries and concerns with my board."

The Velocity Group is led by John Baird. John Baird is a CEO coach in Silicon Valley and has worked—and is currently working—with the CEOs of some very well-known companies. So he knows a thing or two about collaborating with CEOs, management teams, and boards. He and his team are part of the Traction Gap Institute partner ecosystem.

The feedback they heard is consistent with some of the fastest-growing startups in the Valley, where founders state that managing the board is actually one of the most stressful duties of their jobs.

Why is this? Maybe it's because board meetings are the one time every quarter (or every month!) when founders worry about being judged and potentially fired.

The truth is, board members want to "manage you out" as little as you'd like to go. Your skill at running good board meetings is one of the best ways to keep the board "in the tent pissing out, rather than outside pissing in," to quote President Lyndon Johnson.

The following is from a report prepared by Velocity for Wildcat Venture Partners and the Traction Gap Institute. It has some invaluable insights and could help you reduce the stress of working with your board:

Most of the founders we interviewed said that they find building a new product more straightforward than running a board meeting. Lucky for them (and maybe for you), I am going to share with you a rather simple road map to prepare for and manage board meetings.

Using this guide, you can have board meetings that actually add value to the company and leave founders and board members alike feeling that the 3 hours were well spent, rather than a meandering, nerve-racking mess.

The best board/founder relationships are the transparent ones—the ones in which both board members and founders can troubleshoot what's hard, take shared responsibility for growth, and celebrate incremental successes. Nothing is more satisfying for an investor than looking back at a big exit and saying "We really put our all into that one."

HOW TO RUN BOARD MEETINGS
THAT KEEP BOARD MEMBERS "IN THE TENT"

TWO WEEKS BEFORE—Call for Agenda Items

Two weeks shy of the board meeting, reach out to your board members to ask them for topics they'd like to see covered at the meeting. This isn't asking them for the obvious, or asking them to write the agenda. It's simply "In addition to our standard agenda, are there other items you'd like to discuss?"

Think about the following three aspects: the portions of time you want to divide among reporting, leadership, and strategy. Once you review the input of board members, decide which are "boardworthy" topics and which are "subcommittee" topics.

(continues)

Some board members want to micromanage and discuss every hire. You'll want to set very clear standards for what kinds of topics are added to your agenda. When you do not include a board member-requested topic on the agenda, let him/her know "why" you are covering some topics and not others.

▪ Board Topics ▪

BOARD MEETING WORTHY TOPICS	NONBOARD MEETING WORTHY TOPICS
Growth Forecasts and Progress	Specific Growth Tactics
Product Strategy	Individual Product Features
Hiring Plan	Nonexecutive Level Hires
Employee Equity Pool Size	Individual Comp Packages
Fundraising Plan	Day-to-Day Budget

ONE WEEK BEFORE—Share the Board Pack

Four or five business days before the board meeting, send out a four- or five-page document with all relevant information to cover key topics and make important decisions.

Make sure the pack has a cover page that indicates:

- The topics to be covered/discussed
- Why each topic is important
- What action/decision/outcome you want from the discussion
- Frame three or four questions for the board to think about as they are reading the board pack.

Mike Maples from Floodgate Capital says there are really only five questions that need to be answered at a board meeting:[5]

1. Has the market changed since we last met?
2. If so, did it affect us negatively or positively?
3. Has the team changed? For better or worse?
4. Has our position in the market changed?
5. Did we do what we said we would?

We would add three more questions:

1. What's next?
2. What keeps you up at night?
3. What do you think/hope the board can do to help?

Board Pack

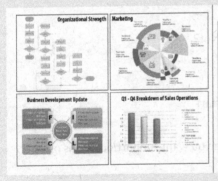 

FIGURE 31[6]

Left Side: Ugly PowerPoint slides that need lots of explanation.
Right Side: An elegant board pack that has all relevant info, but is still easy to read.

(continues)

In consideration of all the above, your board packet should contain the following sections:

- Executive Summary
- Top Highlights (Big Sales, Product News, Customer Stories)
- Top Challenges (Sales, Team, Product, Market Forces)
- By-the-Numbers
- Cash-on-Hand and Runway
- User Growth & Retention
- Relevant Funnel Metrics
- NPS/Customer Feedback
- Changes in the Landscape
- Macro-Level Forces
- Competitive Forces
- Supplier/Vendor Forces
- Product Update
- Status
- What's Working/What's Not?
- Team Update
- Major Hires
- Major Changes to Org Chart
- Major Topic 1
- Summary of the first item you want support/decisions on
- Major Topic 2
- Summary of the second item you want support/decisions on

DURING THE WEEK BEFORE—Board Member 1-on-1s

Meet with or have a call with every board member to discuss what's most important to each of you and get clear on how they will vote on any difficult or uncertain issues. We can't underscore this enough. A board meeting is no place for surprises. So make an effort to get clarity on everyone's positions before you head into the meeting.

TWO DAYS BEFORE—Final Agenda Construction

Board packs are out and being read. You've had pre-meeting meetings with each board member to get clarity on his/her positions on contentious issues. Now it's time to make the final agenda.

MANAGING THE MEETING ITSELF

At the outset, as part of your "Big Picture CEO Update," be sure to overview the agenda, the specific outcomes you would like to achieve, and decisions you would like made. State your interest in having lively and healthy debate. We call these "left-hand column" comments. The right-hand column is the stuff that is easy to say. The left-hand column is harder to say, but that's what makes it important.

Throughout the meeting, capture action items and key decisions made. Don't be afraid to assign specific tasks to specific board members. As stated before, board members are much more likely to remain involved and be helpful when they feel like they are more than just an ATM. Lean on them for actions, not just money and advice.

At the end of the meeting, get feedback from the board on "what worked" and "what didn't work." Make note of their comments and make changes that make sense to you for the next meeting.

MANAGING YOURSELF DURING THE MEETING

First off, sit down at the table with your fellow board members. If you stand at the head, you are mimicking the "founder pitch" scenario and putting the board in the position of listening and

(continues)

judging. Sit down in the middle of the long side of your conference table, so you are as close to as many board members as possible.

Second, try to demonstrate "active listening" as much as possible by letting board members know that you have heard and understood their comments.

Third, don't waste time reviewing information that is in the board packet. If a board member asks for a piece of data that's in the board pack, gently remind him/her that it is in there. It will be obvious to the rest of the board that said board member came ill-prepared, and it will be less likely to happen again.

Fourth, keep an eye on the clock. Be sure to manage your time as you navigate movement between updates, leadership, and more strategic deep dives.

And finally, don't feel you have to have all the answers; use board members during the meeting as needed.

AFTER THE MEETING (Follow-up email)

Although it goes without saying, you should follow up with a summary email after every board meeting. This should include:

- Decisions made
- Action items assigned
- Goals agreed to
- Next board meeting time & place (of course, a calendar invite should be sent, as well)
- Ask what went well and what didn't. This is a request, according to our research, that VERY few founders do well.

SUMMARY

At the end of the day, your relationship with your board will depend much more on how you manage the members than on how you allow yourself to be managed. Smoothly run board meetings show professionalism and inspire confidence. Sharing what's hard, as well as the workload, allows board members to feel like they are "in the tent." Trying to prove your competence or shielding the board from what's actually going on inside the company will only weaken your relationship with them.

PART

SCALING
TO SUCCESS

After Slide 30 "Go-to-Scale"

8

BEYOND THE
TRACTION GAP

You've made it successfully to Minimum Viable Traction!

You have now accomplished more than 80 percent, perhaps 90 percent, of all entrepreneurs. The number is likely even greater than that: it's hard to put an exact number on survivors of the passage from Ideation to MVT because many startups simply come and go without leaving a trace. That means that you are, indeed, part of a very elite group. Take a moment to celebrate.

That's the good news. Now, I'm afraid that you still have a very long journey in front of you, if you intend to remain a viable, independent entity. But, if you followed the steps I've outlined in the previous chapters, you will be far better prepared than most.

You are now soundly in the go-to-scale phase.

• • •

Fortunately, the best practices you've implemented to date should have prepared you well for this phase. They include:

- A market-first product, product process, and market-centric team,
- A culture of high performance, accountability, collaboration, and transparency,
- A management team with deep functional skills and the ability—and processes—to recruit and hire the best talent,
- A governance process designed to quickly make data-driven decisions and to effectively communicate those decisions to every employee, and
- A suite of state-of-the-art back-office and front-office systems that enable cost-effective conversion of awareness and interest into revenue.

At Minimum Viable Traction, you should be at about $6M of Annual Recurring Revenue, or $500K Monthly Recurring Revenue. According to the T2D3 revenue growth model presented in Chapter 7, you now will need to prepare your company to triple, to $18M, over the next year; and then, after that, double year-over-year for the next three years.

To accomplish this goal, you will almost certainly need a fresh round of capital, your third round after your initial seed investment (if you had one). You still will need to calculate how much capital you require to reach that next financial milestone. For that calculation, you should refer back to the end of Chapter 2, where I showed you how much other startups, on average, have raised by the time they reach MVT, at what pre-money valuation, and with what amount of dilution. The amount of capital you will need to reach the next revenue objectives will largely be determined by your Customer Acquisition Cost ratio (CAC ratio); a measure of the effectiveness and efficiency of your growth engine—your marketing and sales organizations; and your churn rates managed by your customer success or customer experience team.

At this point, you will be dealing with true mid- to late-stage investors, who will dive into your financials assiduously and with great detail. In fact, they will expect your investor deck, after explaining what problem you solve—your Minimum Viable Category—to begin with the financials/metrics, not a product overview. And they will expect to know *all* the metrics of your business cold, including:

- Customer Acquisition Costs (CAC),
- CAC Ratio,
- Customer Lifetime Value (CLTV),
- Churn Rates,
- Daily Active Usage Rates,
- Gross Margins,
- Cost of Sales, and
- Average Sales Cycles.

They will not be patient with, or forgiving of, your ignorance.

You should have enough customer and user data on hand that venture investors will now "add value" by telling you how great or lousy you are doing compared to similar companies both in your industry and out of it. You are truly a spreadsheet company, and from now on you will be evaluated by investors on your metrics. So get used to it . . . and good at it.

Ironically, as far as you have come over the past few years, you are still a very young company with a long way to go before you generate some sort of liquidity for yourself, your employees, and your investors through an IPO or M&A event. In fact, it could be another 3 to 4 years before that happens, if it happens at all. This period is no time to rest on your laurels.

A quick story to highlight the unpredictable challenges post MVT.

By 2010, Marketo was firing on all cylinders, four years after its founding. The company was growing rapidly. In fact, Marketo had finished the year at about $14M, up substantially from the prior year. Now, three years after MVP, the company was consistently at or above the T2D3 revenue growth curve.

Although Marketo initially targeted the SMB market, three years after founding the company, marketing teams at some large enterprises had begun to take notice of Marketo and dangled some tantalizingly large deals in front of the company.

The problem? Marketo needed to have some "enterprise-y" capabilities—such as 24/7, follow the sun, global support—if it wanted to engage those enterprise customers. The company didn't have any such programs in place. Indeed, it still needed to commit to building them. Meanwhile, it was becoming increasingly apparent that Marketo needed to include large customers if it was going to continue to maintain its rapid growth.

Ultimately, Phil, the company—and the board—decided it wanted—needed—those deals. So Marketo bit the bullet and added an enterprise team, even though everyone knew it was going to be expensive and difficult. The result? In 2011, Marketo closed about $32M in revenue. So, in retrospect, it was a brilliant and decisive move; but, if you had spoken with the Marketo management team at the time, I suspect they would have told you that adding that enterprise team was extraordinarily difficult.

If you are growing your company correctly, you too will likely face a company-betting moment one to two years after reaching MVT. To keep on the high-growth path, you may be compelled to make one or more existential decisions:

- ▶ Open up a new geography.
- ▶ Move into a new vertical.
- ▶ Add a new product offering.
- ▶ Acquire a company in a new market space.
- ▶ Acquire a competitor in your current market space.
- ▶ Move into a different market segment.

There will be few people by your side—especially ones you trust—to help you make these life-and-death startup decisions. You will "run the numbers" obsessively . . . and you will wake up sweating in the middle of the night with the realization of just how narrow that ledge is that you are walking on. One misstep and you could cripple your company's growth—and all that effort over the years up to this point will have been for nothing.

At this stage, your board most likely consists solely of venture investors, most of whom are smart but may not have ever personally built a large and successful company from scratch. And, if they are less experienced GPs, their investment track record and tenure with their partnership may depend solely on the successful outcome of your startup. You may not realize it, but they may be just as nervous as you—maybe more so—because they are not really in a position to help you. They have no control over what is happening in the company, and their career with their venture firm and in the venture industry is inextricably tied to you.

Some of your venture investors may have some prior operating experience, but few of them will have started or started with a company as an operating executive from its inception and taken it to a large exit. These board members don't possess the operational expertise or experience to help you make key operational decisions based on their personal experience in a similar situation.

This is when having a great board of advisers becomes critically useful.

As startups enter the go-to-scale phase, I highly advise them to bring on two to four advisers; strong, veteran operating execs who've gained wisdom from having been down this path before, know the pitfalls that lie ahead, and can help address many of the questions and issues that you will face. Compensate your advisers with a stock option grant. Advisors for startups at this stage typically receive 0.1 percent to 0.25 percent stock option grants that vest over four years. However, I suggest you limit the time period to just one year to ensure that your advisors are adding value to you and the board.

Therefore, provide them with a stock option grant that ranges between 0.0025 percent and 0.0625 percent of the company, vesting monthly; this amount is just 0.1 percent to 0.25 percent divided by four. By doing this, each year you can decide whether you want to extend the agreement with a specific adviser for another year. If an adviser isn't adding significant value, don't be afraid to replace him or her quickly with others who can. You will not regret investing in this resource.

And remember: no one has traveled the exact path you are creating. Each day, you will be faced with new challenges for which there are no definitive answers—you are living in a bespoke environment.

> ❝ It's all about finding and hiring people smarter than you. Getting them to join your business. And giving them good work. Then getting out of their way. And trusting them. You have to get out of the way so YOU can focus on the bigger vision. That's important. And here's the main thing . . . you must make them see their work as a MISSION."
>
> **SIR RICHARD BRANSON,** Founder, Virgin Group

The best you can hope to do is to surround yourself with top talent, best processes, and wise advisers—and keep an open mind to new ideas. If you've made it this far, you're doing a lot of things right, so have some confidence. Don't become arrogant with success: that attitude has killed many startups. As you grow, each new phase will introduce a new set of challenges that you may not be as well equipped to address. So, find and listen to those with experience for the wisdom of their experience, all while leveraging the processes and skills you've honed during the Traction Gap.

We've now covered a lot of ground:

- ▶ I started out by introducing you to the Traction Gap Framework and its principles.
- ▶ I showed you the key Traction Gap architectural pillars you should be concerned with during each phase of the Traction Gap Framework, and that different pillars must take prominence as you move from one Traction Gap value inflection point to the next.

- I emphasized that without a focus on market-engineering leading to a clear vision and mission statement that defines your category and company, you are ill-prepared to move forward into the go-to-market phase, the domain of the Traction Gap and the cause of the 80%+ failure rate in new startups.

- I explained that developing and defining the category in which you intend to compete to reach Minimum Viable Category is mission-critical and that not nearly enough startups understand or are focused on category creation.

- The "messaging matrix" I provide shows you how to document, store, and share your startup's positioning, messaging, competitive responses, value propositions, etc.

- I suggested that from the inception of your startup, you must become a market-first company, ruthlessly focused on identifying, capturing, and acting on valid market signals. And that you must include into your decision set for new products and features more than just a handful of friends, families, and companies you know personally.

- And I've counseled you that you should never begin to move to the next value inflection point until you are confident that you have satisfied all the product, revenue, team, and systems requirements associated with the current value inflection point.

Though we've looked at a wider space, the true Traction Gap period is from Initial Product Release to Minimum Viable Traction and is primarily concerned with go-to-market issues. That is, I have shown you how you should think about bringing your product to market, rising above the market noise, and preparing your startup to become a category king in the go-to-scale phase.

During your journey, different Traction Gap architectural pillars tend to come to the fore, depending on the stage, and I've pointed them out and discussed them at each stage.

However, there is one dominant Traction Gap architectural pillar that plays a pivotal role at every phase from Ideation through MVT and in perpetuity; it is the *team*. Indeed, every CEO and founder I interviewed for this book said that the team was the most critical factor to success.

In addition, Professor Shikhar Ghosh from Harvard Business School told me that his research validated that the team is the single biggest factor that either enables scaling or constrains companies from scaling. He said that issues with the team plague companies of all sizes—and further, that many, if not most, of the team members who help you successfully navigate one phase are not necessarily well suited for later phases. Those who cannot make the transition will need to be thanked and rewarded for their significant contributions, transferred to new jobs if possible, and replaced as soon as new talent is recruited and promptly installed.

This process means that companies must be prepared to identify and manage executives and others into new positions or out of the business as soon as they show the first signs that they are unable to scale beyond their current roles. Companies must also be equally prepared and able to onboard new executives and managers quickly and effectively so they can come up to speed as rapidly as possible. You do not have time for hesitation. You will live or die by the talent and cohesion of your team.

> " Successful teams struggle, fight, and bicker too. The difference between a successful team and a failing team: when these challenges happen, successful teams acknowledge and resolve them quickly because the vision, harmony, consistent production, and success of the team is more important."
>
> **TY HOWARD,** author, *Untie the Knots That Tie Up Your Life*

Along the way in this book, I also have provided you with hacks—tips/plays—that you might elect to use, depending on where you are along the Traction Gap Framework.

A word of caution, though. You may decide to use one of the hacks I describe, which may have worked well for others, and then execute it "perfectly" . . . only to find that you have limited or no success with it. Why?

The reasons vary. It could be that you're a different company, operating at a different time from when the companies cited here were startups. Your market might be slightly different. Your product might not be as compelling. The overall culture, including consumer tastes, may have changed. There could be many reasons.

The point is that the Traction Gap Framework, the Traction Gap metrics, the suggestions I make throughout the book, and even the hacks I've provided, are meant to be guidelines for your own journey. Your mileage may and will vary. And I cannot guarantee that if you follow the Traction Gap Framework principles that you will be successful. However, if you do not, I believe that your chances of success will be significantly diminished.

When my Wildcat partners and I begin work with an early-stage startup that is a new member of our portfolio, we know up front that each one is bespoke, with its own journey in front of it. And, that journey is seldom consistently "up and to the right." More often than not, there are fits and starts, regressions and setbacks, before things begin to work.

Because of that, we don't supply rote answers to address their issues. Instead, we look at what they are doing and use the Traction Gap Framework to help develop an operating plan and provide a "North Star" that is directionally accurate. But the specific route we take with each company to get to MVT and beyond is as yet unknown, and will depend on changing circumstances.

One of the reasons we are willing to share the information in this book—and not hide it away as the proprietary intellectual property of Wildcat Venture Partners—is that we know the Traction Gap Framework offers guardrails and mile markers, but that most startups will still need additional help to ensure that they arrive safely at their destination. At Wildcat, our track records as entrepreneurs, operating executives, consultants, and investors suggest that we are pretty good helpers! You, too, should find helpers, investors, and advisers who have "been there, done that." Someone—or a group of someones—who you trust and can help you make it through this challenging phase.

So, you might wonder how we—Wildcat—apply these Traction Gap principles and operationalize the Traction Gap Framework with our portfolio companies. The answer is that every early-stage startup that becomes a member of our investment portfolio is eligible to participate in our proprietary *Traction Gap Assessment and Diagnostic* process.

We begin by having each member of the startup's management team take a survey. This survey asks each team member a series of questions designed to determine where each believes the company is positioned along the Traction Gap Framework continuum. This process identifies areas of strength and weakness across product, revenue, team, and systems.

The results from the survey are then evaluated by Geoffrey Moore, along with the Wildcat general partner who made the investment. The two work together to identify areas of misalignment and gaps. They then discuss their analysis in a follow-on workshop with the management team. This workshop typically results in a *Traction Gap Action Plan*, with some prescribed "remedial" work for the startup team to undertake with Traction Gap Institute (TGI) partners.

The TGI partners are typically consulting firms and companies that the TGI has vetted and are willing to provide workshops to help startups remedy issues associated with gaps in product, revenue, team, and systems.

While the Traction Gap Institute is founded and funded by Wildcat Venture Partners, *anyone can join and attend any TGI event at no cost.*

So, even if you aren't a Wildcat portfolio company and may not know Geoffrey Moore or a Wildcat general partner, as a member of the Traction Gap Institute, you still have access to key industry leaders, hacks, and a network of entrepreneurs and consultants off whom you can bounce ideas and from whom you can learn to implement Traction Gap principles.

My partners and I sincerely hope you found this book to be helpful and that you will use and refer to it often, and that it helps you to successfully traverse your way across the Traction Gap.

If you discover new hacks or have other comments you'd like to share with other startups, we'd welcome your input. You can reach us at *traction@wildcat.vc*.

Good luck. Now get out there; work smart, work hard, and change the world.

Bruce Cleveland
& the Wildcat Venture Partners Team

To download a Traction Gap Framework reference sheet that includes all important Traction Gap metrics discussed in this book, visit www.tractiongap.com.

APPENDIX

The following is an example of a Messaging Matrix I originally developed for GreenFig. Although some of the messaging and positioning has changed since I initially created it, the content I developed should serve as an example for you to write your own Messaging Matrix.

Writing this document is not a job to be delegated to a marketing person; it is fundamental to the startup's market-engineering process. Accordingly, while someone may be assigned to make the initial draft, the ideas, words, terms, etc., need to come from the CEO and/or founder and the founding members of the team.

Once the team has completed the Messaging Matrix, everyone in the company should be required to read and internalize it. Failure to do so can lead to branding and positioning issues for the entire startup. If market feedback leads you to change your positioning and messaging, then those changes must be reflected back and captured in this document and then recirculated to every member of the startup.

Messaging Matrix: GreenFig	
Our company is (Strategic descriptor)	GreenFig is a microeducation company offering microdegrees in applied business science, including: customer success, finance, marketing, product, sales, service, and support. GreenFig provides a hybrid training platform that combines live, interactive online and on-premise team-based learning with real-time, hands-on instruction from industry experts to deliver job-ready talent in less than 200 hours.
For (Target customer)	• Higher-ed students augmenting traditional academic programs • Veterans • Professionals in career transition • Lifetime learners seeking new skills and market relevance

(continues)

Why (Compelling reason to buy)	To help people achieve and maintain the skills they need to be "job-ready" in the digital economy.
Technology/ product (Name and category)	The first GreenFig course in Digital Marketing Science will be offered during the 2017 fall semester, with virtual and physical cohorts.
That (Key benefits)	Provides: • **Job-ready** talent with micro degrees in applied business science in **less than 200 hours** • Accelerated experiential learning from a **hybrid training delivery model**—using live, interactive online and on-premise team-based learning • **Hands-on**, real-time **business application software instruction** from industry experts • Work experience gained through **real-world projects** mentored by industry experts • **High-demand certifications** from industry-leading business application software **providers** • **Selective** application process biased toward people who are motivated to learn • Intimate **collaboration** and **networking** between students, instructors, and industry experts
Unlike (Primary competitor)	GreenFig is laser-focused on developing job-ready talent in applied business science. Unlike its competitors, GreenFig's hybrid training platform provides live, interactive online and on-premise team-based learning to accelerate proficiency and job-readiness. GreenFig's competitors do not provide an integrated and comprehensive learning experience, certifications from key business software providers, nor are they hyper-focused on delivering job-ready business science professionals. General Assembly, Udacity, and Coursera are all primarily focused on technical topics, "operational mechanics," and specialization vs. the comprehensive and integrated learning experience needed to acquire proficiency in "the science" of a business function. This is why we use the word "science" in all the names of our courses. This is also why we are calling our students "business scientists." We use the word "applied"—because we are focused on how our students can "apply" what they've learned to drive business and industry vs. "research" science.
Offering (Strategic advantage)	A hybrid training platform that combines live, interactive online and offline team-based learning with real-time, hands-on instruction in business application software from industry experts that delivers job-ready talent in less than 200 hours. The GreenFig microdegree program includes certifications from industry-leading business application software providers such as Marketo, Google, and others.

Tagline (For press release)	A Microeducation Company Offering Microdegrees in Applied Business Science: Preparing People for Jobs in the Digital Economy
Boilerplate (For press release)	GreenFig is a microeducation company offering microdegrees in applied business science, including: customer success, finance, marketing, product, sales, service, and support. GreenFig's hybrid training delivery model combines live, interactive online and offline team-based learning with real-time, hands-on business application software instruction from industry experts. A microdegree program from GreenFig includes practical work experience from business projects where industry mentors help students apply their newly acquired skills. GreenFig's microdegrees can be achieved in less than 200 hours and, when completed, students can be confident that they possess the subject matter proficiency and basic work experience industry demands. GreenFig is currently headquartered in Bend, Oregon and delivers its programs across the US using the GreenFig Education Broadcasting Network. To learn more about GreenFig's applied business science program, visit www.greenfig.net.

Competitive Landscape: Creating the Market	
Key competitors	Online/alternative education providers—Coursera, General Assembly, Udacity, Udemy. These companies aren't really competitors, per se. They are simply alternative forms of education.
Target strategic partners and alliances	We made an announcement with Marketo on April 24 and 25, 2017. If asked, we can accurately state that "we are in discussions with other industry-leading business application software providers to deliver other applied business science courses."
Market trends and other impacts/ changing dynamics	The current educational system is challenged to provide adequate training for the digital economy—jobs that require skills using business application software. **Traditional Education.** Most traditional education programs are not well suited to provide the hands-on and work-related experience students need to master business application software and business science. Industry requirements and business applications change so rapidly that by the time a new curriculum is peer-reviewed and approved, it is already out of date—and few university professors have current industry experience or are skilled in the use of business application software.

(continues)

Market trends and other impacts/ changing dynamics *(cont.)*	**Online Education Programs.** Most online programs are focused on technical subjects, lack real-time, interactive hands-on business application software instruction, and lack business science training, and few offer the real-world work experience companies and government organizations require for even the most basic, entry-level positions. **Application Software Companies.** Application software providers are not in a position to easily address the issue, as one vendor can seldom provide all the necessary functionality for a specific business function. In almost every case, each business function requires a number of application software products from various providers. **Corporate Training.** Due to the rapid pace of change and competition, most employers do not have the luxury of time or the resources to internally train new workers how to use business application software; many current employees are not up to speed with these new applications. Companies are seeking employees already skilled in these operational functions and business applications.
Data and research	**Universities** In the fall of 2016, there were 20.6M students attending US colleges and universities. (Source: NCES Fast Facts—https://nces.ed.gov/fastfacts/display.asp?id=372) Assume 10% penetration = 2M students Assume $3,000 per student TAM = $6B Universities and colleges receiving state and federal funding/aid are coming under increasing pressure to demonstrate that their students are getting jobs. (Source: https://www.newamerica.org/education-policy/edcentral/hold-colleges-accountable-for-jobs/#) More importantly, parents of students attending the non-Tier 1 Universities (e.g., those that aren't Ivy League schools) are increasingly demanding to know what the ROI is from a degree from a particular academic institution. **Veterans** Each year, there are 250,000 veterans returning to the civilian world (source: http://www.economist.com/blogs/democracyinamerica/2014/11/veterans-day). Many are challenged to apply their military experience to civilian positions. Assume that the last 4 years' of veterans returning to civilian world are most likely to be interested in at least 1 business science program. 250,000/year * 4 years = 1M Assume 10% penetration = 100,000 Assume $3,000 per veteran (veterans can use GI Bill to defray most of this expense) TAM = $300M

Data and research *(cont.)*	**Transitioning Workers**
	86% of US workers are seeking a career change (source: http://fortune.com/2014/08/05/job-search-career-change/)
	   In Jan 2017, there were 123M full-time workers in the US. (source: https://www.statista.com/statistics/192361/unadjusted-monthly-number-of-full-time-employees-in-the-us/)
	   86% of 123M = 106M
	   Assume just 1% interested in 1 business science program

Other Considerations: Identifying Key Differentiators

	GreenFig	Udacity	Coursera
Business model	Selective application process $ per course	Open to anyone with $ to pay	Open to anyone with $ to pay
Market category	Microeducation—a hybrid of classroom, online, and on-premise learning	Online Education	Online Education
Customers	Higher-ed students, veterans, lifelong learners, professionals in transition (workers returning to the workforce after prolonged absence, underemployed and unemployed workers)		
Value proposition	1. Job-ready in less than 200 hours. 2. Certificates from industry-leading business application software providers 3. Real-time delivery and hands-on instruction from industry experts 4. Focus on "business science," not just the operational mechanics of how to use a product	Job listings from partners Prepares you for the jobs of tomorrow 3 months / 120 hours	University developed courses 6 courses (1 course / month) (8–10 hours / week) = TOTAL: 240 hrs

(continues)

	GreenFig	Udacity	Coursera
Pricing	$2,500—students currently enrolled in an accredited program, vets, unemployed workers, and workers making under $35,000 per year. $3,800—workers currently employed making more than $35,000 per year	$999—Digital Marketing Nanodegree	7-day free trial $474 each specialization Digital Marketing Specialization This specialization explores several aspects of the new digital marketing environment, including topics such as digital marketing analytics, search engine optimization, social media marketing, and 3D printing.
Core product / service	Microdegrees in applied business science—definitionally, a microdegree includes a formal certificate from industry-leading business application software providers	Nanodegrees, primarily STEM related	Arts and Humanities, Business, Computer Science, Data Science, Life Science, Math & Logic, Personal Development, Physical Science & Engineering, Social Science, Language Learning

	GreenFig	Udacity	Coursera
Features	Live, online/physical instruction and hands-on training combined, with online testing, and real-world project with a real company leading to a microdegree that includes a micro certificate from industry-leading business application software providers. Industry seeks people who possess demonstrated proficiency with real business application software along with relevant work experience.	Primarily time-shifted (pre-recorded) with very little real-time instructor training and interaction, projects are relatively simplistic and provide little interaction with a real company. Certification comes from Udacity, not industry-leading business application software providers. Few companies are seeking people with Udacity nanodegrees.	Primarily time-shifted (pre-recorded) with very little real-time instructor training and interaction, Projects are relatively simplistic and provide little interaction with a real company. Certification comes from Coursera, not industry-leading business application software providers. Few companies are seeking people with Coursera degrees. Project is case study with Grainger.
	GreenFig	**Udacity**	**Coursera**
Customer benefits	Job-readiness in less than 200 hours	New knowledge and potentially new skills	New knowledge and potentially new skills
Top 3 corporate messages	1. Less than 200 hours to proficiency 2. Certification from industry-leading business application software providers 3. Job-readiness	Learn new skills on your own time at your own pace	Learn new skills on your own time at your own pace

(continues)

Corporate Story: GreenFig	
Corporate Name	GreenFig, Inc.
Founded	March, 2017
Headquarters	Bend, Oregon
Other offices	San Mateo, California
Employees	Cari Baldwin—initial employee at founding of company
Financing	Series Seed
Investors	Wildcat Venture Partners
Founders	Bruce Cleveland (Founder), Cari Baldwin (Cofounder)
Story	In early 2015, some of the cofounders of GreenFig created a company called BendPoly (www.bendpoly.com), located in Bend, OR. Over the summers of 2015 and 2016, they held 2 sessions where they successfully trained 35 local and 5 remote students in marketing "science" and how to use business applications such as Google Analytics and Marketo marketing automation software. Each session featured classroom instruction for 5 weeks, 6 hours per day, 4 days per week. The instruction included hands-on application software training by industry experts. For the final 3 weeks, teams of students were formed to develop real marketing campaigns for actual companies. The teams competed against one another and presented their outcomes to an independent panel of industry experts, who acted as judges. The winning team was awarded the president's trophy, and team members were entitled to place this achievement onto their LinkedIn profile. This competition drove teams to perform their very best. After completing the program, the majority of the students seeking a marketing role found positions in industry. This was accomplished in less than 1 year from the students completing the program. Here are two links that help explain the program and its results: **Video:** http://www.bendpoly.com/video-post/bendpoly-program-video-overview/ **Article:** http://www.bendsource.com/bend/training-the-future-workforce/Content?oid=2609069 Based upon BendPoly's success, the BendPoly cofounder decided to create GreenFig to scale the program nationally.

APPENDIX

Something Interesting	Angles we discussed: US politicians, academia, and industry leaders are currently placing a tremendous emphasis on technical training, coding, and other STEM programs. Yet less than 6.5% of the jobs in the US are STEM-related. In addition, the vast majority of people are simply neither interested nor well suited for highly technical degrees and jobs. According to a recent article posted in *The Atlantic*, "Liberal-arts majors are two to three times more likely to be underemployed than those with engineering or nursing majors." The article goes on to states: "The gap between humanities and STEM students is striking. Underemployment afflicts more than 50 percent of majors in the performing arts, anthropology, art history, history, communications, political science, sociology, philosophy, psychology, and international affairs." Yet the US is envied the world over for its creativity, individualism, and innovation. These are precisely what the liberal arts foster. Until now, there have been few programs focused on liberal arts majors—or anyone who is creative and articulate—to make them "job-ready." GreenFig's microeducation program has been designed to address this problem. GreenFig is focused on people who possess critical thinking skills with a desire to learn and who want to become **business scientists**. A business scientist possesses "digital literacy" and understands how to capture, analyze, and utilize customer, financial, market, and product data. People who have gone through a liberal arts program are ideally suited to become business scientists and fill the positions of the 21st century. Reskilling the world for the digital economy was a topic among everyone at the World Economic Forum in Davos in 2016. Helping veterans transition back to civilian life, helping women return to the workforce after child-rearing, helping liberal arts students get great jobs: we have created something that is really impactful. GreenFig's unique focus on job-readiness—in less than 200 hours—and reskilling the workforce to operate the "soft machinery"—business application software—has been tried and tested, and has delivered proven results over the past 2 years.
Key Words	The following are key words and terms that we need to use to reinforce GreenFig's thought leadership and differentiation: **Soft Machinery**—business application software to "power" the digital economy, which relies upon systems of intelligence and significant sources of data. Contrasted against the "hard machinery" (factories, physical machines) that powered the industrial economy that relied upon significant sources of capital. **Business Science**—the "scientific method" uses observation, facts, metrics, and experimentation. "Business science" uses the scientific method to analyze and respond to business transactions and results across all business functions, including but not limited to: customer success, marketing, products, sales, sales operations, service, and support.

(continues)

Business Scientists—people who are skilled in business science and fill key roles in companies of all sizes. Business scientists understand how to capture, analyze, and utilize customer, financial, market, and product data.

Applied Business Science—The act of developing and applying business strategy and tactics using the tools of business science—business application software.

Microeducation—A new education category defined by:
- **Job-ready** talent with microdegrees in applied business science in **less than 200 hours**
- Accelerated experiential learning from a **hybrid training delivery model**—using live, interactive online and offline team-based learning
- **Hands-on**, real-time **business application software instruction** from industry experts
- Work experience gained through **real-world projects** mentored by industry experts
- **High-demand certifications** from industry-leading business application software providers
- **Selective** application process biased toward people who are motivated to learn
- Intimate collaboration and networking among students, instructors, and industry experts

Microeducation—A new education entity that participates in the "microeducation" category.

Microdegree—A student achieves a microdegree when the student successfully masters the material presented in a microeducation course. More importantly, GreenFig's microdegrees prepare students to take an exam leading to a certificate of proficiency by industry-leading business application software providers such as Marketo and Salesforce. This is what employers are looking for: there are tens of thousands of open jobs for people with these skills on jobsites such as Glassdoor.com or Indeed.com.

Job-Readiness—GreenFig is laser-focused on making its graduates "job-ready" by providing a combination of strategy/concept training, skills training (industry-leading business application software), real work experience on real projects, and proficiency certification through "micro certificates" that are endorsed by industry-leading business application software providers.

ENDNOTES

CHAPTER 1

1. (For Figure 2:) Cartoon, "Then a Miracle Occurs…" Used with the permission of ScienceCartoonsPlus.com.
2. (For Figure 3:) Danielle Morrill, "Founder Competition for Series A Deals Is Fierce, Due to Record Number of Seed-Funded Startups in the Funnel," September 8, 2015, https://mattermark.com/founder-competition-for-series-a-deals-is-fierce-due-to-record-number-of-seed-funded-startups-in-the-funnel/.
3. Wildcat Venture Partners.
4. Andreessen, "Product/Market Fit," posted June 25, 2007, https://web.stanford.edu/class/ee204/ProductMarketFit.html.

CHAPTER 2

1. Kurt Schroeder, "Why So Many New Products Fail (and It's Not the Product)," posted March 14, 2017, *The Business Journals*, https://www.bizjournals.com/bizjournals/how-to/marketing/2017/03/why-so-many-new-products-fail-and-it-s-not-the.html.
2. Geoffrey Moore, "A Quantum Theory of Venture Capital Valuations," posted February 7, 2017, https://www.linkedin.com/pulse/quantum-theory-venture-capital-valuations-geoffrey-moore/.
3. (For Figure 10:) Crunchbase, https://www.crunchbase.com/organization/vlocity#section-investors.

CHAPTER 3

1. Interview with Monte Zweben conducted by Velocity Group on behalf of Wildcat Venture Partners, 2017.
2. James Nunns, "He Said What? 5 Things Larry Ellison Actually Said about Cloud," *Computer Business Review* (April 27, 2015), https://www.cbronline.com/cloud/he-said-what-5-things-larry-ellison-actually-said-about-cloud-4563323/.

CHAPTER 4

1. CB Insights, "269 Starup Failure Post-Mortems," August 13, 2018, https://www.cbinsights.com/research/startup-failure-post-mortem/.
2. (For Figure 14:) CB Insights, "The Top 20 Reasons Startups Fail," February 2, 2018, https://www.cbinsights.com/rsearch/startup-failure-reasons-top/.
3. All content from Patrick Campbell's blog (including Figure 15 and Figure 16) sourced from Patrick Campbell, "Customer Research Benchmarks," *ProfitWell* (May 29, 2018), https://www.profitwell.com/blog/customer-research-benchmarks.

4. Quotes in this and the following paragraphs come from, Mat Honan, "Remembering the Apple Newton's Prophetic Failure and Lasting Impact," *Wired* (August 5, 2013), https://www.wired.com/2013/08/remembering-the-apple-newtons-prophetic-failure-and-lasting-ideals/.

5. EMC Digital Universe, "The Digital Universe of Opportunities: Rich Data and the Increasing Value of the Internet of Things," April 2014, https://www.emc.com/leadership/digital-universe/2014iview/executive-summary.htm.

6. All quotes of Sean Ellis are taken from his interview with the Wildcat Venture Partners team.

7. Suite Seven, "The Ultimate Guide to Discovery Interviews," http://suiteseven.com/wp-content/uploads/2014/10/DiscoveryInterviews_SuiteSeven.pdf.

CHAPTER 5

1. Holley Malia, "The Components of Becoming a Category King," posted June 24, 2017, Brey Matter Marketing, https://www.greymattermarketing.com/blog/the-components-of-becoming-a-category-king.

CHAPTER 6

1. Source: Amplero. Used by permission.

CHAPTER 7

1. (For Figure 28:) Neeraj Agrawal, General Partner at Battery Ventures, "The SaaS Adventure," TechCrunch, https://techcrunch.com/2015/02/01/the-saas-travel-adventure/.

2. (For Figure 29:) OpenView Venture Partners https://cdn2.hubspot.net/hubfs/366266/Expansion%20SaaS%20Benchmarking%20Study%20-%20Full%20Report.pdf.

3. Kaiser Mulla-Feroze, *The Missing SaaS Metric: Customer Retention Cost Report*, Totango, *https://drive.google.com/file/d/1x4koxaW12aIM-lxeZ0uxk6cMNqaFBxb0/view*.

4. Gregory Ciotti, "7 Things You Must Understand When Leveraging Social Proof in Your Marketing Efforts," https://neilpatel.com/blog/social-proof-factors-2.

5. Mike Maples, quoted in "The Secret to Making Board Meetings Suck Less," *First Round Capital Management Magazine* (2013), https://firstround.com/review/The-Secret-to-Making-Board-Meetings-Suck-Less/.

6. (For Figure 31:) First Round Capital, http://firstround.com/review/The-Secret-to-Making-Board-Meetings-Suck-Less/.

ACKNOWLEDGMENTS

Writing this book required about a year from start to finish, primarily because I had to do it evenings and weekends. The reality, though, is it took more than thirty years, as a member of the technology community of Silicon Valley, for me to accumulate the knowledge and experience I needed to write it. And none of this would have been possible had I not interacted and worked with some incredibly talented people, many of whom have transformed the world we live and work in.

WILDCAT VENTURE PARTNERS

I owe a deep debt of gratitude to the current and former members of the Wildcat Venture Partners team who provided input and content, performed entrepreneur interviews, offered feedback, and the like. Specifically, thank you: Katherine Barr, Liz Burstein, Bill Ericson, Laura Evans, Abhas Gupta, Nathaniel Krasnoff, Amanda Maestri, Geoffrey Moore, Bryan Stolle, Brett Teele, Jennifer Trzepacz, and Phyllis Whiteley. And, additional thanks to Jennifer for her wonderful project-management skills, Amanda for her graphics skills, and Laura for her interview skills—each of you put in a significant amount of extra effort to help bring this book to life.

When I first introduced the Wildcat team to a very nascent Traction Gap Framework, they immediately saw its value and helped to further develop the key concepts and introduce them to the startup community. Without the Wildcat team's encouragement and support, it would not have been possible to produce this book. Thank you all! You are a great team and I'm proud to be a member of it.

Tom Siebel, former founder, Chairman, and CEO, Siebel Systems; and current founder, Chairman, and CEO, C3

It is difficult to put into words how much I have gained through my professional relationship with Tom Siebel. It began when Tom hired me into Oracle when it was a small private company, and then brought me into Siebel when it too was a small startup. Over the course of ten years, I served as a member of Tom's executive team as the head of marketing, head of alliances, and ultimately head of products. Many of the concepts I share in this book are lessons I learned working for Tom.

Pat House, cofounder and former Vice Chairman, Siebel Systems, and current Vice Chairman and cofounder, C3

Pat is one of the finest marketers and technology executives to come out of Silicon Valley. Few people understand that a lot of what enabled Siebel to grow to a $2B revenue company and $50B in valuation in only five years from startup is due to the contributions of Pat. Before Sheryl Sandberg or any of the other notable women in tech today, there was Pat House. Thanks for teaching me how to be a marketer, Pat. Someday I might be half as good as you.

Flip Gianos, GP, InterWest Partners

Flip convinced me that I should try out venture capital and taught me a lot about how to be a venture capitalist. One of the key principles Flip taught me was: "Do good deals." I haven't always succeeded, but I've done my best to follow that advice, Flip.

Doug Pepper, GP, Shasta Ventures

Doug and I made the investment in Marketo together, and we both served on its board for many years. Along the way, we became more than business colleagues: we became friends. Doug, in fact, is the one who gave me the idea for the Traction Gap. I might have twisted the meaning and taken it a bit further than he might have imagined, but Doug deserves the credit for inspiring me.

ACKNOWLEDGMENTS

Jon Miller, and Dave Morandi, founding Marketo Team

s one of my very first investments as a venture capitalist.
on, and Dave, for letting me be a part of your amazing journey.
shed exactly what you set out to do: you permanently transformed the role of marketing and the role of the CMO. What an extraordinary
feat. Some of the lessons I learned from that experience have found their way
into the Traction Gap principles.

Christopher Lochhead, coauthor of Play Bigger and former Silicon Valley Tech Executive

Chris, thanks for helping the Obo team and me come up with the concept
and definitions—the Fro/Tos—of what it means to be "market-first," one of
the key Traction Gap principles. The "Play Bigger" process we went through
when you hosted us at your awesome home was just outstanding. Here's to
dinosaurs roaming the earth, my friend.

Geoffrey Moore, author and venture partner, Wildcat Venture Partners

Geoff, thank you for encouraging me to write this book. I can only hope it
has a tenth of the positive influence you have had over the entrepreneurial
community.

Michael Eckhardt and Paul Wiefels, The Chasm Group

I want to thank you two for helping me to brainstorm the ideas around the
Traction Gap Framework and its principles. Your feedback was instrumental
in my thinking. Michael, you coined the term "Minimum Viable Traction"
when I was standing at the whiteboard and couldn't immediately come up
with a suitable name for the last Traction Gap value inflection point. It sounds
so obvious now. Thank you!

Michael Malone, author

Mike, you took my ramblings and turned them into entertaining prose. I
really appreciate all the help and advice you provided me—and the prod-
ding—to complete this project. I definitely couldn't have done it without you.

CEOS/FOUNDERS/ADVISERS

A big "Thank You!" to the following people who provided their input, thoughts, and advice to me and the Wildcat team: Tom Chavez, Andrew Chen, Tim Eades, Sean Ellis, Ben Faw, Ed Fields, Harley Finkelstein, Russell Glass, Fred Goff, Athani Krishna, Blaire Krochak, Nathan Latka, Chris Lien, Jamie Miller, Tom Mohr, Megan Niedenthal, Aidan O'Brien, Mark Organ, Kathryn Petralia, Bill Portelli, Amy Pressman, Rajesh Ram, Dale Sakai, Andrew Salzman, Vivek Sharma, Gurjeet Singh, Hari Subramanian, Tom Tunguz, Randall Ussery, Matt Wallach, Bob Wiederhold, David Yarnold, Dave Zabrowski, and Monte Zweben.

Again, thank you all for investing your valuable time by providing feedback on the manuscript, or sitting through the interviews and providing answers to questions about facts long forgotten.

ROBIN CLEVELAND

I want to thank Robin, my wife, mother to Blaire and Megan and "Nonna" to Georgia, Aubrey, AJ, Nat, and Alex. Thank you for putting up with me for all these years, and especially over this past year while this book was coming together. Your willingness to listen and provide constructive feedback along with offering creative insights during our hour-long walks several times each week was indispensable.

JERRY AND ANN CLEVELAND—DAD AND MOM

You provided me with a happy home and strong values growing up. These values continue to serve as my life compass. I can't say that I've always followed the right path initially, but I have always found my way back accordingly. I miss you both very much.

FRIENDS AND BUSINESS COLLEAGUES

And, finally, I want to thank my friends and business colleagues who have had such a positive influence on my life. I am, at the core of it, the sum of those collective interactions. Thank you for being a part of my life and helping to shape it.

INDEX

Vie abrégée de Jean-Claude Colin, fondateur mariste

Justin Taylor sm

Portrait de Jean-Claude Colin assis

Vie abrégée de Jean-Claude Colin, fondateur mariste

Une adaptation de *Jean-Claude Colin, Reluctant Founder*

Justin Taylor sm

FRANCE
2021

© les droits d'auteur restent avec la société de marie

Traductrice:	François Grossin sm
Editeur:	Gabriel Bueno Siqueira
Layout:	Extel Solutions, India
Font:	Minion Pro

ISBN: 978-1-922737-13-7 soft
978-1-922737-16-8 hard
978-1-922737-14-4 epub
978-1-922737-15-1 pdf

Published and edited by

FRANCE

Making a lasting impact

An imprint of the ATF Press Publishing Group
owned by ATF (Australia) Ltd.
PO Box 234
Brompton, SA 5007
Australia
ABN 90 116 359 963
www.atfpress.com

Crédits photos

Frontispiece, pages 1, 7, 8, 13, 15, 31, 39, 46, 47, 53, 59, 62, 63, 67, 69, 74: Ron Nissen sm.

Page 6: *Fourvière: à travers les siècles*, J. Escot, Lyon, 1954.

Pages 21, 54, 68, 81, 82: Society of Mary Archives.

Page 41: Archives of the Catholic Diocese of Auckland.

Page 44: Andrew Murray sm.

Note d'introduction

Cette Petite Vie de Jean-Claude Colin est tirée et adaptée de la biographie complète publiée par l'auteur : 'Jean-Claude Colin, Reluctant Founder' (Hindmarsh, SA: ATF Press, 2018). Elle est produite avec la gracieuse permission de Mme Hilary D Regan et Gabriel Bueno Siqueira, éditeurs de l'ouvrage. Les lecteurs qui souhaitent avoir plus d'informations sur la vie de Jean-Claude Colin ou sur les sources utilisées doivent consulter la biographie complète.

Je remercie vivement Alois Greiler, sm et Ron Nissen, sm, qui ont lu une première version de ce texte et qui ont fait pour l'améliorer des commentaires et des suggestions très utiles.

Chapitre 1
Présentation de Jean-Claude Colin

Jean-Claude Colin et la Société de Marie dont il est une figure fondatrice, s'inscrivent dans le vaste contexte de la réponse du catholicisme français, et plus largement du christianisme européen, au défi présenté par les temps modernes. En France, ces temps modernes sont apparus avec la grande Révolution de 1789, qui a conduit à la persécution de l'Eglise. Mais, même sans le drame et le traumatisme de la Révolution, le catholicisme français aurait été sérieusement mis à l'épreuve par la nouvelle civilisation qualifiée de moderne. Les nouvelles manières de penser appelées commodément les Lumières, l'indifférence religieuse, l'accession des classes moyennes au pouvoir économique et politique, le capitalisme, l'industrialisation et l'urbanisation, la découverte par les Européens de nouvelles terres et de nouvelles populations dans les Mers du Sud : tous ces phénomènes nouveaux appelaient une réponse du christianisme européen. Cette réponse n'a été d'aucune manière seulement négative. Car l'ère nouvelle offrait aussi des possibilités nouvelles et suscitait une vitalité nouvelle.

Colin est né le 7 août 1790, un peu plus d'un an après la chute de la Bastille. Avant qu'il ait eu cinq ans, il avait perdu ses deux parents, victimes, et même martyrs, pensait-il, de la Révolution, suite aux privations endurées du fait

Croix mémoriale aux Barberies

de leur soutien à leur curé réfractaire. Il se souvenait de messes clandestines et de prêtres fugitifs dans son enfance. De telles expériences ne pouvaient que lui donner, ainsi qu'à nombre de ses contemporains, une vision apocalyptique de l'histoire du monde, en contradiction avec la confiance dominante dans le 'progrès'.

La chose intéressante chez lui et non la moindre, c'est qu'il conçut une réponse nouvelle, et semble-t-il, unique en son genre, à ce que nous appelons aujourd'hui la 'sécularisation'. Réponse résumée dans l'expression 'inconnus et cachés en ce monde'. Pour répondre à ce qu'il considérait comme l'orgueil des temps nouveaux—en d'autres mots, son sens caractéristique de l'autonomie humaine—il recommandait l'humilité, l'oubli de soi, pas seulement de l'individu, mais aussi des groupes et de l'institution. En cela, il était inspiré par sa lecture de la présence de Marie dans l'Église naissante. De nos jours son intuition est aussi opportune et nécessaire qu'elle ne l'a jamais été.

Colin appartient à une génération remarquable d'hommes et de femmes représentant la réponse du catholicisme français aux temps nouveaux, avec une floraison vigoureuse et diverse de vie, de spiritualité et d'action apostolique dans l'Église. Une des régions les plus importantes de ce renouveau était celle de Rhône-Alpes, centrée sur Lyon, seconde ville de France à l'époque et siège primatial des Gaules. De fait, cette région formait une certaine unité culturelle autant que géographique ; la langue maternelle parlée dans les campagnes de cette région n'était pas le français mais un patois ou dialecte local francoprovençal, proche mais distinct et du français parlé plus au nord, et du provençal parlé plus au sud. Cette langue, parlée aussi dans certaines régions de Suisse et d'Italie, n'a jamais eu d'expression écrite fixée. Depuis le 16ème siècle, c'est le français qui s'est développé dans la région comme langue de l'administration et de l'enseignement formel.

Lyon garde la mémoire de ses martyrs du 2ème siècle, parmi lesquels on trouve ses premiers évêques, Pothin et Irénée, la servante Blandine, et beaucoup d'autres saints à travers les âges jusqu'aux temps modernes. Parmi les saints hommes et femmes de la période post-révolutionnaire dans le diocèse de Lyon, mentionnons Antoine Chevrier, fondateur de l'Œuvre du Prado ; Pauline Jaricot, fondatrice de l'œuvre de la Propagation de la foi ; Louis Querbes, fondateur des Clercs de Saint-Viateur ; Frédéric Ozanam (Lyonnais d'adoption), fondateur de la Société de Saint-Vincent-de-Paul ; Jean-Pierre Néel, prêtre, missionnaire et martyr.

Dans la partie Est de la région, limitrophe de la Suisse et de la Savoie (autrefois duché indépendant) se trouve le département de l'Ain, avec sa capitale historique (qui n'est plus un centre administratif) et son siège épiscopal de Belley. Avant la Révolution, le diocèse de Belley avait été le berceau de nombreux saints. Après son rétablissement en 1822, cette liste s'est vite allongée avec des saints nés dans le diocèse, ou adoptés ; en premier lieu, bien sûr, le Curé d'Ars, Jean-Marie Vianney ; mais aussi Jean-Baptiste Bottex, une des victimes du massacre du couvent des Carmes, le 3 septembre 1792 ; Gabriel Taborin, fondateur de la congrégation des Frères de la Sainte-Famille de Belley ; Rosalie Rendu, Sœur de la Charité.

Originaire de Saint-Bonnet-le-Troncy (Rhône), Colin, comme nous le verrons, a passé une grande partie de sa vie dans le département de l'Ain. Bien qu'au départ il ne fût pas du tout sûr de sa vocation sacerdotale, il a étudié à Saint-Jodard (Loire) et dans d'autres petits séminaires, puis au grand séminaire Saint-Irénée à Lyon. A l'époque, le diocèse de Lyon, dirigé par le cardinal Fesch, oncle de l'empereur Napoléon, comprenait les trois départements de la Loire, du Rhône et de l'Ain. Ainsi se sont retrouvés ensemble pour étudier des jeunes gens dont les chemins ne se seraient autrement jamais rencontrés. Jean-Marie Vianney était entré une année avant Colin, qui l'a consulté plus tard, plus d'une fois, à Ars. Autre camarade de séminaire, le futur saint Marcellin-Joseph-Benoît Champagnat, né en 1789 à Marlhes, près de Saint-Etienne (Loire), qui allait être étroitement associé à Colin.

Chapitre 2
La Société de Marie

Avant d'être ordonnés le 22 juillet 1816, Colin, Champagnat et quelques autres avaient adhéré à un groupe désireux de former une Société de Marie, dont les membres seraient appelés Maristes. L'initiateur de ce projet était un camarade du séminaire Saint-Irénée, Jean-Claude Courveille, du Puy-en-Velay (Haute-Loire). Agenouillé devant la Vierge noire de la cathédrale, il avait 'entendu' dans sa prière la Vierge Marie lui dire qu'elle voulait une nouvelle société qui porterait son nom, pour faire son œuvre. Cette société, née à un moment de crise dans l'Eglise, équivaudrait en quelque sorte à la Société de Jésus suscitée au temps de la Réforme. Elle favoriserait une vie de prédication, de catéchèse, de confessions dans les paroisses rurales de la région, souvent abandonnées, et serait éventuellement ouverte à des ministères plus larges comme l'éducation et même les missions étrangères.

A la fin du 18ème siècle et au début du 19ème siècle, le nom Société de Marie était 'dans l'air'. Déjà, en 1792, à l'époque où la Société de Jésus avait été supprimée, Bernard Dariès l'avait donné à un nouveau projet circulant parmi des Français exilés en Espagne. A la même période, quelques anciens Jésuites s'étaient regroupés sous le nom de Société de Marie. Il semble toutefois que Courveille et ses compagnons n'étaient pas au courant de cela. En 1817, à Bordeaux, Guillaume-Joseph Chaminade, qui ignorait tout de ce qui se préparait à Lyon, avait fondé une Société de Marie (Marianistes). Le nom Maristes, que Courveille croyait avoir reçu de la Vierge Marie elle-même, n'avait de fait été utilisé par personne.

Pour Jean-Claude Colin, l'appel de Marie était irrésistible depuis l'enfance, quand sa mère mourante avait recommandé tous ses enfants, bientôt orphelins, aux soins maternels de la Sainte Vierge.

Ancienne chapelle de Fourvière

De plus, avant même d'entrer au grand séminaire, il avait pensé à un genre d'institut apostolique placé sous le nom de Marie. De son côté, Marcellin Champagnat avait déjà un plan de congrégation de Frères enseignants, et il avait persuadé les autres aspirants maristes de les inclure dans la Société de Marie, qui comprendrait aussi des religieuses et des tertiaires laïcs. Notons l'origine relativement humble de ces jeunes gens, nés dans des familles de petits propriétaires terriens ou d'artisans. C'est peut-être un effet inattendu de la Révolution et de son principe d'égalité, qu'ils se soient sentis compétents pour fonder une nouvelle congrégation religieuse au lieu de se tourner vers l'un de leurs 'supérieurs' sociaux, un noble, comme l'avaient été jusqu'alors la plupart des fondateurs religieux. Le 23 juillet 1816, le groupe—douze en tout—s'est retrouvé une dernière fois au sanctuaire marial de Fourvière dominant la ville de Lyon. Leur meneur Jean-Claude Courveille célébra sa première messe et donna la sainte communion à ses camarades ; sous le corporal ils avaient déposé un document qu'ils avaient tous signé, par lequel ils s'engageaient à faire tout leur possible pour qu'existe la Société de Marie.

Le nouvel ordonné Jean-Claude Colin fit son apprentissage de prêtre comme vicaire de son frère Pierre à Cerdon (Ain). Situé à l'intersection de trois vallées à l'extrême nord des montagnes du Bugey, à dix-neuf kilomètres de Nantua, Cerdon était un relais sur la route de Lyon à Genève ; en 1832, la population était de 1.745 habitants. Des vignes poussaient sur une des pentes environnantes et Cerdon était—et est toujours—connu dans la région pour son vin agréable, légèrement pétillant.

Cerdon n'avait pas échappé aux effets des événements extraordinaires de 1814–1816. Comme le reste de la région du

Cerdon : Vue du village dans la vallée

Bugey et comme Lyon, le village soutenait Bonaparte. Il avait subi les conséquences des défaites de Napoléon en 1814 et 1815 : l'invasion par une armée autrichienne venue de Suisse, et les réparations de guerre. La région avait aussi souffert d'un été désastreux en 1816 ; durant l'hiver 1817, de nombreux habitants connurent une réelle détresse. Ces événements, dont le maître d'école du village gardait la chronique, auront certainement eu un impact sur les prêtres nouvellement arrivés. Les procès-verbaux de la municipalité nous apprennent que Pierre Colin, en tant que curé, faisait partie d'un Comité de secours organisé par le maire, qui avait décidé d'attribuer à un fonds d'urgence l'argent destiné aux réparations de l'église. Le 3 décembre 1793, l'église, située sur une colline au centre du village, avait été pillée, sa tour détruite et son mobilier brûlé. Après le rétablissement du culte avec le Concordat de 1801, Cerdon avait été desservi par une succession de prêtres. Quand les frères Colin arrivent, la paroisse est, selon toutes les indications, en bon état.

Portait de Jeanne-Marie Chavoin

Sans tarder, Jean-Claude fait adhérer Pierre au projet mariste et commence à écrire une règle pour la Société de Marie. En 1817, Marcellin Champagnat, curé à La Valla (Loire), commence à recruter et à former les premiers 'Petits Frères de Marie', et Pierre Colin invite deux jeunes femmes qu'il connaissait, Jeanne-Marie Chavoin, née à Coutouvre (Loire) en 1786, et Marie Jotillon, à venir à Cerdon et à commencer la branche des Sœurs maristes. En 1819, Jean-Claude fait le vœu d'aller à Rome pour révéler au Saint-Père ce qu'il pense être l'origine surnaturelle de la Société.

Toutefois le projet des aspirants maristes n'avait pas trouvé un accueil favorable de la part des vicaires généraux qui dirigeaient le diocèse de Lyon au nom du cardinal Fesch, exilé à Rome après la chute de son neveu Napoléon. Ils voulaient les garder exclusivement au service du diocèse, et même les fusionner avec les missionnaires de la Croix de Jésus ('Chartreux') nouvellement fondés. Découragés, la plupart des premiers aspirants avaient conclu que le projet ne menait nulle part, et s'en étaient détachés. Dans cette période difficile, Jeanne-Marie Chavoin encourageait et soutenait les deux frères Colin.

En janvier 1822, Courveille, Pierre et Jean-Claude Colin écrivirent au pape Pie VII au sujet de leur projet. Dans sa réponse, le pape leur donna prudemment ses encouragements et les orienta vers son Nonce à Paris. C'est Jean-Claude Colin qui fit deux voyages dans la capitale ; il montra sa règle au Nonce, Mgr Macchi, et aux Pères Sulpiciens, qui lui firent remarquer qu'elle convenait plus 'à des anges qu'à des hommes'.

C'est probable que, si les Maristes avaient soumis un plan simple de congrégation de prêtres engagés dans la prédication de missions et dans l'éducation, et prêts à partir en mission à l'étranger, ils auraient obtenu rapidement l'approbation de Rome. D'autre part, le projet d'une société à plusieurs branches comprenant des prêtres, des Sœurs, des Frères, et des laïcs, s'avérerait inacceptable. De plus, la règle de Colin, dont nous ne possédons aujourd'hui que des fragments, n'était pas du tout du genre de document que les canonistes exigeaient d'un nouveau groupe religieux. Car elle était utopique, à la fois en ce sens qu'elle était hautement idéaliste, mais aussi qu'elle était basée sur une vision de la place de la Société de Marie dans l'Eglise et de fait dans le monde, qu'il est important de bien comprendre si nous voulons saisir la pensée globale de Jean-Claude Colin.

Cette vision utopiste est exprimée dans le sommaire des Règles de la Société rédigé par Colin en 1833 : 'Le but général de la Société est de contribuer de la meilleure manière . . . (à) recueillir tous les membres du Christ . . . de telle sorte que à la fin des temps tout comme au début, tous les fidèles soient, Dieu aidant, *un seul cœur et une seule âme* [*cf* Ac 4,23], au sein de l'Eglise romaine, et que tous, marchant d'une manière digne de Dieu sous la conduite de Marie, puissent atteindre à la vie éternelle.' Colin répétait souvent une parole qu'il attribuait à Marie elle-même : 'J'ai été le soutien de l'Eglise naissante ; je le serai à la fin des temps.' Il a souvent dit que l'Eglise à ses tout-débuts— littéralement 'l'Eglise-qui-était-en- train-de-naître'—était le seul et unique modèle de la Société de Marie. En lisant les Actes des Apôtres, il a trouvé l'état idéal de l'Eglise dans ses premiers temps, quand Marie était son soutien, et que tous les croyants étaient un seul cœur et un seul esprit, partageant leurs biens. Il s'attendait à ce que cela se réalisât 'à la fin des temps', quand Marie aurait été de nouveau le soutien de l'Eglise. Il croyait en cet accomplissement eschatologique ; la Vierge Marie avait un rôle-clé et elle voulait que sa Société jouât ce rôle en son nom. C'était la raison de sa fondation et de son existence. En attendant, la Société devrait s'efforcer de réaliser ce projet et même de modeler la 'nouvelle Eglise' qui ressemblerait à l'Eglise des Actes. Une telle perception du rôle d'une nouvelle congrégation cherchant à être reconnue ne pouvait qu'apparaître irréaliste—peut-être même subversive—à des autorités ecclésiastiques ayant les pieds sur terre. De fait, elle échappa à la compréhension de beaucoup de ceux qui allaient se joindre à la Société de Marie.

En 1822, le diocèse de Belley, qui correspondait au département de l'Ain, était rétabli. Cela signifiait que les futurs Maristes se retrouvaient désormais dans deux diocèses différents, face à deux administrations diocésaines. Le Nonce envoya le dossier mariste au nouvel évêque de Belley.

Alexandre-Raymond Devie, né en 1767 à Montélimar (Drôme), était un homme remarquable et un grand évêque, qui aurait pu honorer des sièges épiscopaux de diocèses plus éminents, mais qui choisit de rester à Belley toute sa vie. Dès le début, il se consacra au bien-être spirituel de son peuple, à l'organisation du nouveau diocèse et à la formation du clergé. Il voyagea inlassablement dans le département de l'Ain dans une voiture qu'il avait fait aménager de manière à pouvoir lire et écrire en se déplaçant. Il vit que les prêtres et religieux maristes pouvaient jouer un rôle dans les plans qu'il avait pour son diocèse, mais il n'avait aucune intention de favoriser leur but d'être approuvés par le pape comme congrégation au service de l'Eglise universelle.

En 1824, Mgr Devie remit un habit religieux à Jeanne-Marie Chavoin et aux jeunes femmes qui vivaient avec elle en communauté, à Cerdon. Il permit aussi à l'un des aspirants maristes restants, Étienne Déclas, de se joindre à Pierre et Jean-Claude Colin à Cerdon, pour commencer à prêcher des missions dans les paroisses voisines. Pendant ce temps, près de Saint-Chamond (Loire), Marcellin Champagnat et ses frères avaient construit un grand bâtiment appelé l'Hermitage, pour servir comme maison-mère et centre de formation des Petits Frères de Marie dont le nombre croissait rapidement, et il avait ouvert des écoles dans de nombreuses paroisses. La Société de Marie à plusieurs branches passait du rêve à la réalité.

Chapitre 3
Prédicateur de missions dans le Bugey

En 1825, Mgr Devie rassembla à Belley les deux communautés de Sœurs et de prêtres. En 1832, six ans après l'arrivée des maristes, la ville épiscopale comptait 4.286 habitants. L'herbe poussait dans les rues. Bien que Belley fût sensiblement à la même distance de Cerdon que de Lyon, les frères Colin et Jeanne-Marie Chavoin n'y étaient jamais allés avant de se retrouver dans ce nouveau diocèse. Plus tard, Colin s'étonna qu'un petit endroit aussi isolé ait été le berceau d'une Société qui s'est développée jusqu'au bout du monde. Il ne pouvait le comparer qu'à Nazareth, lieu improbable où l'Eglise a commencé avec la Sainte Famille.

Le plan pastoral de Mgr Devie pour son diocèse comprenait un programme systématique de missions paroissiales pour renforcer, là où c'était nécessaire, la foi et la pratique catholiques après la tourmente révolutionnaire et ce qui s'en était suivi : la dislocation de l'Eglise, la diffusion de l'indifférence et l'éloignement de la religion. Dans ce contexte, les prêtres maristes qui ne désiraient rien d'autre que de prêcher, catéchiser et confesser, pouvaient former un groupe de missionnaires diocésains. En 1825, le pape Léon XII avait proclamé une année jubilaire, étendue à 1826 - la première depuis 1775. Dans son encyclique *Charitate Christi*, il avait déclaré son désir qu'elle fût une célébration de la miséricorde divine, et qu'elle conduisît le plus grand nombre possible de personnes au sacrement de réconciliation pour obtenir le pardon et l'absolution de leurs péchés.

C'étaient des paroles douces aux oreilles de Mgr Devie, déterminé à utiliser le jubilé pour contrecarrer le rigorisme du clergé français dans l'enseignement moral et l'administration du sacrement de pénitence. Déjà, comme vicaire général du diocèse de Valence (Drôme), il avait introduit la théologie morale et la pratique au confessionnal d'Alphonse de Liguori, caractérisées par le réalisme pastoral et une voie moyenne prudente entre la rigueur excessive et le laxisme. Sa béatification en 1816 avait donné à son enseignement l'estampille de l'approbation papale et l'avait promu en dehors de son Italie natale. Mgr Devie donna suite à l'encyclique de 1825 avec sa propre lettre-circulaire à tous les prêtres de son diocèse, datée du 26 septembre 1826. Le jubilé devait être le moment de redoubler de zèle et d'efforts pour rejoindre ceux qui s'étaient éloignés de l'Eglise par laxisme ou indifférence plutôt que par 'impiété'. Il serait célébré dans le diocèse pendant six mois, à partir de novembre 1826, ce qui permettrait aux fidèles de remplir les conditions pour gagner l'indulgence plénière par la confession, la communion, la visite des églises désignées et les prières prescrites et ainsi obtenir la pleine rémission des dettes restantes de la 'punition temporelle' (opposée à éternelle) encore due pour les péchés pardonnés. Là où c'était possible, des équipes de prédicateurs de mission feraient le tour des paroisses du diocèse et si cela ne l'était pas, le clergé local organiserait une 'retraite' de plusieurs semaines.

L'évêque présenta les thèmes qui devaient être traités durant la mission ou dans les sermons de retraite, dont le Credo des Apôtres, les commandements de Dieu et de l'Eglise, les sacrements et la prière. Lui-même essaierait de venir chaque fois pour donner la confirmation et prendre part aux exercices. En ce qui concernait la confession, il renvoyait ses prêtres à l'encyclique *Charitate Christi*, spécialement à la directive du pape demandant aux prêtres de montrer 'beaucoup de bonté et de charité' envers les pécheurs. Outre la lecture de l'encyclique, les prêtres devront également étudier l'ouvrage d'Alphonse de Liguori, *Praxis confessariorum*, dont des copies seraient mises à leur disposition au séminaire de Brou et au bureau diocésain à Belley.

Comme vicaire de Cerdon, Jean-Claude Colin avait eu l'occasion de se sentir mal à l'aise avec le code de morale rigoriste qu'il avait appris à Saint-Irénée mais il manquait d'assurance pour le mettre en question. Sous la conduite de l'évêque et de St Alphonse il commença progressivement à embrasser pleinement la doctrine et la pratique liguoriennes pour lui-même et pour la Société de Marie.

Le nombre de prédicateurs maristes de missions augmenta lentement avec des prêtres déjà ordonnés qui étaient attirés par leur ministère et la spiritualité mariste. Le territoire missionnaire que leur avait attribué l'évêque était le Bugey, région montagneuse s'étendant entre Cerdon et Belley. La plupart des endroits qu'ils visitèrent étaient de petits villages ruraux, souvent éloignés, avec quelques centaines d'habitants. Tenay faisait exception ; c'était une petite ville industrielle spécialisée dans le tissage, dont la population (1.130 habitants en 1832) comprenait des ouvriers de l'industrie et des propriétaires de moulins, de la classe moyenne. Ils donnèrent aussi des retraites aux séminaires de Belley et de Meximieux.

Village de Lacoux dans un paysage enneigé

Les missions ne pouvaient avoir lieu qu'en hiver quand les fermiers étaient plus libres pour aller à l'église. Le terrain pouvait être ardu, et le climat sévère. Les conditions de vie étaient habituellement des plus simples, et les missionnaires devaient fréquemment 'se faire violence'. Ce qu'ils ont trouvé pouvait varier énormément d'une paroisse à une autre ; cela allait d'églises et de presbytères bien entretenus, à d'autres, sales et négligés ; de communautés vivant la foi avec des pasteurs dévoués, à des communautés indifférentes ou hostiles, où le prêtre (s'il y en avait un) était souvent une partie majeure du problème.

Les maristes firent face à ces différentes situations avec simplicité et détachement d'eux-mêmes. Ils évitaient d'occasionner des dépenses inutiles, acceptaient allègrement ce qu'on leur offrait en matière de logement ou de nourriture, faisaient avec le mobilier ou le matériel qu'ils trouvaient à l'église (pas besoin d'un confessionnal ou d'un pupitre – cela pouvait s'improviser ; deux bougies suffiraient au lieu de six ; les candélabres n'étaient pas indispensables . . .). Par-dessus tout, ils évitaient d'offenser ou d'embarrasser le pasteur ou de prendre sa place à table ou à l'église.

Les missions suivaient un schéma standard, qui pouvait être adapté ou développé. Elles commençaient avec les enfants, une pratique recommandée par Jean-Marie Vianney. On leur faisait le catéchisme, on leur parlait de la mission et on leur demandait de prier pour leurs parents. Ceux qui étaient en âge de recevoir la sainte communion se confessaient. Les plus grands suivaient. L'instruction catéchétique se poursuivait tout au long de la mission, de sorte que l'église était toujours remplie d'adultes aussi bien que d'enfants.

Nous sommes bien informés sur la structure de la mission, les thèmes d'instruction, les différentes cérémonies qui avaient lieu. Le plan révèle une stratégie pour convaincre et convertir, qui semble avoir eu du succès. La parole était illustrée et renforcée par des paraliturgies qui pouvaient être mises en scène par les paroissiens eux-mêmes. La prière était à la base de la mission, car les missionnaires priaient chaque jour et faisaient prier les autres pour la conversion des pécheurs. A leur arrivée dans une paroisse, toujours sans bruit et discrètement, ils s'agenouillaient et priaient pour les âmes du purgatoire du lieu, puis ils se levaient et récitaient le *Memorare*, en confiant la mission à Notre Dame. Chaque instruction commençait par trois 'Je vous salue, Marie'. L'instruction d'ouverture était une invitation à participer à la mission, suivie d'un sermon sur la miséricorde de Dieu. On a encore les mots que Colin leur adressait à cette occasion. Il décrivait les missionnaires comme 'les instruments de la miséricorde divine pour vous', et même 'les instruments les plus indignes'. Il insistait sur le fait qu'ils étaient aussi de simples humains, sujets aux mêmes faiblesses que leurs auditeurs, et qu'en conséquence ils savaient 'jusqu'où peut aller la fragilité humaine'. De sorte que les gens ne devraient pas avoir peur ni se méfier de révéler leurs propres péchés en confession.

Les thèmes de la première semaine - en commençant par le Credo des Apôtres - avaient pour but de gagner la confiance des auditeurs, bien qu'à partir du quatrième jour les prédicateurs commencent à les secouer un peu. Suivait l'explication des Dix Commandements. Là aussi on prenait soin de ne pas décourager les auditeurs. Les

Chaire de l'église de Premillieu

prédicateurs n'entraient pas trop, tout de suite, dans les détails des obligations des commandements, mais ils encourageaient les gens à venir se confesser pour manifester leur bonne volonté et un début de conversion. Cela semble avoir été une pratique régulière de ne pas donner l'absolution à cette première confession, mais de former les pénitents et de leur dire de revenir continuer leur confession au cours de la mission. Après que la plupart des gens se fussent approchés du sacrement de pénitence cette première fois, les missionnaires commençaient à parler de façon plus précise à leurs auditeurs des exigences des commandements et à aborder des sujets tels que la malice du péché et la punition qu'il méritait. A ce stade de la mission, une messe de Requiem était célébrée pour tous les défunts de la paroisse, avec sermons sur la mort et le purgatoire, puis on se rendait en procession au cimetière en portant le drap mortuaire servant à couvrir les cercueils ; au pied de la croix du cimetière, un dernier sermon sur la mort était prononcé.

A mi-parcours de la mission, on donnait un sermon sur la confiance à avoir en la Vierge Marie, suivi d'une procession avec la statue de Notre Dame, avec litanies et hymnes chantés en son honneur.

Intérieur de l'ancienne église d'Innimont

Le lendemain avait lieu une cérémonie particulièrement impressionnante et émouvante. Tous les enfants venaient à la messe, ainsi que leurs parents. Le prédicateur leur demandait s'ils voulaient choisir la

Vierge Marie comme leur mère et leur protectrice. Tous, sans doute, répondaient 'oui'. Le prédicateur continuait en parlant aux enfants du désir de Marie qu'ils soient bons et obéissants. Il leur fallait demander pardon à leurs parents pour toutes les fois qu'ils avaient été désobéissants. Il demandait alors aux parents de retirer toutes les malédictions prononcées contre leurs enfants. A ce stade, beaucoup étaient en larmes. Finalement, parents et clergé étendaient leurs mains sur les enfants et les consacraient à la Sainte Vierge.

Autres thèmes d'instruction : les sacrements, spécialement le baptême, la pénitence et l'eucharistie. A ce moment, la plupart des paroissiens auraient dû être revenus au confessionnal pour poursuivre leur confession à la lumière de leur meilleure compréhension du péché de l'homme et de la grâce divine, et avoir reçu l'absolution. Une cérémonie frappante donnait une impulsion supplémentaire à la conversion, avec une exposition du Saint Sacrement sur un autel spécialement construit au milieu de l'église. Un sermon était donné sur le péché mortel. Puis tous les prêtres présents enlevaient leurs surplis, se prosternaient devant le Saint Sacrement et imploraient le pardon de Dieu.

Le temps fort suivant était centré sur le baptême et les promesses faites par les parrains et marraines au nom de chaque enfant baptisé peu après sa naissance, et sur les obligations qui s'en suivaient. Il leur était demandé de donner leur accord à chacun des articles du Credo en disant 'Je crois' et en levant les cierges allumés qu'ils tenaient. Suivait la promesse d'observer chacun des commandements. La paroisse devait alors être prête à faire une communion générale qui serait annoncée. Dernier acte de la mission, selon la coutume : la bénédiction d'une croix commémorative, comme on peut encore en voir de nos jours dans de nombreux endroits en France. A cause des frais que cela entrainait, la pratique des maristes n'était cependant pas de proposer une plantation de croix ; ils ne le faisaient que si la paroisse le demandait spontanément.

Impressionnantes donc, de telles cérémonies. Mais au cœur de la mission, c'étaient de longues heures passées en chaire et au confessionnal à instruire et à toucher le cœur des gens et à les encourager à se convertir et à faire pénitence. N'oublions pas non plus les nombreuses heures passées chaque jour en prière, à réciter le bréviaire et à faire la méditation personnelle. Au cœur de tout cela : la miséricorde. Quelques années plus tard, réfléchissant sur le ministère de la prédication, Colin se souvenait : 'Nous devons être bons. Après tout, quelle est la différence entre eux et nous ? Ce sont nos frères. Toute la différence entre eux et nous, c'est que nous sommes ceux qui parlent, et eux de pauvres gens qui ne peuvent pas répondre.'

Ces missions maristes et d'autres campagnes similaires d'évangélisation s'exerçaient dans un contexte nouveau. Après la défaite de l'empereur Napoléon, l'ancienne monarchie avait été restaurée en la personne de Louis XVIII, frère de l'ancien roi. Dans l'Eglise, et de façon plus générale dans la société, certains voyaient là une opportunité de restaurer autant que faire se pouvait, l'*ancien régime*. On le savait : certaines missions de renouveau comprenaient de triomphales démonstrations du retour de l'Eglise au pouvoir, main dans la main avec l'Etat ('alliance du trône et de l'autel'). Colin et ses compagnons se réjouissaient personnellement du retour des Bourbons. Mais, sagement, ils évitaient de telles manifestations ou une telle propagande. Colin formula cette politique, qui se poursuivit les années suivantes, dans des déclarations telles que : 'Souvenez-vous, Messieurs, que nous ne sommes pas pour changer le gouvernement, mais pour sauver les âmes.' La Société ne devait pas s'identifier à une quelconque opinion politique. 'En prenant une nuance, nous écartons de nous nécessairement ceux qui ont une autre couleur, et nous sommes pour sauver tout le monde.'

Durant les mois d'été et entre les missions, la petite équipe de missionnaires maristes vivait au petit séminaire de Belley et travaillait sur ses sermons et ses instructions. Leurs conditions de vie étaient loin d'être idéales. Ils étaient logés au grenier, dans des chambres improvisées et contiguës. L'été, ils souffraient de la chaleur, l'hiver du froid. Ils prenaient leurs repas avec les professeurs du séminaire, dont certains se moquaient ouvertement des maristes, traités de 'Tome deux de la Société de Jésus, relié en peau d'âne' ; les élèves suivaient leur exemple. Toutefois ils gagnèrent le respect du supérieur, Monsieur Pichat, qui exprima même son désir de se joindre à eux. Ils reçurent aussi l'aide et le soutien matériel des Sœurs maristes installées à côté, à Bon Repos. Jean-Claude Colin participa à toutes les missions de 1826 à 1829. En 1826, Mgr Devie le nomma supérieur des missionnaires maristes du diocèse.

A la mi-1826, la Société de Marie naissante entra dans une crise profonde. Nous avons suivi la carrière de Jean-Claude Colin et de ses compagnons à Belley. Dans le diocèse de Lyon, Jean-Claude

Courveille s'était occupé à établir des communautés de frères et de sœurs enseignants, dont les relations avec ceux de Marcellin Champagnat et celles de Jeanne-Marie Chavoin, n'étaient pas claires. Il se considérait aussi comme le supérieur général de la Société de Marie tout entière, revendication acceptée par certains, dont Marcellin Champagnat, mais pas par tous. La relation entre les deux Jean-Claude n'a, semble-t-il, jamais été chaleureuse, et les deux Colin avaient agi occasionnellement indépendamment de Courveille, tout en reconnaissant son leadership *de facto*.

En mai 1826, Courveille commit à l'Hermitage un acte sexuel non spécifié avec un postulant frère, presque certainement un mineur, et partit faire une 'retraite' à l'abbaye trappiste d'Aiguebelle (Drôme). Le fait fut porté à la connaissance d'Étienne Terraillon, un des signataires restant de la promesse de 1816, qui vivait aussi à l'Hermitage, et qui informa les autorités diocésaines. Champagnat, entre-temps, avait reçu une lettre de Courveille, d'Aiguebelle, parlant longuement de son indignité à être mariste en des termes pouvant être compris comme une démission du groupe. Terraillon recommanda à Champagnat, et à Colin aussi, qui venait d'arriver à l'Hermitage de façon inattendue, d'accepter la démission de Courveille, avec effets immédiats. Comme ils hésitaient, car ils étaient encore dans le noir sur ce qui était arrivé, Terraillon dut leur en dire suffisamment sur ce qu'il savait pour les décider à suivre son conseil. A partir de ce moment, Courveille fut exclu de la Société naissante, et empêché d'y revenir quand, quelques années plus tard, il demanda à le faire.

Cela laissait la petite Société de Marie avec la question troublante : Comment le message originel pouvait-il être réellement de Marie si celui qui l'avait reçu, et qui était le fondateur et le chef du groupe, s'était montré si indigne ? Les maristes continuèrent à croire que Marie avait, de fait, 'parlé', mais en même temps ils firent tout leur possible pour effacer Courveille de leur mémoire collective. Ils se trouvèrent ainsi désormais sans leader reconnu par tous, et ils le restèrent pendant quelques années.

En mars 1829, Jean-Claude Colin dirigea sa dernière mission à Ruffieu, dans le Valromey. L'évêque vint lui-même à la fin du mois et confirma 600 enfants dont beaucoup venaient des paroisses voisines. L'église était petite. Un autre missionnaire, installé dans la tribune, relayait le sermon de Colin par une fenêtre vers la foule qui était à l'extérieur. L'évêque apportait avec lui la nouvelle du décès du supérieur du petit séminaire, M. Pichat. Il demanda à Colin de retourner immédiatement à Belley pour aider son frère Pierre à préparer les élèves à Pâques. En fait, il avait décidé de mettre fin à la vie itinérante de Jean-Claude. Le soir de Pâques, 9 avril, Mgr Devie le fit venir et lui dit de prendre la direction du séminaire le lendemain. Cette nomination, inattendue, surprit Colin profondément. Il demanda trois jours pour faire une retraite et prier pour que l'évêque changeât d'avis. Mais Mgr Devie lui intima simplement de prendre ses fonctions immédiatement.

Pour beaucoup de personnes qui pensent à leur passé, il y a une période de leur vie qu'elles considèrent comme une 'époque héroïque' ; certes, elles ont lutté contre des difficultés, mais cela avait été 'la meilleure' époque de leur vie. Pour Jean-Claude Colin, la période de sa vie qui a été 'le bon temps', malgré ses épreuves, ce furent ces années de janvier 1825 à mars 1929, où il a prêché des missions dans les montagnes du Bugey.

Chapitre 4
Directeur d'école

L'établissement dont Colin prenait la direction avait été fondé en 1751 comme collège tenu par des prêtres religieux. Il avait été rouvert en 1803 après la Révolution, sous la direction des 'Pères de la Foi ' (ex-Jésuites, et leurs émules plus récents). C'est à cette époque qu'y étudia l'écrivain, poète et homme d'état, Alphonse de Lamartine, qui a donné son nom à l'école. En1808, elle était passée sous le contrôle de la commune mais elle commençait à décliner. Elle était sur le point de fermer en 1823 quand Mgr Devie obtint l'autorisation de la placer sous le contrôle du diocèse comme petit séminaire. Elle continua toutefois à garder un caractère mixte, en accueillant en plus des séminaristes des garçons qui ne se destinaient nullement à la prêtrise.

Photo ancienne de la façade du bâtiment à Belley

La nomination de Colin tomba à une période sensible dans les relations entre l'Eglise et l'Etat en France. Au début de 1828, le gouvernement conservateur avait senti le besoin de faire des concessions au courant libéral et décidé de le faire dans le domaine de l'éducation où il y avait une forte opposition au contrôle de l'Eglise. Certaines des mesures prises touchaient l'établissement de Belley. Le 16 juin, après moult examens de conscience, le roi Charles X, avait signé deux ordonnances plaçant les petits séminaires sous le contrôle plus étroit du gouvernement. Le premier décret plaçait huit séminaires jusqu'alors tenus par les Jésuites sous l'"Université", c'est-à-dire le système public d'éducation. Il demandait aussi à tous les supérieurs et enseignants de petits séminaires de déclarer qu'ils n'appartenaient à aucune congrégation religieuse non établie légalement en France. Le second fixait le nombre de séminaires et de leurs étudiants, et les bourses d'études pour les financer. Il exigeait aussi la reconnaissance de la nomination des supérieurs par le gouvernement. Comme les autres évêques, Mgr Devie avait protesté contre ce qu'ils considéraient comme un empiètement de leurs droits. Mais après que le gouvernement eût donné des explications apaisantes, il décida de se conformer aux nouvelles dispositions. Le 24 avril 1829, Mgr Devie écrivit au Ministre des Affaires Ecclésiastiques pour solliciter l'accord pour la nomination de Jean-Claude Colin comme remplaçant de Monsieur Pichat, décédé. L'accord fut donné le 3 mai. Comme les maristes n'étaient pas encore une congrégation, la nomination de Colin répondait strictement à l'exigence du gouvernement. Il avait trente-huit ans—âge mûr à l'époque—et était dans la fleur de l'âge.

On a une idée de l'école dont est chargé Colin par les réponses faites par Mgr Devie le 27 février 1828 à un questionnaire du Ministère des Affaires Ecclésiastiques. Elle comptait 200 étudiants, dont vingt ne payaient rien, la plupart des autres entre dix et vingt francs par mois, et quelques-uns entre trente et cinquante francs. L'établissement n'avait pas de revenus. En plus des pensions payées par les étudiants, ses seules ressources étaient les 'sacrifices' faits par l'évêque et le clergé du diocèse. Il y avait trente externes, essentiellement des choristes et des servants d'autel de la cathédrale. Les matières enseignées couvraient l'ensemble du curriculum, du primaire avec l'apprentissage de la lecture et de l'écriture, au secondaire le plus élevé, avec des classes de français, grec, latin, rhétorique, philosophie et mathématiques. Le plain-chant était aussi enseigné, mais pas la musique, ni la danse ni l'escrime. Certains étudiants avaient réussi le baccalauréat universitaire. En 1827, quarante-trois diplômés avaient été admis au grand séminaire de Brou. Les étudiants portaient habituellement des habits ordinaires ; le dimanche et les jours de fête, ils étaient en uniforme : pardessus sombre coloré pour les plus jeunes, soutane pour les aînés se préparant à la théologie. Le corps enseignant, jeune, comptait douze membres : des prêtres diocésains et des clercs destinés au ministère sacerdotal dans le diocèse.

Le fait que le collège était aussi un petit séminaire signifiait que le clergé de la cathédrale se sentait libre d'exiger la participation des étudiants aux célébrations liturgiques certains jours de fête et de faire appel de temps en temps aux prêtres du collège. Colin réussit à réduire la présence des étudiants à la procession annuelle de Corpus Christi. Il mit fin aussi aux 'emprunts' de professeurs par la cathédrale les jours de classes. 'Quand vous m'enverrez des professeurs pour faire la classe, je vous enverrai des chanoines pour officier', fit-il remarquer. Les dignitaires de la cathédrale se plaignirent à l'évêque, mais ce dernier soutint son directeur.

Jean-Claude accepta sa nomination à condition que le collège fût confié aux maristes. En tout cas il avait réalisé que sa nomination au collège et celle de son frère comme directeur spirituel, signifiaient beaucoup plus que boucher des trous ou accomplir une tâche au nom de l'évêque. Déjà, dans la lettre adressée au pape Pie VII, les maristes avaient déclaré qu'un des buts de la Société de Marie était de 'former la jeunesse au savoir et aux vertus par tous les moyens'. L'heure était venue pour les prêtres, aussi bien que les frères, de transformer leurs aspirations en réalité. Au fur et à mesure que leur nombre augmenta, des maristes furent nommés au collège de Belley.

Les années précédentes, Colin avait pu observer l'école de près et réaliser qu'il existait des tensions à la fois entre les étudiants mais aussi dans son personnel. Il devait établir rapidement son autorité dans la maison. Le corps estudiantin était composé d'au moins trois groupes assez distincts. La plupart étaient des séminaristes qui avaient commencé leurs études à Belley et qui les poursuivaient. Un second groupe était celui des étudiants en philosophie qui avaient jusqu'alors été formés dans l'autre petit séminaire, à Meximieux. Bien qu'ils se préparent à exercer le ministère dans le même diocèse, ils manifestaient apparemment une 'répugnance marquée' à devoir passer un an ou deux avec leurs camarades de Belley et ne formaient pas avec eux une 'communauté homogène'. Enfin, il y avait les étudiants laïcs, survivants de l'ancien collège municipal, qui avaient gardé leur esprit de 'collégiens', et qui le passaient aux séminaristes. Colin a rappelé que, bien que la tenue des étudiants le reste de l'année après sa prise de fonction eût été 'assez bonne', il en avait expulsé six ou sept ; aux autres, il avait demandé de se décider sur ce qu'ils voulaient faire. Quand la nouvelle année scolaire commença à la Toussaint 1829, une quarantaine environ ne revint pas. D'un autre côté, les inscriptions étaient nombreuses. La 'piété et la bonne tenue' furent notable cette année-là.

Ses collègues, dira-t-il, lui causèrent plus d'ennuis que leurs élèves. De fait, une des plus grandes épreuves qui advint à la Société fut de vivre avec des 'collègues qui pensaient que nous étions fous, qui n'entraient pas dans nos manières de penser, qui agissaient contre nous'. Le premier mois, 'chaque professeur' vint le voir pour lui donner des conseils : 'Vous devez faire ceci, vous devez changer cela'. Finalement, à une réunion du conseil, il fit connaître sa pensée : il n'avait aucune intention de se démarquer des manières de son prédécesseur et il ne voulait plus entendre parler de changements. A la fin de l'année, il dit à un des professeurs de ne plus revenir. Et durant les vacances d'été, il opéra un certain nombre de changements dans le personnel.

Quand, à la Toussaint 1829, le staff se réunit après les grandes vacances, le nouveau directeur leur présenta un bref Traité de quinze pages sur l'éducation qu'il avait composé en combinant des principes généraux et des commentaires adaptés à la situation du collège. En agissant ainsi, Colin montrait une remarquable assurance. Il avait pris ses fonctions de directeur sans aucune expérience de l'enseignement : un fait bien connu des anciens membres de son personnel qui étaient prêts à le lui rappeler. Outre ses propres observations et idées de 'la meilleure pratique', Colin avait consulté et lu soigneusement ceux qui étaient considérés comme les meilleurs auteurs. Durant l'été, il avait passé une partie de son temps à lire un ouvrage bien connu sur l'éducation, du début du 18ème siècle, le *Traité des études*, de Charles Rollin, publié à Paris entre 1726 et 1731, et considéré en France tout au long du 18ème siècle et jusqu'au 19ème siècle comme une autorité majeure en matière d'enseignement. En fait, ce livre n'est pas un traité sur l'éducation', au sens où nous l'entendons aujourd'hui. Globalement, c'est plutôt un manuel d'enseignement des humanités et de la rhétorique, traitant du contenu du curriculum classique, et de la manière de l'enseigner. Rollin commençait et terminait son livre par des remarques pédagogiques dont Colin s'inspira beaucoup.

Ce court traité de Colin est en fait le seul ouvrage substantiel composé par lui qui ne soit pas une règle religieuse. Il montre son pouvoir d'assimilation et de synthèse. Ce n'était pas un réformateur éducatif. Nous ne devons pas chercher de l'originalité dans le contenu de son ouvrage. Ce qu'il écrit dedans pourrait être trouvé ailleurs, chez des auteurs plus anciens, ou parmi ses contemporains, dont certains étaient des innovateurs d'une manière qu'il ne prétendait nullement imiter. Mais sa synthèse personnelle et l'intégration de ses sources révèlent quelques traits originaux, et indiquent bien sa perception fine du monde de l'enseignement.

On trouve tout de suite un exemple frappant de sa perspicacité dans le titre donné à son avis : *Avis à messieurs les professeurs, préfets, directeurs et supérieur du petit séminaire de Belley*. Ainsi ne s'adresse-t-il pas seulement au staff—professeurs, préfets, directeurs—mais aussi au supérieur (c'est-à-dire lui-même), exprimant ainsi dès le début sa solidarité avec eux. En cohérence avec lui-même, le pronom qu'il utilise le plus fréquemment tout au long de l'ouvrage est 'nous'. Il n'écrit jamais 'vous'. Il ne dit pas au staff ce qu'ils ont à faire : nous sommes tous ensemble dans cette entreprise. Un coup d'œil au plan du document montre que les instructions de Colin concernent essentiellement les relations entre personnes et groupes de personnes. Dans son Introduction il déclare qu'éduquer une personne est déjà une 'tâche sublime', et que l'éduquer à la manière chrétienne est un 'travail céleste'. Les éducateurs ont pour tâches principales de faire de leurs élèves des 'chrétiens, des hommes honnêtes et polis, et des savants'.

Cinq qualités sont requises chez l'éducateur : l'autorité, la compréhension des élèves, une bonne instruction, l'exemple et la vigilance. L'autorité doit être gagnée par le respect plutôt qu'inspirée par la peur. La discipline, spécialement les récompenses et les punitions, doit prendre en compte la mentalité de l'élève, y compris son sens de l'équité. Dans la gamme des punitions disponibles, les châtiments corporels ne sont pas mentionnés, ce qui contraste avec les coups de fouet habituels dans les écoles anglaises de l'époque. Les membres du staff doivent former une communauté, vivant ensemble et partageant prières et repas.

Ce qui précède montre clairement que les instructions de Colin n'étaient pas écrites spécifiquement pour la formation de candidats à la prêtrise, et qu'elles pouvaient convenir à toutes les écoles. De sa pensée sur l'éducation on peut distinguer trois aspects particuliers : une gaieté saine, pas trop d'observances religieuses et une attention à chaque individu. Une école dirigée dans l'esprit des instructions de Colin devait être un espace sûr et accueillant, où les jeunes pouvaient grandir et apprendre les valeurs religieuses, morales et humaines tout en suivant leurs programmes d'études.

Chapitre 5
'Centre d'unité'

Depuis que Courveille s'est éclipsé en 1826, les aspirants maristes—sœurs, frères et prêtres—vivaient et travaillaient dans les deux diocèses de Belley et Lyon, sans aucun leader commun, reconnu au moins par eux. Le résultat le plus probable aurait dû être la scission des maristes en deux groupes affiliés à leurs diocèses respectifs. Ce processus était déjà en train de se produire sous la pression de la réalité et des autorités diocésaines qui voulaient les maristes, mais comme leurs propres instruments. Les maristes, eux, voulaient rester unis. Aussi, à l'automne 1830 – cela faisait quatre ans que Courveille était parti—les prêtres des deux groupes diocésains, se réunirent à Belley et élurent Jean-Claude Colin comme 'centre d'unité', ou, comme on l'appela aussi, 'supérieur central'. Ce n'était pas la reconnaissance ou l'officialisation d'une position que Colin avait déjà. Comme tous les prêtres maristes du diocèse de Belley vivaient ensemble au collège-séminaire, il était en fait le supérieur. Mais il l'était par nomination de l'évêque. S'il y avait eu d'autres communautés de prêtres maristes dans le diocèse, il n'aurait pas nécessairement été leur supérieur. Quant à Lyon, Colin n'avait, bien sûr, aucune autorité sur les prêtres et les frères de l'Hermitage, qui étaient sous celle de Marcellin Champagnat.

Pourquoi, alors, Colin a-t-il été choisi ? Il avait montré son attachement à la Société de Marie : il avait rédigé un avant-projet de règle et s'était juré à deux reprises d'aller à Rome ; avec son frère Pierre et Courveille, il était le cosignataire d'une lettre au pape Pie VII ; il avait présenté la règle au Nonce à Paris. De fait, le choix était limité. Des signataires du formulaire de la promesse de 1816, ils ne restaient plus que quatre ; deux seulement auraient pu être réellement pris en considération, c'est-à-dire Colin et Champagnat. Marcellin était occupé à plein temps avec les frères ; Colin était le seul réel candidat restant. Dire cela n'est pas déprécier Jean-Claude Colin, mais mettre en relief et en perspective ce qu'il avait réalisé. La grandeur de Colin consista à se lever et à prendre la responsabilité de l'avenir d'une œuvre qu'il n'avait pas commencée, tout en croyant et en insistant sur le fait qu'il n'était rien de plus qu'un supérieur provisoire qui occupait le poste jusqu'à ce que quelqu'un de plus qualifié que lui pût prendre la suite.

A ce point de sa vie, faisons une pause et demandons-nous à quoi il ressemblait. Tout d'abord, son apparence. Jean-Claude Colin était petit (1 m 64 de haut), légèrement corpulent. Il avait un visage de forme ovale et un large front haut. Ses cheveux, qui descendaient sur ses oreilles, avaient dû être bruns au départ, à en juger par ses sourcils, mais ils étaient devenus prématurément blancs. Son teint était clair et ses yeux bleu-gris. Il avait un nez aquilin et un menton déterminé.

Ce dernier trait exprimait un fort caractère, en quelque sorte contredit par une manière qui pourrait aisément le faire paraître, comme le notait un observateur, comme 'l'un de ces bons petits vieux curés de campagne, tout simples, tout timides, ne sachant où se mettre pour prendre moins de place'. De plus, il ne se souciait guère de son apparence. Il suivait la mode de sa jeunesse en se rasant de près, plutôt que de se laisser pousser la barbe comme le faisaient beaucoup de clercs au 19ème siècle. Souvent, cependant, son menton exhibait des poils de plusieurs jours, et sa soutane portait des taches de tabac à priser. Il avait un défaut d'élocution, qu'il maitrisa largement, et avait tendance habituellement à prononcer toutes les consonnes sifflantes comme des 'ch'. Néanmoins tous ceux qui l'ont connu reconnaissaient sa maîtrise intellectuelle et son ascendant personnel qui faisaient de lui un meneur d'hommes.

D'autre part, l'impression de timidité et de manque d'assurance correspondait au comportement qu'il avait eu dans son enfance et dans son adolescence. Ceux qui l'avaient connu alors auraient été très surpris de rencontrer plus tard l'homme qui, disait-on, 'faisait les choses à une grande échelle . . . [et] marchait non pas à pas mesurés, mais à enjambées géantes qui - c'était garanti - tendaient à éclabousser celui qui était à côté de lui'. Mais en même temps, même quand il fut placé à la tête des maristes, Colin hésitait fréquemment à prendre des décisions qui semblaient évidentes aux autres, et attendait d'être certain que c'était la volonté de Dieu. Même des admirateurs ont été forcés de se demander s'il était 'peut-être trop gêné dans la gestion de ses affaires', notant qu'il 'a eu des difficultés avec beaucoup de personnes qui ont eu à faire avec lui, à l'intérieur et à l'extérieur (de la Société)'. De façon caractéristique, des périodes de grande énergie étaient suivies de moments d'inaction. Toute sa vie, il a aspiré à la solitude, et fait des tentatives répétées de renonciation à sa charge.

L'élection de Colin comme 'supérieur central' des maristes avait eu lieu sur fond de la Révolution de juillet qui a renversé Charles X et porté sur le trône Louis-Philippe d'Orléans. Vers le début de la nouvelle année scolaire, en novembre 1830, l'agitation politique et sociale permanente commença à avoir un impact énorme, même au collège-séminaire de Belley. Avec le recul, Colin considérait comme son 'chef d'œuvre' d'avoir gardé l'école ouverte pendant toute l'année 1830–1831. Il sortit de cette période éprouvante comme un leader ayant fait ses preuves et qui était reconnu.

Julien Favre, qui devait succéder à Colin comme supérieur général, était un étudiant en rhétorique au collège de Belley en 1830–1831. Il se souvenait de la vie à cette époque. Les élèves avaient commencé à protester contre l'autorité par la passivité et la non-coopération. Si l'un d'eux était puni, tous se mettaient de son côté. Le mot circulait : 'Pas de chant aux Vêpres', et personne n'ouvrait la bouche. Si l'un osait briser l'embargo, il était frappé. Pour montrer leur mécontentement, ils paradaient en silence autour des bâtiments de l'école en traînant bruyamment leurs pieds sur les dalles. Puis, comme en 1790, les paysans descendirent de la montagne avec des fusils—réels ou imités. Cela mit les élèves dans une réelle ferveur révolutionnaire, qui se répandit aux professeurs. Un jour de congé, pour la promenade récréative habituelle, les étudiants enlevèrent leurs uniformes, se saisirent de haches en bois et marchèrent comme un bataillon, en chantant la Marseillaise et d'autres chants révolutionnaires, 'avec une sorte de frénésie comme s'ils avaient bu'. Un des professeurs prit part aussi à cette manifestation. Ils arrivèrent dans une forêt où ils commencèrent à hurler et se comporter de telle sorte que Pierre Colin, qui était avec eux, craignit d'être tué.

Nous n'avons pas beaucoup de détails sur la manière dont Colin géra l'insurrection au collège. Il eut largement à y faire face seul. En effet, pendant la plus grande partie de cette période, Mgr Devie, qui venait d'être opéré de la cataracte, était hors service car il récupérait d'une opération qui, en ce temps-là, requérait l'immobilisation du patient pendant une longue période, le temps que la plaie guérisse ;

il y avait danger de mort, et la guérison totale était lente. Colin se retrouvait donc sans soutien actif de l'évêque au moment où il en avait besoin, et il semble avoir trouvé dans les interventions du vicaire général une entrave plutôt qu'une aide. Quant à ses collègues, à quelques exceptions près, notamment son frère Pierre, il semble qu'il ait reçu d'eux peu de soutien ; certains étaient même en révolte ouverte. Plusieurs montrèrent qu'ils adhéraient aux nouvelles tendances en souscrivant publiquement—et malgré la désapprobation formelle de l'évêque—à *L'avenir*, un journal catholique libéral édité par le comte de Montalembert, qui militait pour la séparation de l'Eglise et de l'Etat.

Une rumeur de complot circula parmi certains membres du personnel pour évincer Colin en ce moment favorable où il était isolé et vulnérable. Ces collègues qui étaient particulièrement rebelles pensaient qu'était venue leur chance de renverser l'autorité tandis que d'autres pouvaient imaginer qu'en sacrifiant Colin ils pourraient calmer les étudiants. En ville, on s'attendait même, jour après jour, à apprendre, l'assassinat de Colin. Lui restait calme et contrôlait la situation. Favre était quasiment certain que, sans Colin, le collège-séminaire n'aurait pas survécu à la crise. Le diocèse de Belley lui dut beaucoup ; Mgr Devie le réalisa sans doute et lui en fut reconnaissant. Toutefois Colin eut un prix à payer, en termes de santé personnelle : ses cheveux blanchirent, et il se fit vieux prématurément. Colin parla des dommages causés à sa santé par l'anxiété constante et le manque de sommeil.

Ayant réussi à faire traverser la crise au collège, Colin avait gagné le droit de dicter ce qu'il voulait : que ce fût un établissement mariste. Il écrivit aux confrères de l'Hermitage en leur disant qu'il pensait lui donner 'une nouvelle marche correspondant à notre but'. A la rentrée scolaire prochaine tous les professeurs devront avoir été affiliés à la Société, et il y aura un vice-supérieur qui sera aussi le maître des novices. De nouvelles structures seront mises en place : selon leurs âges, les élèves seront séparés en trois divisions, chacune ayant son étude, son dortoir et ses promenades propres ; les maîtres auront leur propre réfectoire. L'année qui débuta en novembre 1831 vit d'autres changements dans le personnel ; ceux qui avaient souscrit à *L'avenir* ne sont pas revenus.

Une des manières pour les prêtres maristes des deux diocèses de développer un sens d'unité était de se réunir pour une retraite commune. A la fin de la retraite qui s'est tenue en septembre 1831, tous les participants—staff du collège de Belley inclus—signèrent un acte de consécration à Notre-Dame pour signifier leur affiliation à la Société de Marie. Parmi les nouveaux signataires se trouvait le P. Pierre Chanel. Prêtre du diocèse de Belley depuis 1827, il s'était senti une vocation pour les missions étrangères. Un moment, avec d'autres collègues, Claude Bret et Denis Maîtrepierre, il avait pensé se porter volontaire pour partir en Amérique, destination de nombreux missionnaires français. Qu'il se soit joint aux maristes est peut-être dû au fait qu'on s'attendait à ce qu'ils acceptent de travailler en mission, une chose qu'ils envisageaient certes, mais en direction de laquelle ils n'avaient fait aucun pas jusqu'à présent. A la même époque où il se joignit aux prêtres maristes du collège de Belley, sa sœur Françoise entra au couvent des sœurs maristes, à Bon-Repos. Chanel fut nommé d'abord professeur, puis successivement directeur spirituel (automne 1832) et vice-supérieur (automne 1834). Ce dernier poste faisait de lui le responsable effectif de l'administration quotidienne du collège au nom de Colin, qui restait le supérieur mais avait désormais beaucoup d'autres soucis qui occupaient son temps et son attention.

Marches dans la chapelle de La Capucinière

Porte d'entrée de l'ancien
bâtiment de La Capucinière

Jusqu'alors les prêtres maristes de Belley manquaient de maison à eux. Les derniers mois de 1832, Colin fut très occupé par le projet de reprendre un ancien couvent capucin à Belley, connu justement sous le nom de la 'Capucinière'. La propriété, nationalisée en 1791, avait été acquise en 1826 par Mgr Devie, qui voulait en faire la résidence du groupe de missionnaires diocésains qu'il voulait fonder sur le modèle des 'Chartreux' de Lyon. C'est probablement à la fin de 1831 qu'il proposa aux maristes d'utiliser la maison. En novembre 1832, une communauté de trois prêtres et de plusieurs frères coadjuteurs (appelés d'abord 'frères Joseph') put s'y installer. Les maristes avaient enfin leur propre maison où ils pouvaient vivre la vie religieuse et recevoir des candidats en formation. Les prêtres qui travaillaient au collège-séminaire continuèrent à y vivre. Colin, qui n'avait pas encore obtenu de l'évêque l'autorisation de s'installer à la Capucinière, faisait des allers-retours entre les deux maisons, qui 'ne faisaient qu'une', dit-il à Champagnat, et dont il était bien sûr le supérieur.

Le couvent capucin formait un rectangle autour d'une cour intérieure. Un côté était occupé par une chapelle publique, ou église, avec une chapelle attenante plus petite ou chœur, où les religieux récitaient l'office divin. L'église n'avait plus servi de lieu de culte depuis la Révolution. Avant son acquisition par Mgr Devie, elle avait servi de théâtre et de salle de danses. Initialement, les maristes ont utilisé seulement l'aile sud du bâtiment et une moitié de la cour, pendant qu'un locataire sur place occupait le reste. L'année suivante ils avaient la maison tout entière pour eux.

Dès le début, les maristes de la Capucinière continuèrent à prêcher des missions dans le diocèse. Après 1834, l'ancien couvent capucin commença à servir aussi de maison de formation. A l'époque, la plupart des candidats pour la branche cléricale de la Société, étaient déjà ordonnés ; il n'y avait pas encore de noviciat formel. La formation offerte par La Capucinière était donc destinée seulement à un très petit nombre d'étudiants. Après l'approbation de la Société en septembre 1836, qui impliquait la permission de prononcer les vœux de religion, un noviciat canonique devint nécessaire, également pour ceux qui étaient déjà prêtres avant d'entrer.

Colin décida également d'ouvrir un petit internat à la Capucinière, qui fonctionna jusqu'en 1840. Ce fut la première maison d'éducation appartenant aux prêtres maristes, distincte du collège-séminaire qu'ils encadraient mais qui appartenait au diocèse. Il commença très modestement. En fait, aucune tentative ne fut faite pour donner des cours sur place. Les internes suivaient les cours au collège-séminaire. Par la suite, la maison admit un petit nombre d'internes de familles aisées locales, et donna des cours aux plus jeunes, tandis que les plus grands allaient au collège.

Qu'il s'agisse de la maison de formation ou de l'internat, les débuts ne furent guère brillants. L'établissement ou, peut-être mieux, l'expérience était très fragile et n'inspirait pas confiance à première vue. Les confrères étaient découragés et même effrayés. 'Que va-t-il se passer si tout le monde part ?', demanda un jour Claude Bret à Jean-Claude Colin, qui répondit aussitôt et avec force : 'Si tout le monde part, je chanterai le *Te Deum* et je recommencerai.'

Un incident concernant l'internat de Belley illustre très bien l'idée de Colin sur les maristes appelés à être des 'instruments des miséricordes divines'. Un des garçons était le fils du général Louis Carrier, qui vivait à Belley, et qui était bien connu pour être un catholique non-pratiquant. Quand il tomba malade, Colin avait espéré que Jean-Marie Millot, préfet de l'établissement, pourrait le réconcilier avec l'Eglise. Mais le général ne voulait pas de viatique (communion donnée aux mourants) apporté publiquement comme c'était l'habitude ; il demanda qu'il lui fût apporté en privé, la nuit tombée. Colin croyait que le général avait manifesté suffisamment de bonne volonté pour qu'on lui concédât cela, mais le vicaire général ne fut pas d'accord. Alors Colin alla voir l'évêque, qui lui dit de faire comme M. Carrier demandait. Avant de mourir le 30 octobre 1838, le général avait non seulement reçu les sacrements mais il avait publiquement béni son fils et demandé aux domestiques de prier pour lui. Commentaire de Colin : 'Il a fait bien plus que ce qui lui avait été demandé.'

En ce temps, l'autorité de Jean-Claude sur toute la Société était plus morale que légale. Néanmoins il croyait qu'une responsabilité et une autorité lui avaient été données—même si c'était seulement de façon provisoire. Dans son esprit au moins, il n'était pas un simple négociateur ou intermédiaire pour conseiller ou persuader, mais pas pour commander. D'autre part, ni les limites de son autorité ni sa manière de travailler n'étaient définies ; seules l'expérience, et occasionnellement l'erreur, pourraient les lui indiquer. Il pourrait invoquer l'obéissance, mais les autres se considéreraient-ils tenus à obéir ? Les maristes avaient déjà eu avec Courveille la mauvaise expérience d'un prétendu 'supérieur général' qui avait essayé d'exercer une autorité que les autres ne lui reconnaissaient pas. Ils seraient très sensibles à toute tentative de Colin de dépasser les limites. Le supérieur central et ses confrères allaient avoir besoin de largeur et de flexibilité. Il y avait de la place pour beaucoup d'incompréhensions. Et il y en eut.

Il y avait aussi la question de la position de Colin vis-à-vis des autorités diocésaines de Lyon. A leurs yeux, il n'était qu'un simple prêtre d'un autre diocèse, sans droit d'intervention dans le diocèse de Lyon, même si cela concernait les maristes de chez eux. En d'autres mots, ils ne reconnaissaient rien en lui d'un supérieur religieux. Le souci immédiat de Colin était de garder ensemble les prêtres des deux diocèses, dans un même esprit et avec des manières de vivre similaires. Bien sûr, il était plus intimement lié aux prêtres de Belley, dont il partageait la vie et le ministère, et dont il était le supérieur. Il était moins bien connu de ceux de Lyon, mais pour le bien de l'unité, il exerçait maintenant un contrôle sur eux aussi. Peu de temps après l'élection de Colin comme supérieur central, Marcellin Champagnat fut élu supérieur ('provincial') des prêtres de Lyon, position ratifiée par les autorités diocésaines de Lyon. La relation entre les deux allait être cruciale. Heureusement, ils se connaissaient bien, avaient beaucoup de respect l'un pour l'autre et avaient depuis longtemps l'habitude de communiquer.

Bien sûr, Champagnat était également le supérieur des frères enseignants. Jusqu'à présent, Colin avait eu tendance à considérer les frères de manière assez marginale dans la Société de Marie ; c'était essentiellement l'affaire de Champagnat. Marcellin, de son côté, l'avait toujours tenu informé de leurs affaires. Désormais Colin admit qu'ils faisaient intégralement et pleinement partie de la Société et qu'il devait leur porter une attention plus grande, pas seulement par intérêt fraternel mais aussi—dans un sens pas facile à définir et à articuler particulièrement avec l'autorité de Champagnat—en tant que leur supérieur majeur. Il y avait ensuite les sœurs maristes. Dès le départ, elles avaient été considérées comme une branche de la Société de Marie. Le supérieur central était aussi responsable d'elles, mais elles avaient leur propre supérieure, Mère Saint-Joseph (Jeanne-Marie Chavoin). Tout cela contribuait à rendre la situation considérablement complexe.

En ce temps-là, Colin travaillait à la reconnaissance de la Société de Marie comme congrégation supra-diocésaine. De son côté, Mgr Devie voulait que les maristes de Belley fussent entièrement sous son contrôle. Pendant des années, l'évêque fit tout son possible pour convaincre Colin. Mais Jean-Claude lui opposa une résistance inébranlable et sentit que l'évêque exerçait sur lui une pression injuste. Un jour, il réalisa qu'il ressentait une grande antipathie pour lui et décida de prendre une mesure héroïque pour la résoudre. Il courut dans les rues de Belley vers la résidence de l'évêque, frappa à la porte, entra, se jeta à ses genoux, avoua ses sentiments d'hostilité et demanda pardon. L'évêque, pris par surprise, le reçut paternellement et l'embrassa. Ce fut la fin de la 'tentation' de Colin, mais pas encore du conflit entre eux.

En dépit de leurs divergences, Mgr Devie ne perdit pas la haute estime qu'il portait à Colin. Au contraire, c'était précisément parce qu'il l'estimait tant qu'il était déterminé à le garder dans son diocèse. Au cœur de leurs heurts les plus violents, il lui confiait pourtant des missions importantes et confidentielles ; il lui proposa même le poste de vicaire général. L'évêque tenta aussi plusieurs fois de le créer chanoine honoraire. Une fois, il utilisa la ruse et lui demanda d'apporter à sa résidence le camail de chanoine de Monsieur Pichat, avec l'idée de le déposer sur ses épaules, mais Colin avait anticipé la manœuvre et il l'avait déjouée en envoyant quelqu'un porter le camail. Chez Colin, le soin d'éviter ces nominations devrait être vu non pas simplement comme des exemples édifiants du refus d'accepter honneurs et dignités, mais aussi et spécialement comme des échecs dans le jeu de l'évêque de l'impliquer inextricablement dans la machine du diocèse. Pour sa part, Colin n'a jamais manqué de respect ni d'obéissance à son évêque ; il semble qu'il le voyait comme un père. Il est probable qu'il ait reconnu la grande chance qu'il avait eu de travailler pour un grand chef dont il avait accepté, le moment venu, des postes de responsabilité et de leadership. En interagissant avec Mgr Devie, Colin a acquis à la fois la dureté et l'art de la diplomatie. Tout cela l'a préparé à la mission qui l'attendait.

Quand Mgr Devie fut sur son lit de mort en 1852, il demanda à voir Colin. Celui-ci vint de Belley faire ses adieux à son mentor. Le mourant donna sa bénédiction à la Société de Marie. Il donna aussi à Colin quelques conseils et recommandations personnels, et lui demanda, dans ses rapports avec les autres, de ne pas risquer de blesser leurs sentiments en ne contrôlant pas ses humeurs momentanées.

Chapitre 6
Reconnaissance de Rome et Océanie

Vers la fin de 1830, les pensées de Jean-Claude Colin recommencèrent à se tourner vers Rome, avec le vœu de présenter au pape le projet de Société de Marie et d'expliquer son origine surnaturelle. Au début de l'année suivante, le 2 février 1831, se produisit un événement qui devait avoir un effet déterminant sur le destin de la Société de Marie. Ce fut l'élection d'un nouveau pape pour succéder à Pie VIII qui avait régné brièvement après la mort de Léon XII en 1829. C'était le cardinal Mauro Cappellari, qui avait pris le nom de Grégoire XVI. Cappellari était un moine camaldule, qui combinait une grande piété personnelle et une simplicité de vie à une politique profondément conservatrice en matière ecclésiale et temporelle. Cardinal, il avait été préfet de la Sacrée Congrégation de la Propagation de la Foi, (*'de Propaganda Fide'*, ou simplement *'Propaganda'*), de nos jours 'Evangélisation des Peuples'. A ce poste, il s'était beaucoup intéressé à relancer l'effort missionnaire de l'Eglise, interrompu par les tumultes et les confiscations des décades précédentes. En tant que pape, son intérêt allait se maintenir.

Quand Mgr Devie apprit le désir de Colin de se rendre à Rome, il l'en découragea. Apparemment Colin ne fit rien durant le reste de 1831 ni au cours de l'année 1832 pour faire avancer le projet. Les choses bougèrent à nouveau l'année suivante. Il fut décidé d'approcher la curie de Rome par le biais du cardinal Vincenzo Macchi, avec lequel Colin avait traité quand il était nonce apostolique à Paris. En avril 1833, Jean-Claude et six autres aspirants maristes dont son frère Pierre et Pierre Chanel, signèrent une pétition à présenter au Saint-Père, lui demandant implicitement d'approuver la Société. D'autres pétitions présentaient un projet de Constitutions et une demande d'indulgences pour les tertiaires maristes laïcs. Colin avait aussi besoin de lettres de recommandation des deux diocèses où les maristes étaient présents. Il finit par les obtenir de Mgr Devie, de Belley, et de l'Administrateur de Lyon, Mgr Gaston de Pins, qui exprimaient leur estime des maristes mais se gardaient bien de recommander leur approbation par Rome en tant que congrégation pontificale.

En août 1833, Jean-Claude et deux compagnons, Pierre Chanel, du diocèse de Belley, et Antoine Bourdin, de Lyon, se préparèrent à partir à Rome pour présenter le projet mariste au Saint-Père. C'était la toute-première fois que Colin, âgé de cinquante-trois ans, voyageait hors de France. C'était même son premier voyage aussi long depuis ses deux déplacements à Paris dix ans plus tôt. Quelle qu'ait pu être la largeur de sa vision—au point d'embrasser une grande partie du globe—son monde physique resta extrêmement limité tout au long de sa vie. Il n'avait simplement aucun goût des voyages ou de la découverte de nouveaux horizons, et, comme ses ancêtres paysans, il ne s'est jamais éloigné loin de chez lui, sauf nécessité.

Premier arrêt : Lyon, où les maristes déposèrent au pied de Notre Dame de Fourvière leur projet de voyage et demandèrent sa bénédiction et sa protection. Puis Marseille, où ils trouvèrent un bateau prêt à traverser la Méditerranée jusqu'à Civitavecchia, le port de Rome. Le nom du navire présageait bien : Notre Dame du Bon Secours, mais c'était un bateau de marchandises côtier, sans cabines pour les passagers. Les trois maristes dormirent à même le pont ; Colin et Chanel souffrirent du mal de mer. Des tempêtes entravèrent la traversée, et le bateau prenait l'eau. Finalement il atteignit Civitavecchia, pour s'entendre dire qu'il allait être mis en quarantaine. Cependant les maristes furent autorisés à partir à Rome. Ils arrivèrent avant l'aube, à la Porta di San Pancrazio, sur le Janicule, le 15 septembre, et trouvèrent un logement dans le centre historique, près de l'église nationale Saint-Louis-des-Français. En atteignant enfin la Ville Eternelle, Jean-Claude a-t-il ressenti quelques émotions intenses ? Il ne nous l'a pas dit.

La Rome que Jean-Claude Colin a vue en 1833 était une ville beaucoup plus petite qu'aujourd'hui, avec une population de moins de 150.000 habitants contenus dans d'anciens remparts, et pas du tout une ville moderne, même selon les critères de l'époque, presqu'entièrement ecclésiastique, tournant autour de la cour pontificale. En ce temps-là, l'administration de l'Eglise n'était pas aussi centrée au Vatican qu'elle l'est aujourd'hui. Le pape vivait habituellement au Palais du Quirinal où se trouvaient aussi les Offices centraux du gouvernement civil des Etats pontificaux. C'est là que se tenaient les audiences ainsi que les conclaves pour élire un nouveau pape. D'autres réunions de cardinaux pouvaient se tenir au Quirinal ou au Vatican. Tous les départements ecclésiastiques de la curie romaine n'avaient pas leurs propres bureaux permanents comme de nos jours, et leurs officiers travaillaient souvent au palais du cardinal titulaire.

Les trois maristes découvrirent qu'ils étaient arrivés juste au moment où tout fermait pour les grandes vacances. Colin avait déjà prévu de rester jusqu'à Noël. En attendant, les pèlerins maristes contactèrent plusieurs fois le cardinal Macchi et virent d'autres prélats qui étaient encore à Rome. Ils firent le pèlerinage touristique habituel. Chaque jour ils célébraient la messe dans une église différente. Comme tous les pèlerins d'hier et d'aujourd'hui, ils achetèrent des chapelets, des médailles et des livres pieux. Comme tous les touristes, ils étaient épuisés en fin de journée. Il leur restait toutefois encore une visite à faire, et la plus importante, celle qui était de fait l'objet du vœu de Colin : voir le Saint-Père et lui 'ouvrir son cœur' sur la Société de Marie et sa règle. Peut-être commençait-il à ce moment-là à percevoir la façon dont les choses marchaient réellement à Rome. C'était hautement improbable qu'il ait la chance d'avoir cette sorte de conversation cœur à cœur avec le pape qu'il avait imaginée. Aux multiples demandes d'audience adressées au camerlingue du pape il lui avait été répondu que trop d'audiences étaient déjà inscrites dans le court laps de temps qui restait au pape avant son départ pour Castel Gandolfo. Finalement le cardinal Macchi obtint une audience pour le 28 septembre.

Introduits en présence du pape, ils trouvèrent devant eux une silhouette courte, vêtue de blanc, d'apparence quelconque mais aux manières bienveillantes, assise sur un trône. Selon le protocole de l'époque, ils s'agenouillèrent, embrassèrent d'abord sa pantoufle puis sa main ; après quoi, le pape les fit se lever et resta debout avec eux jusqu'à la fin de l'audience. Il y avait un problème de langue. Chanel dit quelques mots en italien, hésita puis s'arrêta. Bourdin ne fit pas mieux en

Escalier du Quirinal

latin. Colin pensait que le pape comprendrait au moins le français et commença à parler dans cette langue, mais d'un regard on le fit arrêter. A la fin le pape parla en latin tandis que les trois Français répondaient dans leur langue. Grégoire XVI avait été bien informé. Il les orienta vers les officiers de Curie concernés. L'audience était terminée ; il ne restait plus qu'à recevoir la bénédiction finale du pape. Les trois maristes présentèrent les chapelets et médailles achetés sur le chemin du palais. C'est alors que se produisit un incident embarrassant. S'étant inclinés et sortant à reculons, ils trébuchèrent sur la traîne de leurs soutanes et perdirent leur chemin. Le pape leur cria : 'Tournez à droite', et sonna une cloche pour qu'on guidât ses visiteurs vers la sortie. A ce moment-là Colin tourna le dos au pape et se précipita vers la porte, suivi par les autres. Ils étaient dehors, transportés de joie par leur expérience. Plus tard Jean-Claude vit le côté amusant de leur sortie embarrassante. Ils partirent aussitôt raconter à Macchi ce qui s'était passé et, selon Bourdin, celui-ci fut 'charmé'.

Il était temps pour Bourdin et Chanel de retourner à Belley car l'année scolaire allait commencer en novembre. Colin les accompagna jusqu'à Lorette, où ils vénérèrent la Sainte Maison qui y aurait été apportée de Nazareth. Il retourna ensuite à Rome, qui commençait à revivre après la fête de Saint Martin, le 11 novembre. Installé au couvent des Franciscains attenant à la basilique des Saints Apôtres, Colin passa l'hiver à rencontrer des cardinaux et des monsignori susceptibles d'être impliqués dans l'approbation de la Société de Marie et de sa Règle, et à étudier à la *Biblioteca casanate*, une bibliothèque publique attachée au couvent dominicain de Santa Maria sopra Minerva. C'est là qu'il tomba pour la première fois sur un exemplaire des constitutions jésuites qui allaient exercer une influence importante sur le développement des constitutions maristes.

Les prélats de la curie rencontrés par Colin furent impressionnés par sa sincérité et sa dévotion, mais ils le découragèrent dans son projet qu'ils trouvaient 'un peu vaste', et même 'monstrueux'. Le 31 janvier 1834, la Congrégation des Evêques et Réguliers se réunit au Vatican ; sur un rapport négatif du cardinal Castruccio Castracane, elle vota contre l'approbation de la Société. Néanmoins, en prix de consolation, elle recommanda d'accorder les indulgences requises. Colin n'avait plus de raison de rester à Rome plus longtemps. Il arriva à Belley plus tôt que prévu, le 21 février. Les élèves célébrèrent son retour au collège-séminaire avec la sonnerie de la cloche, des chants, des pâtisseries, du vin et un congé pour le reste de la journée. Peu après, Mgr Devie autorisa Colin à vivre à la Capucinière. Et les affaires maristes en restèrent là.

En 1835, les choses commencèrent à bouger. La Congrégation *Propaganda Fide* avait décidé d'établir un Vicariat de la Polynésie occidentale en plus du Vicariat de la Polynésie orientale confiée

Portrait de Mgr Pompallier

à la congrégation des Sacrés-Cœurs de Jésus et de Marie ('Pères picpuciens'), fondée par Pierre Coudrin en 1817. En fait, sur le papier, le nouveau vicariat incluait aussi la Mélanésie et une partie de la Micronésie. La Mission catholique du Pacifique Sud était considérée comme extrêmement urgente car les missionnaires protestants, qui avaient une longueur d'avance de plusieurs décades, s'établissaient rapidement dans toute la région.

La question qui se posait maintenant était de trouver un chef de mission et des missionnaires. La recherche orienta la Congrégation de *Propaganda* vers Lyon et Jean-Baptiste-François Pompallier, qui avait appartenu pendant quelques années au groupe des aspirants maristes—un atout supplémentaire car ils pourraient fournir les missionnaires dont on avait besoin. Pompallier et Colin furent contactés. Le 10 février 1836, Colin accepta l'invitation à fournir du personnel pour le nouveau vicariat. En retour, il reçut un Bref papal reconnaissant (seulement) les prêtres de la Société de Marie et les autorisant à prononcer les vœux de religion et à élire un supérieur général. Toutefois ce ne fut pas avant le 24 septembre que Colin fut élu supérieur général, et que lui et ces compagnons prononcèrent leurs vœux de pauvreté, chasteté et obéissance. A cette époque, Pompallier avait déjà été nommé vicaire apostolique et consacré à Rome comme évêque titulaire de Maronée. Il présida l'élection de Colin mais il ne fit pas profession ; à la place, il fit une déclaration d'adhésion à la Société de Marie. Sur le moment, personne—y compris Colin—ne semblait avoir pensé qu'il était très important que Mgr Pompallier ne fût pas un profès mariste. Il se considérait lui-même, et le P. Colin le considérait comme un mariste, nonobstant le droit canon. Cela voulait dire que le chef de la nouvelle mission dans le Pacifique n'appartenait pas réellement à la congrégation religieuse qui lui avait été confiée.

A Rome, Mgr Pompallier avait été prévenu de s'attendre à ce que les missionnaires eussent leur propre supérieur religieux, et il avait été informé des sphères respectives d'autorité de chacun : la sienne en tant que vicaire apostolique et celle du supérieur religieux. A sa grande surprise, Colin lui délégua les pouvoirs de supérieur religieux. Ce qui était beaucoup plus important pour l'avenir, c'était l'idée de l'autorité du supérieur religieux que se faisait Pompallier, restrictive selon lui : s'assurer de l'observation de leur Règle par les religieux ; tout le reste les concernant, y compris leur bien-être spirituel et matériel, relevait de son autorité de vicaire apostolique. Le P. Colin semble avoir adhéré à cela au départ ; après tout, il n'avait aucune autre information sur les pouvoirs respectifs d'un supérieur religieux et d'un vicaire apostolique que celle donnée par Pompallier ; de plus il n'avait qu'une expérience limitée de supérieur. C'est important de réaliser que la délégation de Colin à Pompallier n'était qu'une simple délégation. Il n'était pas question que le vicaire apostolique *en tant que tel* fût le supérieur religieux. Colin pouvait—et de fait il le fit, déléguer l'autorité à d'autres. Il y avait là une source supplémentaire de conflits entre eux, à l'avenir.

Chapitre 7
Supérieur Général

Quand Jean-Claude Colin s'assit à son bureau à la Capucinière, à Belley, pour la première fois après son élection comme supérieur général, peut-être le soir même du 24 septembre 1836, il put faire le point sur sa situation et la responsabilité qui lui avait été donnée. Il avait été choisi comme premier supérieur général d'une congrégation qu'il n'avait pas fondée. Non seulement çà : il s'en retrouvait le chef, contre sa volonté. Dans son esprit, il était un bouche-trou jusqu'à ce qu'un autre de meilleur et de plus adéquat pût assumer la responsabilité. En même temps il réalisait que personne d'autre n'était disponible pour cette tâche.

L'ascension de Colin vers la fonction suprême est exceptionnelle et a peu de parallèles. Il était prêt à vouer toute son énergie à une cause en quelle il croyait mais qu'il n'avait pas commencée ; sans avoir désiré le poste, il fallait prendre d'importantes initiatives et en assumer la responsabilité. Mais il restait convaincu qu'il n'était pas fait pour la tâche que ses collègues lui avaient imposée, et il chercherait la première occasion pour démissionner. Chez lui, il n'y avait clairement ni ambition personnelle ni intérêt propre. Ses protestations, qu'il n'était pas réellement celui qui devait diriger la Société, vont beaucoup plus loin que les hésitations normales de quelqu'un entrant dans une fonction qui risque de dépasser ses capacités. Elles semblent représenter ce qu'il pensait vraiment de lui. Il ne jouait pas l'humble ni le faux modeste. Pas besoin non plus de recourir à des hypothèses psychologiques. Mais la réticence n'implique pas nécessairement un manque d'engagement. Comme précédemment au collège-séminaire de Belley, une fois installé, Colin n'a pas hésité à remplir sa mission et s'est donné tout entier. Il allait diriger la Société les dix-huit années suivantes. Mais durant tout ce temps, il a continué à considérer sa fonction comme temporaire, et il a fait plusieurs tentatives, ou projets du moins, de démission de supérieur général jusqu'à ce qu'il fût finalement autorisé à le faire en 1854.

En attendant, il y avait du travail à faire. Le plus important était, bien sûr, d'envoyer les premiers missionnaires dans le Pacifique. Il fallait le faire le plus tôt possible. La nouvelle Société n'avait donc pas le temps de s'organiser et se retrouvait seule pour se préparer à cette mission dans un vaste territoire à l'autre bout du monde, avec une population nombreuse et dispersée dans une multitude d'îles, aux cultures très différentes, dont on connaissait peu de choses en Europe. Qu'il y ait eu, au début, des moments de confusion, d'hésitation et d'incertitude, ce n'est guère étonnant.

A la fin de cette année capitale 1836, Mgr Pompallier partit pour le Pacifique avec quatre prêtres maristes et trois frères maristes. Les frères avaient été formés par Marcellin Champagnat à l'Hermitage. Avant de quitter Lyon, les missionnaires gravirent une nouvelle fois la colline de Fourvière pour confier la mission à la Vierge Marie. Leurs noms avaient été inscrits sur un rouleau, qui a été déposé dans un cœur votif en argent ; au fil des ans, les noms de leurs successeurs ont été ajoutés.

Rivière Hokianga

Après avoir changé plusieurs fois de plans *en route*, Pompallier décida d'installer en Nouvelle-Zélande la base de sa mission. Le 10 janvier 1838, après plus d'une année de voyage, l'évêque, accompagné d'un prêtre et d'un frère, arriva au Hokianga Harbour, dans le nord du pays, où ils devaient trouver une grande partie de la population maorie et des colons européens. En cours de route, ils avaient déploré le décès de Claude Bret et ils avaient laissé deux prêtres et deux frères sur les îles de Wallis et de Futuna où ils étaient les premiers missionnaires chrétiens. Laissons-les à leurs nouveaux postes, mais notons la difficulté extrême du territoire de la mission qu'ils entreprenaient, et l'existence précaire qu'ils eurent souvent à mener. Notons aussi la distance énorme les séparant de Rome et de Lyon, avec pour résultat la lenteur et le hasard des communications. Au début, une lettre d'Europe pouvait prendre un an pour arriver en Nouvelle-Zélande ; de même pour la transmission de l'argent, des informations et des instructions. A propos d'argent, la nouvelle mission avait reçu une subvention de démarrage à la fois de la Congrégation de *Propaganda* et du diocèse de Lyon. Mais l'aide financière à venir dépendrait de la Propagation de la Foi, dont la fondatrice, Pauline Jaricot, était originaire de Lyon aussi. Avec Paris, Lyon continuait d'être le centre administratif de cette remarquable organisation dirigée par des laïcs. Ces fonds étaient acheminés vers le Pacifique en passant par Colin. En 1839, il décida d'ailleurs de transférer la maison-mère de la Société de Marie de Belley à Lyon, dans une propriété appelée 'Puylata', située sur les pentes au-dessus de la Saône, en-dessous de Fourvière. De la terrasse, les beaux jours, on peut voir le Mont Blanc.

Colin était directement responsable des prêtres maristes et des frères coadjuteurs en Europe, du recrutement, de la formation, des missionnaires en Océanie, et également, en tant que leur autorité suprême, des frères, des sœurs et des laïcs maristes. Jusqu'en 1839, il avait gouverné seul la Société. Une fois installé à Puylata, il mit en place une administration générale, avec des procédures et pratiques administratives régulières.

Marcellin Champagnat faisait partie de cette première administration, chargé spécialement des Petits Frères de Marie. Mais à partir du milieu de 1839, sa santé donna de vives inquiétudes. La question de sa succession et du futur gouvernement des frères maristes devint urgente. Colin pensa que le temps était venu pour les frères d'élire l'un des leurs pour diriger leur institut. Le 12 octobre

1839, il était à l'Hermitage pour présider l'élection du 'frère directeur général' en accord avec le règlement qu'il avait rédigé. Le frère François Rivat, un des premiers compagnons de Marcellin Champagnat, fut élu pour diriger un institut de 139 frères dans quarante-cinq maisons en France, en plus de ceux envoyés en Océanie. Toutefois Marcellin restait 'provincial' des frères et continuait à correspondre avec Colin pour les affaires importantes telles que les réponses à donner aux évêques qui, de toute la France et de plus en plus nombreux, demandaient des frères pour leurs diocèses, et que Champagnat ne pouvait satisfaire.

Portrait du Père Champagnat

Le mercredi des cendres 4 mars 1840, Marcellin fut affligé d'une violente douleur aux reins, qui dura jusqu'à sa mort. Il se mit alors à prendre ses dernières dispositions. Le 18 mai, il dicta son 'testament spirituel'. C'est un document qui respire la sainteté de l'homme. S'adressant à ses 'très chers frères', Champagnat mourant souligna l'unité de la Société de Marie en plusieurs branches, sous l'autorité d'un supérieur général.

Du 24 au 25 mai, Colin alla à l'Hermitage lui faire ses adieux. Le 6 juin 1840, Marcellin mourut à l'âge de cinquante et un ans. Il fut enterré deux jours plus tard. Pierre Colin et plusieurs autres pères maristes assistèrent aux funérailles, mais pas Jean-Claude. Du groupe originel, Champagnat était le seul d'une stature égale à celle de Colin. Les deux hommes avaient travaillé ensemble de nombreuses années, échangé sans arrêt, n'avaient pas toujours été d'accord mais avaient un unique but à l'esprit : l'œuvre de Marie'. Le provincial des frères n'hésitait pas à exprimer une opinion contraire à celle du supérieur général qui cédait—parfois—mais qui, à d'autres moments, lui demandait de se soumettre. Une confiance totale régnait entre eux. Pour Colin, c'était la fin d'un partenariat solide qui, au-delà des formalités de l'âge, manifestait une estime, et même une affection authentique. Pour la Société de Marie, un âge s'achevait. Un grand arbre était tombé, et le vide n'a jamais été comblé.

La Société de Marie commençait à croître rapidement. Nombreux étaient les prêtres diocésains attirés par les missions d'Océanie. En

1839, il y eut une seule entrée, mais c'était un futur saint canonisé : Pierre-Julien Eymard, prêtre du diocèse de Grenoble, qui fondera plus tard la congrégation des Prêtres du Saint Sacrement.

En Océanie, la plus grande partie du personnel et de l'argent était investie en Nouvelle-Zélande, qui était de loin l'archipel le plus grand et le plus peuplé des îles du Pacifique. Là, les maristes rencontrèrent de nombreux problèmes, en plus de ceux dus aux distances, qui aggravaient les autres. D'abord, les missionnaires protestants qui évangélisaient le peuple maori depuis 1814, habituellement avec succès, même si beaucoup n'avaient pas encore embrassé le christianisme. Eux et leurs convertis étaient fréquemment hostiles à l'arrivée de missionnaires catholiques. Les maristes trouvèrent aussi un large groupe de colons européens, en croissance rapide, dont bon nombre, souvent des vétérans de l'armée britannique, était catholiques ; leurs besoins et leurs attentes entrèrent rapidement en compétition avec l'attention portée par les missionnaires à leur appel premier à évangéliser les maoris. En 1840, deux ans après l'arrivée des missionnaires catholiques français, le gouvernement britannique établissait son autorité sur le pays tout entier, déjouant ainsi l'espoir d'une colonie française en Nouvelle-Zélande. Mgr Pompallier et les maristes craignirent les effets que cela pouvait avoir sur leur présence en Nouvelle-Zélande. Des frictions apparurent entre l'évêque et nombre de ses prêtres. Finalement, le supérieur général décida d'intervenir personnellement.

Le P. Chanel avait été déposé sur l'île de Futuna, en Océanie centrale, avec le F. Marie-Nizier Delorme. Sur l'île voisine d'Uvea ou Wallis, se trouvaient le P. Pierre Bataillon et le F. Joseph Luzy. Vers la fin de 1841, pratiquement tous les habitants étaient convertis. A

Vitrail du martyre du Père Chanel

Futuna, le progrès était beaucoup plus lent, en fait presque inexistant. En plusieurs années Chanel n'avait réussi à baptiser que quelques bébés mourants, et quelques autres. Mais sa générosité inlassable et sa bonté lui avaient valu de la population locale le surnom d' 'homme au bon cœur'. En avril 1841, on comptait quinze adultes catéchumènes, dont l'un était le fils d'un des deux rois de l'île. Sa conversion provoqua la colère de son père et un complot contre le missionnaire, qui fut brutalement assassiné le 28 avril 1841. Mais à Futuna aussi, 'le sang des martyrs est la semence de chrétiens' ; en 1845, l'île était entièrement chrétienne.

La nouvelle de la mort de Chanel ne parvint en Europe qu'une année plus tard. La réaction immédiate de Colin à ce second décès d'un mariste qu'il avait envoyé en mission, fut le choc et la peine. 'Son cœur, sensible à l'excès,' nota un observateur, 'fut attendri et accablé de cette perte [autant que pour Bret]. C'était comme s'il avait été frappé par un coup de foudre.' Suivit une réaction de soumission à la volonté de Dieu : 'Il tomba à genoux et dit au Seigneur : 'Soyez béni ! . . . Que votre volonté soit faite !'

Le supérieur général annonça à la Société le meurtre de Chanel comme un martyre. 'Chantons un cantique de louange en l'honneur de Marie, notre mère, la Reine des Martyrs. L'un de ses enfants et notre frère a mérité de verser son sang pour la gloire de Jésus-Christ'. La mort violente du P. Chanel comme martyr a été reconnue par l'Eglise, qui l'a béatifié en 1889 et canonisé en 1954.

Les années suivant le martyre de Pierre Chanel, les maristes ont établi des missions précaires, mais durables à long terme, à Tonga et à Fidji, qui toutes deux avaient déjà été évangélisées par des Méthodistes, et à Samoa. Un premier essai d'implantation en Nouvelle-Calédonie s'était heurté à l'hostilité de la population locale et avait causé la perte d'une vie ; un second essai dut être abandonné ; le troisième fut le bon. La mission mariste aux Salomon et en Nouvelle-Guinée s'avéra trop difficile ; elle greva les ressources de la Société. Elle fut confiée aux missionnaires de la Société des Missions de Milan, qui ne purent pas tenir non plus. Les maristes revinrent éventuellement aux Salomon en 1897. L'histoire des premières missions maristes dans le sud-ouest du Pacifique est une histoire héroïque, qui n'a pas encore été totalement racontée.

Colin n'a jamais visité l'Océanie. Néanmoins il s'est profondément impliqué dans la mission mariste dans le Pacifique sud. La distance donne parfois une perspective large. En partenariat avec la Congrégation *Propaganda Fide*, il fut capable de planifier le développement de la mission en Océanie, y compris l'érection de nouveaux vicariats.

Au cours de son mandat de supérieur général, Colin organisa quinze départs de missionnaires, pour un total de cent dix-sept maristes : soixante-quatorze prêtres, vingt-six Petits Frères de Marie et dix-sept frères coadjuteurs. Ce nombre représente un gros sacrifice pour ce qui était encore une petite congrégation. Colin avait un profond souci de ses hommes dont il se sentait responsable devant Dieu. Il insistait sur le besoin des missionnaires de vivre en communauté, et d'une manière générale sur le droit du supérieur religieux d'assurer leur bien-être spirituel et temporel. Ce fut la cause de conflits avec Mgr Pompallier et plus tard avec d'autres évêques de mission qui voulaient que les missionnaires fussent entièrement sous leur contrôle, et cela l'amena à réfléchir sur les rôles respectifs des supérieurs ecclésiastiques et religieux.

Une des manières essentielles dont Colin soutint les missionnaires, ce fut en tant que guide spirituel. Il commença à le faire en donnant une règle de vie et une spiritualité réaliste au premier groupe qui partit en Océanie, et que leurs successeurs appliqueront par la suite jusqu'à aujourd'hui.

A la retraite annuelle de septembre 1841, Colin tenta une première fois de démissionner. Il y pensait depuis plusieurs mois, et il l'avait anticipé en brûlant ses papiers personnels. Il croyait que le moment était venu de passer à un autre le gouvernement de la Société. Mais ses confrères ne furent pas d'accord. Colin accepta leur décision et se mit de nouveau à la tâche.

Chapitre 8
La Mission en Océanie

Nous sommes arrivés à une crête dans la vie de Jean-Claude Colin, spécialement dans son gouvernement comme supérieur général de la Société de Marie. Les décisions prises et les orientations confirmées au printemps et à l'été de l'année 1842 ont façonné les événements et les choix encore à venir, comme l'eau dévalant d'un bassin dans les montagnes. Pour le moment, au moins, il n'était plus question de démission. Colin était au travail et il avait des choses qu'il voulait réaliser.

En avril 1842, les maristes tinrent une 'assemblée', qui peut bien être considérée comme leur premier chapitre général. Un certain nombre de questions nécessitait des décisions. La principale affaire était de discuter et approuver un projet de constitutions sur lequel Colin travaillait depuis un certain temps. Il y avait aussi des questions urgentes concernant l'Océanie, où les relations avec Mgr Pompallier étaient particulièrement tendues. Toutefois, celles-ci ne furent pas discutées en assemblée, mais Colin fit sur plusieurs d'entre elles des commentaires informels. Et il y avait la demande imprévue des Frères maristes d'une union permanente des prêtres et des frères dans une même Société de Marie, sous l'autorité d'un même supérieur général.

Le texte de constitution approuvé par l'assemblée d'avril 1842 fut le texte le plus complet produit jusqu'à ce moment par Jean-Claude Colin. Toutefois il ne le considérait pas comme l'expression définitive de la 'règle' ; de fait, son dernier chapitre resta inachevé. Bien que ce soit loin d'être seulement de très grandes lignes générales des conditions de la vie religieuse mariste, Colin s'est abstenu d'y inclure de nombreuses prescriptions détaillées qu'il considérait comme appartenant à la règle et qu'il insérera dans les constitutions de 1872.

Colin avait refondu le corps de la législation mariste dans un cadre qui était fondamentalement celui de la Société de Jésus. Néanmoins, une comparaison, même brève, des deux documents révèle qu'il n'y a pas une simple correspondance entre le contenu des chapitres. D'une part, Colin n'a pas hésité à utiliser largement le texte de Saint Ignace, jusqu'à de longues sections empruntées mot à mot, notamment au sujet du noviciat et du supérieur général. D'autre part, il n'a pas seulement adapté ses sources, mais il a aussi introduit beaucoup d'éléments propres à la Société de Marie, et exprimé souvent ses propres intuitions. Ainsi, par exemple, au portrait ignatien d'un supérieur général évoquant d'entrée une armée à structure pyramidale d''officiers subalternes' commandés par un 'officier supérieur', il ajouta la 'sollicitude maternelle' pour les malades, la confiance en Marie, l'opposition à l'esprit du monde et à l'avidité de l'argent et des biens. Colin restait fondamentalement indépendant d'Ignace.

Maintenant ses pensées se tournaient surtout vers Rome et le voyage qu'il allait bientôt entreprendre. Il avait déjà écrit une lettre au cardinal Fransoni, préfet de la congrégation *Propaganda Fide,* pour lui révéler le désaccord grandissant entre Mgr Pompallier et les maristes en Nouvelle-Zélande et leur supérieur général à Lyon. Fransoni était soucieux de remédier au différend qui mettait en péril la Mission tout entière du Pacifique. A ce stade, il chercha à calmer les sentiments blessés, et à réconcilier les parties. Mais Colin était convaincu qu'il fallait de Rome beaucoup plus que des mots apaisants. Au cours de sa prochaine visite là-bas, il avait l'intention de soulever la question des responsabilités respectives dans une mission, de l'évêque et du supérieur, concernant les religieux de cette mission confiée à l'évêque.

Autre sujet qui occupait l'esprit de Colin depuis quelque temps : la réorganisation de la mission de l'Océanie occidentale. Au départ, c'était un seul et vaste vicariat confié au seul Mgr Pompallier. Différents plans de division du vicariat avaient déjà été suggérés. Colin avait maintenant des idées précises et des propositions concrètes à faire. Il avait rédigé un 'Mémoire sur les Iles de l'Océanie occidentale', de six pages, destiné à fixer les limites des nouvelles missions qui pourraient être établies. Il traçait les coordonnées de la zone du Pacifique-Sud tout entier formant le vicariat de l'Océanie occidentale, et identifiait les principaux groupes d'archipels : Nouvelle-Zélande ; Fidji, Tonga, Samoa, Wallis et Futuna ; Nouvelle-Calédonie, Nouvelles-Hébrides (aujourd'hui Vanuatu), Salomon ; Nouvelle-Guinée, Nouvelle-

Croix et palmes de cocotiers à Tutu

Bretagne, Nouvelle-Irlande, Iles de l'Amirauté, etc. ; Carolines enfin, distinctes des Mariannes qui dépendaient déjà de l'Eglise aux Philippines. Chaque groupe, à son tour, était décrit avec une attention particulière portée au climat, aux ressources naturelles, aux populations et au potentiel de développement. Des propositions de futurs arrangements ecclésiastiques étaient faites pour la région. La

Nouvelle-Zélande, à cause de sa taille et de sa population, et de l'intérêt déjà porté par les missionnaires protestants, nécessitait deux vicariats. Un troisième vicariat regrouperait Fidji, Tonga, Samoa, ainsi que Wallis et Futuna, Rotuma, les Gilbert (aujourd'hui Kiribati) et d'autres îles. La Nouvelle-Calédonie, les Nouvelles-Hébrides et les Salomon constitueraient le quatrième vicariat, et la Nouvelle-Guinée et les îles adjacentes le cinquième. Les îles micronésiennes des Carolines, au nord de l'équateur, pourraient être un riche terrain de mission et requérir aussi un vicaire apostolique. Ces recommandations étaient si bien fondées que, quand Colin se retira de la direction de la Société en 1854, toutes avaient été ou allaient être mises en œuvre par Rome.

Le 28 mai, Jean-Claude Colin, avec Victor Poupinel pour compagnon, quitta Lyon pour Marseille puis Rome, où ils arrivèrent le 2 juin. Beaucoup de choses avaient changé depuis sa première visite dans la Ville Eternelle neuf ans plus tôt ; le voyage de 1842 à Rome était fait dans des circonstances assez différentes de celui de 1833. A l'époque, c'était un prêtre obscur d'un petit diocèse français cherchant une reconnaissance papale pour une congrégation religieuse nouvelle qui avait laissé beaucoup sceptiques, même s'ils avaient tous été impressionnés par sa sincérité et par sa foi. Les

Portrait du Père Poupinel

recommandations qu'il avait obtenues de deux évêques étaient plutôt tièdes et il ne connaissait personne à Rome sinon le cardinal Macchi qu'il avait rencontré dix ans plus tôt à Paris. Maintenant c'était le supérieur général d'une congrégation qui avait été approuvée par le pape et qui était responsable d'une entreprise missionnaire à l'autre bout du monde. Il avait environ cent prêtres directement sous ses ordres et il était aussi considéré officieusement par beaucoup comme le supérieur général de branches de frères enseignants et de sœurs, et de divers groupes de laïcs. Depuis plusieurs années il entretenait des relations épistolaires régulières avec le cardinal Fransoni, et il était connu d'autres cardinaux, notamment Castracane, qui, tout en continuant à s'opposer au concept d'une société à plusieurs branches, était venu à apprécier et estimer Jean-Claude Colin. Maintenant les portes lui étaient grand ouvertes. Aux yeux de la curie romaine il était devenu un personnage important.

Poupinel raconte que ceux qui à Rome rencontraient le P. Colin pour la première fois étaient impressionnés par son 'air de sainteté et de simplicité', par sa modestie et son humilité ; l'un d'eux s'attendait même à ce qu'il fût canonisé un jour et que sa statue occupât la niche alors vacante à Saint-Pierre, à côté d'Alphonse de Liguori. En dépit de sa répugnance pour les visites de courtoisie, Colin rendit visite à un certain nombre de cardinaux. Bien sûr, il eut aussi des réunions d'affaires régulières avec Fransoni et Castracane. Ce dernier se força à être aimable avec lui ; il l'accueillit avec une grande attention. Un jour, alors qu'il avait dépassé Colin dans la rue sans le voir, il se pencha par la portière de sa voiture et lui fit signe de la main. Une autre fois, alors que le cardinal était lui-même à pieds, il doubla le pas pour l'atteindre et s'entretenir avec lui. Colin, bien sûr, se déplaçait partout à pieds, ce qu'il trouva très fatiguant ; jusqu'à ce qu'il fût pressé par Castracane et d'autres de suivre l'exemple de Philippe Neri et de prendre une voiture de temps à autre. Ils lui dirent qu'il n'avait pas besoin d'être plus saint que le saint, qui aimait à dire qu'à Rome 'tout est vanité, hormis aller en voiture.'

Comme Castracane venait à mieux connaître Colin, son admiration pour lui augmentait. Il dit à un autre prêtre : 'C'est le *vir simplex et rectus* (l'homme simple et droit) dont parlent les Saintes Ecritures [Job 1,1]. M. Colin est un saint. Il a compris son âge.'

La visite la plus importante qu'il avait à faire à Rome était bien sûr la visite au pape, toujours Grégoire XVI. Toutefois, Colin n'était pas pressé de demander une audience et il ne le fit que vers la fin de son séjour dans la Ville Eternelle. Il avoua à Poupinel qu'il s'en exempterait volontiers s'il le pouvait, car 'c'est aller recevoir des compliments du Saint-Père pour ce que la Société fait en faveur des missions étrangères'. Il savait maintenant qu'il ne pourrait pas traiter des affaires avec lui, et qu'il serait renvoyé aux officiers appropriés de la curie. Vers la fin juillet, il se décida enfin à demander une audience. Elle fut fixée au 3 août mais elle n'eut lieu que trois jours plus tard. Le protocole fut malmené. Le pape ne voulut pas laisser Colin lui baiser les pieds, et le supérieur général hésita à prendre la main que Grégoire lui tendait. Il apparut que le pape avait été une nouvelle fois 'bien prévenu' au sujet de son visiteur. Il lui parla des missions d'Océanie, du P. Chanel, d'un projet de mission en Afrique du sud et de la protection du gouvernement français. A la fin, Colin demanda la bénédiction apostolique pour toute la Société. 'Bien volontiers', répondit le Saint-Père, 'de grand cœur, afin qu'elle croisse toujours.' Cela avait été, après tout, bien plus qu'une simple visite de courtoisie.

Comme la fois précédente, Colin était aussi un pèlerin et un touriste à Rome. Comme la fois précédente, il consacra aussi du temps à étudier, le droit canon en particulier. Tout le monde félicitait la Société d'avoir déjà un martyr en la personne du P. Chanel. On lui expliqua comment faire pour introduire sa cause de béatification. Il écrivit en France et demanda de rassembler toutes les informations possibles sur la vie de Chanel en France, avant son départ en Océanie.

Bien sûr, la plus grande partie du temps de Colin était consacrée aux affaires pour lesquelles il était venu à Rome. Cela impliquait la préparation et la rédaction de lettres et d'autres documents, la consultation d'experts, ainsi que de nombreuses réunions. Mais, de façon caractéristique, cela impliquait aussi beaucoup de temps passé en prière. Maintenant il pensait qu'il ne devrait pas chercher à faire approuver par le pape son texte de constitutions, mais plutôt recueillir des avis et la confirmation qu'il procédait de la bonne manière. Le point difficile pour la Société de Marie allait toujours être sa structure à plusieurs branches, en particulier l'incorporation de frères enseignants comme un corps largement autonome, avec sa propre administration, ses propres maisons et ministères, sous le supérieur général des pères. Deux experts consultés lui répondirent qu'il n'y aurait aucune difficulté à obtenir du pape l'approbation des frères enseignants comme institut indépendant. L'obstacle à la reconnaissance des frères comme partie intégrante de la Société de Marie élargie était l'opposition montrée précédemment par le cardinal Castracane et son insistance sur la seule approbation possible des prêtres.

Colin alla voir Castracane. Comme prévu, celui-ci avança le décret de 1836. Le supérieur général remarqua que le cardinal ne comprenait pas suffisamment la situation en France, où les frères, sans reconnaissance de l'Etat, étaient dans une position vulnérable ; leur union avec les prêtres leur donnait une certaine protection et un statut assuré. Une fois ce point saisi, Castracane commença à chercher la manière dont les frères pourraient être approuvés sans remettre en cause le décret existant, peut-être comme tertiaires. Mais il avait toujours des réserves sur l'idée d'ensemble. Il ne doutait pas que cela pourrait marcher aussi longtemps que Colin resterait le supérieur général. Mais ensuite ? Il était moins sûr, et craignait des difficultés à venir entre prêtres et frères. Il ne lui avait certainement pas échappé que les frères étaient déjà beaucoup plus nombreux que les prêtres, et il prévoyait qu'un jour ils demanderaient leur indépendance. Colin était d'accord, spécialement si les frères rencontraient des difficultés avec les prochains supérieurs. Une sage législation pourrait éviter cela mais on ne pouvait pas légiférer sur tout, spécialement sur des choses qui pourraient ne pas se produire avant longtemps. De fait, il n'était pas trop inquiet si les branches se séparaient un jour. Ce qui était plus important, c'était le présent, alors que les frères avaient besoin d'être unis aux prêtres, sous leur supérieur. Maintenant, semble-t-il, les 'branches' étaient devenues pour lui moins une question de principe que de convenance pratique.

Bien sûr, il y eut aussi d'importantes discussions entre Colin et Castracane au sujet de l'Océanie. Pour régler le différend en Nouvelle-Zélande, Colin maintenait qu'il fallait clarifier l'autorité légitime d'un supérieur religieux sur les sujets composant le personnel d'un vicariat missionnaire. Le préfet de *Propaganda* finit par donner son accord. Il invita Colin à formuler ce qu'il pensait du contenu d'un décret de la Congrégation. Colin demanda quatre choses : établir un provincial en Nouvelle-Zélande, qui représenterait le supérieur général de la Société de Marie et qui, sans préjudices des droits et de la juridiction du vicaire apostolique, 'veillerait sur chaque missionnaire' ; en cas de besoin, pouvoir retirer et remplacer un missionnaire, après notification préliminaire à *Propaganda* ; exiger que les missionnaires ne fussent pas isolés, de façon ordinaire ; faire venir un missionnaire tous les quatre ou cinq ans pour faire un rapport à *Propaganda* et au supérieur général de la Société sur tout ce qui concerne le bien-être de la mission et de chaque missionnaire. La Congrégation donna son accord à ces dispositions, mais dans une seconde version de son décret, qui devait s'appliquer plus largement à d'autres missions que les missions maristes du Pacifique, ajouta un cinquième article selon lequel les communications entre le vicaire apostolique et Rome devaient passer par le supérieur général. Colin ne l'avait pas demandé et il prévoyait que cela pourrait mener à des difficultés ultérieures. Ce qui fut le cas. En 1846, Rome annula le décret entier.

Sujet suivant à l'ordre du jour de Colin durant sa visite à Rome en 1842 : le début de la restructuration de la mission catholique dans le sud-ouest Pacifique. Avec succès, il demanda au cardinal Fransoni d'ériger un nouveau vicariat de l'Océanie centrale comprenant Tonga, Fidji, Samoa, ainsi que Wallis et Futuna. Pour le supérieur général il était urgent d'agir pour empêcher la croissance grandissante de la présence protestante à Fidji, Tonga, et Samoa.

Début août 1842, Jean-Claude Colin avait terminé ses affaires à Rome. Il espérait pouvoir partir avec le P. Poupinel le soir du 15 août, fête de l'Assomption de Notre Dame. Mais entre-temps il contracta le paludisme – un fléau commun à Rome à cette époque. Un médecin fut appelé ; il ordonna la purge habituelle, et lui prescrivit de la quinine, plus efficace. Colin fut suffisamment impressionné par la sévérité de sa maladie pour demander à Poupinel de faire venir son confesseur si le mal empirait et lui donner ses instructions sur ce qu'il devrait faire avec ses papiers.

Finalement ils purent quitter Rome le soir du 28 août. Poupinel se demandait comment le supérieur général allait bien pouvoir supporter le voyage de retour en France. Colin arriva à Lyon complètement épuisé. Il s'exclama : 'Ah! il est temps. Je n'en peux plus.' La fièvre était revenue, et il partit se coucher.

Chapitre 9
La Société en Europe

Comme la Société grandissait, il devenait urgent d'avoir des constitutions dans une version finale approuvée par le Saint-Siège. En fin de compte, La Société en Europe

Colin n'avait pas demandé l'approbation de son texte de 1842. Les années suivantes, il continua à travailler sur la Règle. Il était aussi occupé à rédiger des constitutions pour les sœurs, pour le Tiers-Ordre, et, un temps, pour les frères maristes. Cela le conduisit à envisager de donner sa démission de supérieur général pour se consacrer totalement au travail de rédaction des constitutions. Il soumit sa démission au chapitre de 1845, qui refusa de l'accepter mais lui donna un congé du gouvernement de la Société.

1848 fut de nouveau une année de révolution en France, et plus largement en Europe. Le 24 février, à Lyon, la chute du roi Louis-Philippe donna le signal à des bandes d'ouvriers, notamment des tisserands en soie, de se précipiter dans les rues, d'entrer dans des institutions religieuses et de briser tous les métiers à tisser qu'ils trouvaient. Leur grief était que ces maisons, souvent des orphelinats ou institutions

Escalier à Puylata

similaires, employaient leurs pensionnaires comme main d'œuvre gratuite et maintenaient ainsi à un bas niveau le salaire des autres ouvriers.

Les maristes de Puylata, qui n'avaient pas de métiers à tisser la soie, s'attendaient à voir leur maison également envahie et craignaient violence et pillage. Colin apprécia la situation. Une fois de plus il garda la tête froide, comme en 1831 quand il avait maintenu l'ordre à l'école de Belley. Le soir du 26, il fit à la communauté l'exposé de ce qui s'était passé en fait à Paris et à Lyon ; c'était la meilleure façon de répondre aux rumeurs et aux spéculations, et de calmer les esprits. Jusqu'alors, la seule violence faite l'avait été aux métiers à tisser la soie, pas aux religieux eux-mêmes. Les maristes, leur dit-il, devaient s'attendre à avoir de la visite la nuit prochaine. Il leur expliqua alors comment recevoir les visiteurs. Un père et deux frères feront la garde. Il faudra conduire les 'envoyés de la République' immédiatement au réfectoire, où ils trouveront du pain, des fruits et du vin, qu'il avait donné l'ordre d'apporter de la cave en quantité. Un coup de cloche avertira tous les maristes de se tenir prêts, lampe allumée. Ils devront recevoir—'fort poliment'—ceux qui viendront inspecter leurs chambres—sans doute à la recherche de métiers à tisser. On lui suggéra d'enlever une statue bien visible de Notre Dame : 'Je m'en garderai bien, et que dirait la sainte Vierge ? C'est elle qui est notre gardienne.' Et de plus, sa vue adoucira ceux qui viendront.

La visite attendue arriva. Des ouvriers armés enrôlés dans la Garde Nationale furent reçus par Colin et un compagnon ; ils mangèrent et burent tout ce qu'ils voulaient, demandèrent un certificat de bonne conduite et s'en allèrent. Ils étaient manifestement contents de la réception des maristes et ils revinrent neuf fois dans les deux jours qui suivirent. Finalement, le 28, la maison fut officiellement chargée de nourrir les révolutionnaires, et un garde fut posté à la porte pour prévenir toutes incursions. Résultat : les maristes purent continuer leurs tâches normales sans avoir besoin de se cacher, comme d'autres prêtres religieux le firent.

La crise immédiate avait été surmontée. Malgré sa préférence personnelle pour la vieille monarchie des Bourbons, Colin croyait que lui et les maristes pouvaient s'entendre même avec une république. Mais il prit conscience qu'un grand changement allait se produire en France, qui ne serait pas sans grandes conséquences pour l'Eglise et pour la Société de Marie. Le 11 mars 1848, le commissaire provisoire de la république à Lyon proclama la dissolution de toutes les congrégations religieuses non autorisées, dont les maristes faisaient partie. Ce décret ne fut pas appliqué mais quatre jours plus tard, Colin craignant la dispersion forcée des religieux et la confiscation de leurs biens, s'arrangea pour louer Puylata à des amis, avec un bail pour trois ans, et muta ailleurs la plus grande partie des maristes qui étaient là ou dans d'autres grosses communautés (repérables, donc). Il dit à ceux qui étaient à Paris de se tenir prêts à quitter la capitale, si nécessaire. Il répéta aussi avec insistance que les maristes ne devaient pas attirer une attention hostile sur eux, mais être littéralement 'inconnus et cachés en ce monde'. Au lieu de s'opposer ouvertement à des idées 'fausses' comme le communisme qui commençait à prévaloir, les maristes devraient travailler au salut de ceux qui les professent.

En l'occurrence, l'ordre fut bientôt restauré, et une Seconde République conservatrice installée, qui se transforma en Second Empire sous Napoléon III. Même ainsi, la révolution de 1848 avait bouleversé plus d'un projet, comme l'organisation d'un 'second noviciat' pour ceux qui avaient déjà quatre ou cinq ans de ministère.

Les remarques de Colin trahissent parfois un pessimisme croissant sur le temps dans lequel vivait la Société. Il n'a jamais proclamé la fin imminente du monde mais il semble qu'en privé il croyait qu'elle pouvait être proche. Mais ce n'était pas une cause de peur ou de consternation puisque Marie avait promis d'être le soutien de l'Eglise à la fin des temps. En fait, le temps était venu pour sa Société de jouer sa partition : 'Marie se servira de nous, ses fils'. Il insistait toujours davantage sur le besoin de la foi et de la prière qui 'seules peuvent convaincre les esprits, éclairer les intelligences et toucher les cœurs'. La Société de Marie était un 'corps avant tout actif' mais elle ne réalisera rien 'si nous n'unissons pas en nous l'homme d'oraison à l'homme d'action'.

En dépit de sa préoccupation constante pour l'Océanie, Colin présidait aussi à une période de croissance de la Société de Marie en France. La prédication continuait d'être un apostolat majeur. Le travail des missions paroissiales se poursuivait. D'autres formes de prédication s'y ajoutaient, telles que des séries de sermons et d'instructions pour l'avent, le carême ou Corpus Christi. La prédication de retraites aux prêtres, aux séminaristes ou aux religieux devenait une activité de plus en plus importante. En 1838, une nouvelle œuvre émergea quand les maristes furent invités à prendre en charge le centre de pèlerinage de Notre-Dame de Verdelais, près de Bordeaux (ce qui donna aussi l'occasion de sortir pour la première fois des diocèses de Lyon et de Belley). En 1846 et en 1847 Colin accepta deux autres centres de pèlerinage : Notre-Dame-des-Grâces, à Rochefort-du-Gard dans le sud de la France, et Notre-Dame de Bon-Encontre, près d'Agen, au sud-est de Bordeaux. Durant la 'haute saison' de ces sanctuaires, les maristes étaient occupés par les besoins spirituels et temporels des pèlerins. Entre deux hautes saisons, ils étaient libres d'organiser des missions paroissiales. A Verdelais et à Agen des paroisses étaient attachées

Eglise de Verdelais et sa flèche

aux sanctuaires. Néanmoins le P. Colin était résolument opposé à l'acceptation régulière de paroisses par les maristes car, selon lui, elles étaient contraires à leur vocation missionnaire.

De plus en plus, Colin promouvait l'éducation comme œuvre majeure de la Société de Marie. En 1845, les maristes avaient fini par quitter le collège-séminaire de Belley. Mais, la même année, ils ouvrirent un nouveau collège à Valbenoite (Loire), dans les bâtiments d'une ancienne abbaye bénédictine. En fait, les maristes y étaient depuis 1831, comme vicaires du curé qui avait acheté le site et qui avait l'intention de le laisser à la Société. Quand il mourut en 1844, Colin décida d'y ouvrir un pensionnat, qui eut bientôt toutes les classes secondaires et quatre-vingt-dix élèves environ. Toutefois une contestation survint sur l'état dans lequel la propriété avait été laissée, et la Société perdit le procès. Le supérieur général décida alors d'accepter l'invitation de la municipalité de Saint-Chamond, proche de l'Hermitage, à reprendre le collège communal dans lequel il transféra l'établissement de Valbenoite. Semblable invitation vit l'arrivée des maristes dans la petite ville de Langogne (Lozère), où ils relevèrent le collège décadent avant de le rendre au clergé diocésain.

Toulon (Var) était - et est toujours - une base navale française importante. En 1845, les maristes avaient ouvert une résidence pour les missionnaires à La Seyne-sur-Mer, tout proche. L'idée germa d'y installer un pensionnat. Mais il fallut attendre 1849 pour avoir l'autorisation d'ouvrir l'école. Elle commença avec un tout petit nombre d'élèves, mais graduellement ce nombre augmenta ; en 1854, ils étaient 140, principalement des fils d'officiers de marine.

Les deux derniers collèges ouverts durant le généralat du P. Colin furent Brioude (Haute-Loire) en 1853-1854, et Montluçon (Allier) également en 1853.

Une autre œuvre importante d'éducation entreprise par la Société au cours du généralat fut la fourniture de personnel aux grands séminaires diocésains où les candidats clercs étudiaient la théologie et se préparaient au sacerdoce. Le premier séminaire fut celui de Moulins (Allier, en 1847), puis ceux de Digne (Alpes-de-Haute-Provence, en 1849) et de Nevers (Nièvre, en 1852). Les maristes prirent aussi la direction du petit séminaire de Digne en 1853.

Naturellement, à cette étape de son histoire, la plupart de ceux qui étaient entrés dans la Société de Marie étaient des citoyens français. Toutefois, il est intéressant de noter que, même alors, sa composition commençait à se diversifier, avec pas moins de dix-neuf natifs de Savoie qui, à l'époque, n'étaient pas des nationaux français mais des citoyens du royaume de Piémont-Sardaigne. Il y avait aussi une poignée de représentants d'autres pays européens.

Tout au long de son généralat, des suggestions et des offres furent adressées au P. Colin pour établir une présence mariste soit en Angleterre, soit en Irlande. L'intérêt premier, bien sûr, était la possibilité d'apprendre l'anglais, mais aussi de recruter du personnel anglophone pour les missions du Pacifique qui comprenaient aussi des territoires anglais et français. Mais Colin ne pensa pas que les ressources limitées de la Société lui permettaient d'accepter de telles offres.

Bâtiment et église adjacente Sainte-Anne

Néanmoins, en 1850, la Société de Marie fit sa première fondation européenne hors de France. Ce fut à Londres, une ville déjà familière à beaucoup de maristes qui y transitaient en partance pour l'Océanie, ou au retour. A la fin mars de cette année, Mgr Nicholas Wiseman, vicaire apostolique du district de Londres et bientôt, avec la restauration de la hiérarchie catholique en Angleterre et au pays de Galles, cardinal-archevêque de Westminster, interrogea les maristes sur la possibilité d'ouvrir une maison à Spitalfields, dans l'East End de Londres, pour travailler parmi les immigrants irlandais qui arrivaient de plus en plus nombreux après la récente famine, et dont les besoins surchargeaient l'Eglise anglaise. Ils étaient pris en charge jusqu'alors par Joseph Quiblier, que Colin avait connu à Rome, quand il était supérieur des Sulpiciens à Montréal, et c'est sans doute lui qui avait suggéré les maristes à Wiseman et qui avait servi d'intermédiaire.

Sans tarder, Quiblier en personne vint à Puylata ; Colin accepta d'envoyer trois prêtres et deux frères. Il n'y avait pas d'église catholique ni de presbytère à Spitalfields. Les maristes auraient à les construire eux-mêmes. Colin demanda de l'aide à l'Association pour la Propagation de la foi. Le fruit des négociations, ce fut une présence mariste missionnaire dans l'East End de Londres, qui s'est occupée de vagues successives d'immigrants, jusqu'à une époque récente.

Chapitre 10
L'avenir de la Société

Colin pensait aussi au profil futur de la Société. De plus en plus il sentait que l'opposition constante de Rome à l'approbation d'une Société à plusieurs branches pouvait signifier, après tout, que ce n'était pas selon la volonté de Dieu. Il commença à préparer les frères maristes à la séparation d'avec les pères. Un moment-clé de ce développement fut l'approbation des frères par l'Etat comme congrégation enseignante en 1852, ce qui signifiait qu'ils n'avaient plus besoin du 'parapluie' que leur offraient les pères. En 1854, année de la démission de Colin comme supérieur général, les frères étaient pleinement indépendants.

Si la séparation des frères s'est faite sans douleurs, celle des sœurs fut tout autre. En un mot, Colin croyait que les sœurs maristes devaient, elles aussi, devenir une congrégation indépendante de droit diocésain en attendant l'approbation pontificale. C'était une position qui pouvait se défendre. Moins facile à comprendre, par contre, était son insistance pour qu'elles cessent de s'appeler elles-mêmes sœurs maristes et adoptent le nom de 'Religieuses du Saint Nom de Marie'. Jeanne-Marie Chavoin, qui n'était plus supérieure générale, soutenait avec éloquence que, quel que fût leur statut canonique, c'était la volonté de Dieu qu'elles restent une branche de la Société. Beaucoup d'autres facteurs compliquaient la situation, dont l'accession dans la congrégation à des postes de responsabilité d'une nouvelle génération de sœurs dont les idées étaient différentes de celles de la fondatrice. Finalement Colin perdit patience avec Jeanne-Marie et coupa, un temps, les relations. Ce fut une triste fin à une longue et, un temps, une profonde amitié. En fin de compte, les sœurs maristes gardèrent leur nom, adoptèrent les constitutions écrites par Colin et devinrent pour finir une congrégation de droit pontifical.

Jusqu'à présent il a été peu question de la troisième branche de la Société telle que prévue initialement, celle des laïcs. En fait, Colin ne s'y est directement impliqué qu'à l'occasion seulement. Vers la fin de 1845, la nomination du P. Pierre-Julien Eymard par Colin comme directeur du Tiers-Ordre de Marie fut un moment important de l'histoire de la branche laïque. La direction donnée par Eymard fut décisive, à la fois pour la croissance du nombre de tertiaires et la formation de groupes particuliers s'adressant à différentes catégories de personnes, ainsi que pour l'orientation qu'il leur donna. Le 8 décembre 1846, il reçut dans le Tiers-Ordre de Marie son plus illustre membre, Jean-Marie Vianney, le saint curé d'Ars. La règle qu'il composa en 1847 suivait la tradition classique des 'tiers-ordres', comme celle des Franciscains, des Dominicains et des Carmélites, de laïcs qui n'étaient pas seulement étroitement associés aux religieux, mais qui vivaient aussi dans le monde un genre de vie religieuse assouplie, avec un fort accent sur la prière et la vie intérieure.

Cette conception de la branche laïque contrastait avec la vision très différente de la 'Confraternité des croyants des deux sexes qui vivent dans le monde' que Colin avait esquissée dans le *Summarium* de 1833. Elle était ouverte potentiellement à tous les catholiques et prescrivait seulement quelques prières et exercices pieux. Néanmoins – au moins à ce stade – Colin ne protesta pas contre la règle d'Eymard. Peut-être laissait-il tout simplement l'affaire à la personne qu'il avait nommée ; de toute façon, en dépit de ses intentions déclarées, il n'avait pas encore écrit la règle du Tiers-Ordre. Il est possible aussi que la prudence et l'expérience tenaient une part dans ce changement de direction. L'idée de 1833—une organisation ouverte à tous avec une mission universelle, qui serait soumise au supérieur général mariste—n'était pas acceptable pour le cardinal Castracane et la curie romaine qui craignaient qu'elle fût perçue comme subversive par les dirigeants civils. Les autorités ecclésiales et publiques seraient beaucoup plus à l'aise avec un tiers-ordre traditionnel aux contours familiers. L'idée initiale de Colin sur le laïcat - comme tant d'autres concernant la Société - devra attendre son heure.

Concernant les œuvres de la Société, Colin devenait de plus en plus pessimiste sur l'avenir des maristes dans le Pacifique. La situation en Nouvelle-Zélande avait été résolue avec la création de deux diocèses ; l'un à Auckland avec Mgr Pompallier, tandis que les maristes s'étaient retirés dans l'autre à Wellington sous Mgr Philippe Viard. La question des relations entre les supérieurs ecclésiastiques et religieux dans les vicariats apostoliques a été finalement réglée en 1851, mais dans un sens totalement opposé aux idées de Colin : dorénavant, dans un territoire de mission confié à une congrégation ou un ordre religieux, le chef de mission devait être regardé également comme le supérieur religieux *ex officio*. L'expérience des difficultés rencontrées par Colin avec les évêques des pays de mission le faisait douter de la pertinence même pour des religieux de fournir en personnel un vicariat apostolique.

De toute façon, il semble que Colin ait estimé trop élevé le coût humain de l'engagement mariste en Océanie. Sur les missionnaires qu'il avait envoyés là-bas, vingt et un étaient décédés de mort violente ou de maladies avant 1854. Il était temps de marquer au moins une pause et de faire le point. Après 1849 il n'envoya plus de missionnaires en Océanie, mais il continua à soutenir ceux qui y étaient. Les envois en mission seront repris par son successeur.

En même temps qu'il repensait la mission mariste en Océanie, le P. Colin engageait la Société de façon décisive dans l'éducation qu'il considérait comme un 'territoire de mission' à part égale. Comme nous l'avons vu, il avait ouvert de nouvelles communautés à la fois dans des écoles existantes où la Société avait été demandée, et dans de nouveaux endroits. La retraite annuelle de 1848 fut suivie d'une semaine d'étude sur l'éducation, ce qui attestait de l'importance grandissante de ce ministère dans la branche des prêtres. L'année suivante, il convoqua une réunion des supérieurs des établissements scolaires pour préparer un plan d'études commun pour les collèges maristes.

Les années suivant 1848 virent aussi l'émergence d'une nouvelle aventure mariste. En 1841, alors qu'il attendait dans la cour du collège-séminaire de Belley une voiture pour le ramener à Lyon, Colin avait révélé à ses compagnons qu'il pensait à une branche contemplative. L'idée semble être venue de certains tertiaires laïcs de Lyon qui voulaient

Bâtiment au milieu de arbres à Marcellange

mener une vie de prière et de recueillement. Colin y était favorable ; il aurait même aimé une telle vie. Il en avait parlé à l'évêque de Belley, qui avait donné son accord. Une propriété était disponible. Colin était sous pression pour établir un genre de communauté contemplative qui vivrait sous une règle moins exigeante que celle des trappistes ou des chartreux. Une nouvelle communauté fut établie à Marcellange (Allier) en juin 1842. Deux ans plus tard, elle était fermée mais Colin n'abandonna pas l'idée.

Vieille photo du bâtiment et de la colline, La Neylière

En1850, le P. Colin trouva une propriété plus convenable, appelée 'La Neylière', dans les Monts du Lyonnais. Cette maison allait beaucoup l'occuper—en temps et en attention—dans les mois et années à venir. Entre temps, le projet avait un peu évolué, passant d'une 'Trappe mitigée', essentiellement pour des laïcs, à un lieu dans lequel les pères maristes seraient aussi impliqués. Un autre changement important vint de l'extérieur de la Société. L'adoration eucharistique était depuis longtemps une dévotion centrale dans l'Eglise catholique. A Paris et ailleurs, un mouvement prenait forme pour organiser l'adoration perpétuelle ; Antoine Bertholon, un père mariste, y était très impliqué. Mère Marie-Thérèse (Théodelinde) Dubouché, fondatrice des Sœurs de l'Adoration Réparatrice, le prit comme directeur spirituel. D'autres maristes eurent l'occasion de la rencontrer.

Pendant ce temps, à Lyon, lors de la fête de Corpus Christi 1845, Pierre-Julien Eymard avait ressenti un attrait très fort pour faire de Jésus Eucharistie le centre de son ministère sacerdotal. En janvier 1849, alors qu'il était à Paris, il rencontra le groupe eucharistique. Il rentra à Lyon avec l'idée de promouvoir la dévotion eucharistique parmi les maristes. La même année, le cardinal de Bonald avait demandé aux pères maristes de s'occuper de la dévotion de l'adoration nocturne dans la ville. En 1849 aussi, Mère Marie-Thérèse avait eu une extase dans laquelle elle vit des prêtres en adoration et comprit que c'étaient des maristes.

A la retraite de septembre 1850, Colin parla de la nouvelle propriété acquise à La Neylière, 'dans les intérêts de la Société et pour d'autres motifs très puissants concernant la gloire de Dieu et le bien des âmes'. Il donna quelques détails sur le but de la maison et les espoirs qu'il mettait en elle, et s'exclama : 'Ah, si on pouvait mettre dans cette maison l'esprit de saint François de Sales à la Visitation !'.

En mai 1852, après des transformations importantes de la maison, Colin put y installer une communauté. Au cours de la retraite d'ouverture, il parla plusieurs fois de la nouvelle œuvre, donnant des détails sur la règle à observer. Maintenant, il ne pensait pas seulement à une simple maison, mais à une 'œuvre' plus grande, et même à une 'nouvelle branche' avec plusieurs maisons sous l'autorité du supérieur général.

Colin présenta ensuite les deux buts qu'il souhaitait voir la maison poursuivre : d'abord, offrir un 'refuge' aux nombreuses âmes pour qui le monde était plein de dangers et qui voulaient se donner sincèrement à Dieu – pour cette raison, elle serait 'probablement' placée sous le patronage de Notre Dame de Pitié, ou de Compassion ; ensuite, offrir aux membres actifs de la Société de Marie une maison de retraite où ils pourraient renouveler leur zèle et se préparer à la mort à la fin de leur vie active. A ce stade, semble-t-il, l'adoration

Statue et fenêtres, à La Neylière

eucharistique serait une part importante de la vie de La Neylière, mais pas le seul ni le principal but.

Le 24 juillet 1853, le P. Colin bénit la chapelle de Notre Dame de Compassion, à La Neylière. A la retraite annuelle de cette année-là, il parla longuement de la maison. Il désirait maintenant qu'elle fût une 'maison de prière où il souhaitait voir établir l'adoration perpétuelle'. Ce n'était pas le seul changement dans sa pensée. Il envisageait aussi l'heure où une partie de la Société serait occupée à prêcher, à courir après les pécheurs pour les convertir, tandis que l'autre aurait continuellement 'les bras levés vers le ciel' pour attirer sur les missionnaires les grâces célestes. Et ce ne seront pas ceux qui courront qui seront le plus missionnaires, mais ce seront ceux qui prieront.

Colin partagea avec Dubouché ses espoirs et ses projets sur l'œuvre eucharistique mariste et s'intéressa à la sienne. Vers la fin de 1853, il pouvait envisager que 'les prêtres qui, en France, s'occupent de l'œuvre de l'adoration du Saint Sacrement' puissent un jour 'former une corporation uniquement occupée à cela, presque sur le même modèle que les sœurs réparatrices.' Néanmoins, pour le moment, il ne regardait pas au-delà de La Neylière. Il semblerait que sa vision de l'œuvre eucharistique était très large, englobant les différentes formes sous lesquelles elle se manifestait en France parmi les prêtres, les religieuses et les laïcs, et en lesquelles il voyait 'plusieurs branches se répandant de tous côtés', sans qu'une branche dépendît d'une autre. Son idée, dit-il à Dubouché, était d''encourager toutes ces œuvres qui tendent au même but : réparer les outrages faits à Notre Seigneur', et il lui conseilla de suivre la même ligne. C'est clair qu'il était bien loin de vouloir se placer lui-même à la tête de cette œuvre multiforme, et de placer ses différentes 'branches' sous l'égide de la Société de Marie. En fait, les maristes devaient rester 'inconnus', et ils ne voulaient pas que son nom ou le sien fussent prononcés.

Au début de l'année 1854 le projet eucharistique mariste était toujours 'en cours'. Colin – plus prudent que jamais – refusait d''aller trop vite' et se méfiait de se laisser entraîner dans des schémas grandioses. En janvier, et de nouveau en mars (à deux reprises), il eut l'occasion d'écrire au P. Eymard, mais il ne fit aucune mention de La Neylière ou de l'œuvre eucharistique. L'évolution de leurs idées respectives semble avoir été un cas de développement parallèle. Quoiqu'il en soit, Colin disait à Dubouché que 'La Neylière est toujours mon œuvre favorite. Je ne désire rien de plus que de terminer mes jours au pied des saints autels'. Et il espérait que Dieu lui accorderait bientôt la 'liberté'.

Chapitre 11
'Père fondateur'

Depuis 1851 Jean-Claude Colin préparait sa démission. Déjà, depuis son élection comme supérieur général le 24 septembre 1836, il avait attendu le moment où sa fonction pourrait être confiée à d'autres mains et il avait tenté deux fois de démissionner, en 1841 et en 1845. A ces deux occasions ses confrères ne lui avaient pas permis de le faire. Nul doute qu'ils avaient une opinion de sa capacité de les gouverner plus haute que la sienne. Il avait toujours souffert des effets physiques et émotionnels du stress. Maintenant il sentait ses forces décliner. De plus, il devait terminer le travail sur les constitutions. Cette fois, ses confrères étaient enclins à accepter son propre jugement sur ses capacités de continuer ; il semble qu'ils aient senti qu'était venu le temps d'un changement à la tête de la Société. Certains, toutefois, craignaient que le renoncement de Colin à ses fonctions conduisît à une division dans la Société. On se demandait aussi si Colin, une fois qu'il ne serait plus supérieur général, aurait encore l'autorité de donner à la Société ses constitutions D'autre part, Jean-Claude croyait que son autorité venait de plus haut et qu'elle était indépendante d'un poste choisi.

Avant de pouvoir démissionner, Colin dut préparer le terrain légal. La Société de Marie manquait d'une procédure, acceptée et approuvée, pour élire le supérieur général, qui serait, bien sûr, fixée dans ses constitutions. Aussi Colin dut-il imaginer un processus électoral formellement accepté par les membres de la Société et approuvé par Rome. Enfin, tout était prêt. A un chapitre réuni à Lyon le 5 mai 1854, Jean-Claude Colin quitta les fonctions du supérieur général de la Société de Marie.

La Société que Colin remettait à son successeur comptait 221 prêtres et 33 frères en Europe, répartis en deux provinces. La plus nombreuse, Lyon, comprenait—outre la maison-mère de Puylata et la nouvelle maison de La Neylière - un noviciat à Lyon, un scolasticat à Belley, un troisième noviciat-scolasticat, cinq collèges (Brioude, Langogne, Montluçon, Saint-Chamond et La Seyn), trois grands séminaires diocésains (Digne, Moulins, Nevers) et un petit séminaire (Digne), quatre résidences missionnaires (Moulins, Riom, Rochefort, Toulon), trois aumôneries de frères maristes (l'Hermitage compris) et une aumônerie de sœurs maristes.

La province de Paris était plus petite. Ses novices et ses scolastiques étaient formés dans la province de Lyon, et elle n'avait à l'époque aucun collège. Il y avait cinq grosses communautés à Paris, Bon-Encontre (missions), Valenciennes (missions), Verdelais (sanctuaire marial, paroisse, missions) et Londres.

Des missionnaires envoyés par Colin dans le Pacifique, cinquante-trois (quarante-quatre prêtres et neuf frères) étaient encore en Océanie. Sur les soixante-huit qui n'y étaient plus, vingt et un étaient décédés en mission, certains de mort violente, d'autres étaient retournés en Europe ou avaient quitté la Société. En Nouvelle-Zélande, les maristes avaient quitté les quatorze missions fondées dans ce qui est maintenant le diocèse d'Auckland, et ils en avaient fondé quatre dans le nouveau diocèse de Wellington. En Océanie centrale, il y avait quatre missions à Futuna et Wallis, trois à Fidji, trois à Samoa et deux à Tonga. En Nouvelle-Calédonie il y avait quatre missions. Enfin, il y avait une procure à Sydney, en Nouvelle-Galles du Sud.

Colin avait aussi refusé beaucoup d'invitations en France et ailleurs, car les ressources de la Société, pensait-il, ne lui permettaient pas de les accepter. Pour des raisons similaires, il n'avait pas accepté d'autres missions que l'Océanie ; pendant longtemps il avait hésité avec une mission en Afrique australe, mais finalement il l'avait refusée.

L'exploit de Colin est d'avoir pris une entreprise religieuse qu'il n'avait pas démarrée et de l'avoir solidement établie. Quand il était devenu supérieur central en 1836, on pouvait douter de la survie de la Société de Marie. Les vingt-quatre années suivantes, il a guidé—non sans difficultés ni contradictions—les groupes débutants de prêtres, frères et sœurs qui se considéraient eux-mêmes comme des branches d'un même arbre, en marche vers la maturité et la reconnaissance, et éventuellement vers l'indépendance en tant que congrégations religieuses. Pour cette raison, il méritait éminemment le titre de 'Père fondateur' qui lui fut bientôt conféré.

Le 10 mai, le chapitre général choisit Julien Favre comme second supérieur général de la Société de Marie. Agé de quarante et un ans, il était originaire de Hotonnes (Ain) ; en 1836, il avait été ordonné prêtre du diocèse de Belley. Peu après, il était entré dans la Société de Marie nouvellement reconnue, et avait commencé à enseigner la théologie à la Capucinière. Il était resté à ce poste jusqu'à 1852, quand Colin l'avait nommé provincial de Lyon et de ce fait numéro deux dans la hiérarchie mariste. Comme Colin se préparait maintenant à partir, Favre pouvait être considéré comme son successeur désigné. Quoiqu'il en fût, le chapitre l'élut au premier tour de scrutin.

Un commentaire attribué au P. Maîtrepierre, après que Julien Favre eût succédé à Jean-Claude Colin comme supérieur général de la Société de Marie, peut être pris comme un résumé – au risque de la caricature – du contraste entre les deux hommes : ' Nous avions un fondateur ; maintenant nous avons un organisateur.' Une telle remarque peut être prise, bien sûr, de plusieurs façons. Elle peut exprimer le regret de la fin du temps de l'inspiration et de l'innovation ; elle peut aussi exprimer la satisfaction du passage à la normalité et à la prévisibilité. Maîtrepierre, qui avait été un temps associé de près à Colin comme son bras droit, réalisa qu'un changement profond avait lieu. Peut-être y avait-il une pointe de nostalgie de ce qui s'était passé. Néanmoins il y avait peu de doute que, globalement, lui et probablement beaucoup de maristes, aient été satisfaits et même soulagés de s'installer dans une phase nouvelle de consolidation et de croissance régulière, avec un homme de méthode et d'ordre, bref, un 'organisateur'.

Dans beaucoup de congrégations et d'ordres religieux – en fait dans beaucoup d'autres organisations – la transition de la personne fondatrice et de sa génération à la suivante, est notablement délicate car les nouveaux-arrivants veulent aller de l'avant, parfois avec des manières s'éloignant plus ou moins nettement des précédentes. Pas étonnant donc si le passage de Colin à Favre ne s'est pas fait sans difficultés, et a donné lieu à des blessures et à des incompréhensions des deux côtés. Si la dispute qui s'en suivit ne dépassa pas la Société et fut résolu sans schisme ni scandale, nous le devons en grande partie à la modération montrée par les deux hommes, à leur commun attachement à la Société et à leur désir partagé de faire passer les intérêts de celle-là avant des considérations personnelles.

Colin avait quitté ses fonctions sans résoudre la question de savoir si 'les Pères maristes du Saint Sacrement' (comme il les appelait souvent lui-même) devaient devenir une œuvre externe à la Société de Marie, ou être une branche interne, et, si c'était le cas, quelle serait sa relation précise avec son tronc. C'étaient des questions qui inquiétaient les membres de la Société. En cessant d'être supérieur général, Colin avait renoncé à son droit de les régler. Bientôt une crise éclata à propos de l'implication des maristes, spécialement de Colin lui-même, dans l'œuvre eucharistique. Le P. Favre intervint et signifia son 'opposition formelle' à l'entreprise de La Neylière. Le P. Colin comprit que l'œuvre eucharistique devait être juridiquement séparée du reste de la Société de Marie, sans penser pour autant, semble-t-il, que cela l'empêcherait de ne plus rien à voir avec elle. En août 1855, Favre décida qu'il était temps pour lui d'intervenir explicitement. Nous n'avons pas de compte-rendu direct de ce qui s'est passé entre les deux hommes. Le résultat fut que, en obéissance à son successeur, Colin renonça à son projet de communauté contemplative eucharistique à La Neylière, qui lui tenait tant à cœur.

Néanmoins il continua à s'intéresser et à soutenir d'autres personnes qui, à l'intérieur ou à l'extérieur de la Société, étaient impliquées dans des projets eucharistiques. L'un d'eux était le P. Pierre-Julien Eymard, dont les affaires touchaient à l'heure décisive. Au cours de plusieurs réunions avec lui, Favre s'était exprimé clairement. Il avait de l'estime pour l'œuvre eucharistique en elle-même, mais il la voyait comme quelque chose d'extérieur à la Société. Il estimait aussi beaucoup

Bureau et chaise, à La Neylière

Eymard et souhaitait le garder dans la Société. Pour cette raison, il voulait qu'il se retirât de l'œuvre eucharistique. Eymard, toutefois, croyait que sa mission eucharistique était prioritaire. Le 14 mai 1856, il fut dispensé de ses vœux dans la Société de Marie et il s'en alla à Paris commencer la Société du Saint Sacrement. Après avoir été accepté par l'archevêque de Paris, il écrivit à Favre. Il lui demanda de lui garder son amitié, et en toute correspondance avec Rome, de parler seulement de 'l'œuvre', et non pas de sa propre 'indignité'. Favre l'assura que 'la séparation qui s'est opérée entre nous ne nous empêchera pas de nous aimer toujours dans les cœurs de Jésus et de Marie.' Il mit les maristes au courant du départ d'Eymard : il parla de sa grande générosité et pria pour qu'il puisse 'faire connaître, aimer et glorifier notre Seigneur dans le sacrement de son amour—et nous nous réjouirons de tout notre cœur'.

Une des raisons pour lesquelles Colin avait donné sa démission de supérieur général, c'était la rédaction des constitutions de la Société de Marie. Il vint à Belley en novembre 1855 et commença à travailler sur celles des sœurs, et sur le règlement des frères coadjuteurs. Il ne savait pas qu'à ce moment-là Favre avait commencé à écrire la 'Règle fondamentale' des prêtres. Ce fut le début d'une crise prolongée, qui prit plus tard des proportions telles qu'elle menaça l'unité de la Société de Marie.

Favre dit plus tard à Colin qu'il avait composé sa règle 'plutôt malgré moi, cédant aux demandes pressantes du conseil et d'un très grand nombre de mes confrères.' Cette explication ne procédait pas simplement de la volonté de s'excuser, ou de déplacer la responsabilité sur les autres. La nouvelle administration sentait le besoin d'une règle faisant autorité pour le gouvernement des maisons et des œuvres maristes. Favre ne pouvait pas, comme Colin, assurer les maristes que tel ou tel point était 'dans la règle' ou 'serait dans la règle'. Les candidats potentiels à la Société, qui demandaient à voir les constitutions, étaient 'étonnés et même déçus' d'apprendre qu'il n'y avait pas encore de règles définitivement écrites. De fait, ils étaient invités à s'engager à quelque chose qui était non définie. Pour toutes ces raisons, on n'a pas de mal à voir pourquoi le conseil de Favre le poussait à fournir à la Société—non pas des constitutions définitives qu'ils espéraient toujours recevoir de Colin—mais une série de règles de base provisoires faisant autorité, qui guideraient son gouvernement interne et seraient remises aux candidats et aux novices. Favre et un assistant travaillèrent rapidement et efficacement. Le 6 janvier 1856, ils produisirent un texte, les *Regulae fundamentales Societatis Mariae ex illius constitutionibus excerptae*, que Favre publia le 2 février suivant. Le titre exprime l'intention de compiler seulement les 'règles fondamentales' 'extraites' des constitutions de la Société. Pour les non-initiés, elles ont dû ressembler à un simple vademecum tiré d'un texte présumé existant et approuvé.

La vraie question n'est pas de savoir pourquoi Favre et ses conseillers ont produit un tel texte—la logique est claire—mais pourquoi ils ont agi sans en parler à Colin. Mieux encore, pourquoi le nouveau supérieur général n'a pas simplement offert à Colin de l'aider à terminer le travail sur les constitutions des prêtres ? S'il avait agi ainsi, n'aurait-il pas évité à lui-même et à la Société de Marie beaucoup d'ennuis, à la fois à moyen et à long termes ? Il semble que la décision de Favre de ne pas approcher Colin—une décision certainement prise avec l'avis de ses conseillers les plus proches, et peut-être à leur instigation—était motivée par l'expérience et l'observation de la difficulté croissante de travailler avec lui. Mieux valait faire face à sa colère après coup que de s'engager dans de probables arrangements prolongés, sans promesse de résultats fructueux.

Quand en février 1856 on remit à Colin un exemplaire des 'Règles fondamentales' de Favre, il n'eut pas besoin d'aller plus loin que la première page pour voir comment, en dépit de la proclamation qu'elles étaient 'extraites des constitutions', le nouveau supérieur général était en fait—peut-être sans le réaliser pleinement—en train d'opérer quelques ruptures radicales. Etait-ce encore la même Société ?

Colin a-t-il jamais pensé alors suivre Eymard avec qui il avait eu de longues conversations à Lyon en mars 1856 ? On l'a affirmé plus tard. Si oui, il a dû être enclin à penser que la nouvelle direction que le P. Favre semblait donner à la Société de Marie lui donnait raison. S'il ne reconnaissait plus en elle la société pour laquelle il avait donné sa vie, ne valait-il pas mieux trancher net et rejoindre la nouvelle société qu'il avait appelée la 'porte gauche' de son cœur ? En fin de compte, nous le savons, il est resté dans la Société qui était la 'porte droite' de son cœur.

En avril 1856, Favre soumit ses 'Règles fondamentales' à la Congrégation romaine pour les Evêques et Réguliers. La congrégation les confia à un consulteur, qui fit un certain nombre de commentaires. On notait que, puisque les constitutions de la Société de Marie n'avaient jamais été approuvées, il était inapproprié de déclarer dans le titre que ces règles fondamentales étaient 'extraites des constitutions' (de la Société). Favre se mit à réviser le texte, qui serait désormais simplement appelé 'Règles fondamentales de la Société de Marie'.

Le P. Colin pensa qu'il avait été contourné. La dizaine d'années qui suivirent furent largement des années de retrait et de silence. Il ne prit aucune part aux affaires de la Société et ne participa à aucun chapitre ni à aucune retraite commune. Son seul engagement public fut pour les sœurs maristes : il continua à les accompagner et à travailler sur leurs constitutions. Peu à peu il prenait de l'âge. Des problèmes de santé se faisaient plus fréquents et l'affaiblissaient progressivement. Il continua encore à voyager dans des endroits familiers, mais tendit à passer de plus en plus de temps à La Neylière. Là, sa vie adopta un mode régulier qu'il nous est possible d'observer à travers les yeux de ses compagnons et visiteurs. Il avait plus de temps maintenant pour ses relations, spécialement ses frères et sœurs encore en vie, un neveu et deux nièces qui étaient maristes. Il continua à correspondre aussi avec Mère Marie-Thérèse Dubouché, jusqu'à sa mort, en août 1863.

Entre temps, le 13 juillet 1856, Jean-Claude souffrit la perte de son frère Pierre, dont la vie avait été si liée à la sienne. Il se trouvait avec lui à Puylata quand il est mort. En quelque sorte, Pierre Colin a nécessairement vécu dans l'ombre de son jeune frère. Il était néanmoins une figure importante et très aimée dans la Société, où il était connu sous le titre de 'Père directeur', porté depuis l'époque où il avait été directeur spirituel au collège-séminaire de Belley. Au début, à Cerdon, avec Jean-Claude, il avait joué un rôle significatif dans les efforts faits pour établir la Société. Comme curé, au moins formellement, il avait pris les devants pour plusieurs actes officiels. On peut le considérer comme le co-fondateur des sœurs maristes car c'est lui qui avait connu Jeanne-Marie Chavoin et qui l'avait fait venir avec Marie Jotillon à Cerdon, où il avait continué à les guider et à les protéger. Il était resté l'un des collaborateurs les plus proches de Jean-Claude—une position qui n'a pas toujours été facile, même pour la fratrie. Jean-Claude ressentit profondément la perte de son frère.

Deux années plus tard, le 30 juin 1858, Jeanne-Marie Chavoin mourut à Jarnosse (Loire). Jean-Claude avait voulu s'y rendre pour la voir, mais il ne l'a jamais fait. C'était maintenant le seul survivant des temps héroïques de Cerdon et de Belley, où elle et les deux frères Colin s'étaient soutenus dans leurs projets et leur travail pour la

Société de Marie. En dépit de leurs divergences récentes, les relations entre Jean-Claude et Jeanne-Marie avaient été un temps étroites et profondes. Cela explique peut-être le brin d'amertume quand il réagit au refus de Jeanne-Marie à suivre ses dernières idées sur les sœurs. Quoiqu'il en soit, c'était un autre vide irréparable dans le cercle de ses vieux amis et camarades d'armes.

Au début de 1860, les relations glaciales entre le P. Jean-Claude Colin et le P. Julien Favre commencèrent à se réchauffer. Le supérieur général avait envoyé ses vœux de nouvel an à son prédécesseur. Colin lui avait répondu de façon aimable et l'avait assuré de sa prière constante pour lui et pour la Société. Au milieu de l'année, le 15 juin 1860, le Saint-Siège approuva la règle de Favre, appelée maintenant 'Constitutions des prêtres de la Société de Marie', à l'essai pour six ans. Colin en conclut qu'il avait été 'relevé de la mission de fournir des constitutions aux yeux de Dieu et de la Société', et que son seul devoir maintenant était de se préparer à la mort.

Tous les maristes, cependant, ne partageaient pas cette évaluation. Un nombre croissant pensait que seul Colin avait le droit de composer les constitutions définitives de la Société. Un chapitre général fut convoqué pour 1866. Le P. Favre conseilla vivement à son prédécesseur d'y participer pour 'mettre le sceau de votre sagesse et de votre autorité sur votre propre travail', et il demanda pardon pour 'tout ce qui avait pu le plonger dans la détresse'.

Quand le chapitre s'ouvrit le 5 juin, Jean-Claude Colin était là, assis à côté de Julien Favre. Les débats et l'état d'esprit respiraient l'unité et l'harmonie. Le jubilé d'or (légèrement anticipé) d'ordination sacerdotale de Colin fut célébré solennellement. Plus significatif encore : le chapitre lui confia 'la rédaction de nos règles'. Tout le monde, Colin lui-même y compris, présuma que cela signifiait prendre le texte de Favre comme base et le réviser. Entre temps, une demande avait été faite au Saint-Siège pour rallonger de six années la période d'essai.

Même avec l'aide d'assistants, Colin progressait lentement car il n'était pas à l'aise avec un texte de base qui n'était pas le sien. Un tournant décisif se produisit en avril 1868 quand, en visite à Belley, il apprit l'existence d'un exemplaire de ses constitutions de 1842, qu'il pensait ne plus exister. A partir de ce moment-là, il se décida à revenir à ce texte qui exprimait le mieux ses idées, comme base des constitutions attendues par la Société.

C'était une décision potentiellement discutable. D'une part, elle permettait au travail d'avancer facilement et rapidement. D'autre part, elle équivalait à abandonner le mandat donné par le chapitre général, qu'il avait essayé loyalement de remplir, et à assumer—ou plutôt reprendre—un mandat qu'il pensait avoir reçu du ciel. La question était : La Société reconnaitrait-t-elle ce mandat ?

Il apparut rapidement que l'opposition à ce retour aux constitutions de Colin ne reposait pas seulement sur le fait que la règle de Favre avait été approuvée provisoirement par Rome. Des doutes étaient émis sur le droit de Colin de se considérer comme le fondateur de la Société de Marie, et sur l'inspiration de sa règle. Désormais beaucoup de maristes avaient entendu parler de Courveille. N'était-il pas réellement le fondateur ? De toute façon, quelles étaient les origines de la règle primitive ? Les controverses sur ces points ne furent pas résolues avant 1870.

Un chapitre général fut convoqué pour le 5 août de cette année-là. Le P. Favre dit à l'assemblée : 'Nous nous sommes réunis non pas pour nous diviser, mais pour nous unir'. Il lui demanda d'avoir 'un esprit de paix et d'union' et d'éviter le 'le triste exemple de certaines sociétés nouvelles où le général et le fondateur n'étaient pas unis et avaient chacun leurs propres partisans'. Il 'préférerait plutôt mourir' que se trouver lui-même dans une telle division. Afin de lever les derniers doutes, ambiguïtés ou suspicions qui restaient sur sa position concernant ses propres constitutions et celles de Colin, il déclara que 'des circonstances particulières' l'avaient obligé à publier 'les règles que vous connaissez.' Mais maintenant 'le Très Révérend Père Fondateur nous donne son travail. Je l'accepte de tout mon cœur.'

Une commission capitulaire reconnut que 'le R. P. Colin est notre seul et vrai fondateur', en ce sens qu'il est 'celui qui a non seulement pensé l'œuvre, mais qu'il l'a organisée et lui a donné vie'. Elle recommanda que le chapitre se résolût à accepter 'en principe' les constitutions qu'il lui présentait. Le chapitre adopta aussi une déclaration selon laquelle la Bienheureuse Vierge Marie est vraiment la fondatrice de la Société qui porte son nom et que la Société la choisit comme sa 'première et perpétuelle supérieure'.

Cette déclaration à ce moment et dans ce contexte avait une grande signification : elle symbolisait la pleine réconciliation de Colin et de Favre dans un acte où chacun 'disparaissait' et reconnaissait, avec tous les maristes, Marie comme leur fondatrice et leur supérieure.

Mettre ainsi l'origine et le gouvernement de la Société à un plan surnaturel élevé ne dispensait pas les maristes, bien sûr, de mener des investigations historiques sur le rôle joué par les 'instruments' humains que Marie avait utilisés pour établir la congrégation, ni de concevoir des formes appropriées de gouvernance en son nom. Mais cela signifiait qu'il n'y avait plus de raisons désormais de prendre le parti du fondateur ou du supérieur général, l'un contre l'autre, et cela faisait disparaître la menace du schisme. C'était un bel exemple de l''inconnus et cachés' en acte.

Le 2 septembre, le chapitre dut être suspendu, par peur d'une révolution suite à la défaite de la France face à la Prusse et à ses alliés allemands. Quand il reprit en janvier-février 1872, il acheva le travail d'examen et d'approbation du texte. Il ne restait plus aux constitutions maristes qu'à être approuvées par Rome. Ce que fit le pape Pie IX le 28 février 1873.

Le 25 mars 1873, en la fête de l'Annonciation, le supérieur général annonça à la Société tout entière la bonne nouvelle : 'Nos constitutions sont définitivement approuvées par le Saint-Siège.' Pour Colin, cette approbation signifiait la fin de sa mission envers la Société. Un nouveau pas devait être franchi. Le 9 juillet, le P. Favre convoqua un chapitre général spécial pour recevoir et promulguer les constitutions de la Société de Marie approuvées par le Saint-Siège. Le chapitre se réunit le 12 août 1873. Jean-Claude Colin était là pour assister à l'achèvement final du travail de sa vie. Toutefois il ne prit part à aucune des sessions plénières.

Le lundi 25 août, le départ de Colin pour La Neylière prit certains maristes par surprise, bien que la rumeur eût circulé qu'il était sur le point de s'en aller. La nouvelle se répandit. Ceux qui étaient dans la maison descendirent, chacun avec un exemplaire des constitutions. Colin entra dans la salle du chapitre et se laissa choir dans un fauteuil. On demanda au fondateur de dire un dernier mot. Il s'efforça de prononcer quelques phrases, mais ses forces l'abandonnèrent. Il demanda de l'aide pour se lever. Quand ceux qui étaient près de lui comprirent qu'il voulait se mettre à genoux et leur demander leur bénédiction, ils protestèrent et le firent rester assis. Colin voulait toujours recevoir leur bénédiction. Ils commencèrent, mais Colin les interrompit et leur demanda pardon pour les mauvais exemples qu'il leur avait donnés ; il leur demanda de prier pour que le Bon Dieu lui pardonnât toutes les fautes par lesquelles il avait entravé 'l'œuvre de la

Sainte Vierge'. Ils insistèrent pour qu'il leur donnât sa bénédiction. Il s'exécuta dans une formule latine un peu longue englobant la Société tout entière, ses ministères, les parents et bienfaiteurs des maristes et tous les membres du Tiers-Ordre. Ils voulaient recevoir de lui leurs volumes des constitutions, mais il insista pour ce fût le supérieur général qui en fît lui-même la distribution. Ils voulaient qu'au moins il touche et bénisse les volumes.

A ce moment-là, les novices, d'autres prêtres et quelques frères entrèrent dans la salle et lui demandèrent sa bénédiction. Sa voix était si faible qu'on l'entendit à peine ; il était en larmes. Les plus proches l'embrassèrent ; tous les autres voulurent avoir le même privilège. Il était temps de partir ; la voiture attendait. Ignorant les protestations de Colin, ils l'enlevèrent sur le fauteuil et le portèrent dans la voiture. Ainsi prit-il congé du chapitre et de Lyon, pour ne plus jamais revenir.

Jean-Claude pouvait maintenant chanter son Nunc Dimittis. Mais il n'avait pas encore tout à fait terminé son travail. Malgré ses forces chancelantes, il passa les dernières années de sa vie à travailler sur la règle de la branche laïque de la Société. C'était un retour à ses premières intentions exprimées en 1833. Pendant cette période c'est le Frère Jean-Marie Chognard qui s'occupa de lui ; depuis quelques années déjà il lui servait de secrétaire et d'assistant personnel ; graduellement il devint son soignant et son infirmier. Comme la vue de Colin baissait, Jean-Marie écrivait sous sa dictée et lisait pour lui, notamment un passage quotidien de la Bible – habitude observée par Colin depuis le temps du séminaire. Il s'affaiblissait de plus en plus. Quand, à l'automne 1875, ils commencèrent le livre de Job, il nota que Colin pensait qu'il ne vivrait pas assez longtemps pour le terminer. Colin s'endormit paisiblement le 15 novembre à l'âge de quatre-vingt-cinq ans. Ses restes reposent à La Neylière.

Photo ancienne de l'autel et de la tombe, à La Neylière

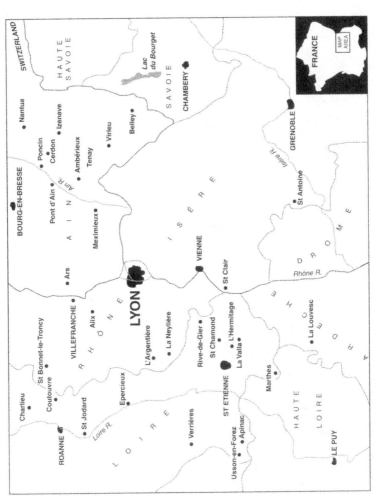

Carte des lieux des Origines maristes

table des matières

CPSIA information can be obtained
at www.ICGtesting.com
Printed in the USA
LVHW092325111221
705969LV00001B/50